The Public and Private Management of Grief

Caroline Pearce

The Public and Private Management of Grief

Recovering Normal

palgrave
macmillan

Caroline Pearce
King's College London
London, UK

ISBN 978-3-030-17661-7 ISBN 978-3-030-17662-4 (eBook)
https://doi.org/10.1007/978-3-030-17662-4

This Palgrave Macmillan imprint is published by the registered company Springer Nature Switzerland AG
The registered company address is: Gewerbestrasse 11, 6330 Cham, Switzerland

Preface

On completing a research project, it can be difficult to recall the initial reasons that motivated one to pursue that particular area of study. In the course of carrying out the research that fills the pages of this book I was often faced with the question: Why did you choose to research this topic? This seemingly innocent question felt fraught and complex as my topic of choice was something which made many people feel uncomfortable. Having spent at least ten years intellectually preoccupied with grief, bereavement, death, and illness, the question became a personal bugbear of mine. Answering such queries often opened up an inquiry into my personal motivations and private life in a way that made me feel exposed. It seemed that my interest in grief could be explained only by some traumatic event in my own life, as though my intellectual preoccupations were directed by my emotional disposition; a demonstration of my own unresolved mourning.

In this process of speaking about grief, the grief became attached to me. Or, borrowing the words of Sara Ahmed, in speaking about a problem, I became the problem. For me this caused considerable frustration, as though my scholarly work was a thinly disguised attempt to figure out my own problems. It made my choice of research topic feel small and individual, feminine even, in a way that felt negative, as though I was stuck within the realm of the domestic and intimate. Though my interest in the notion of recovery was to an extent borne out of my own grappling with it, this book moves out and beyond, to a place where I stopped taking it personally, yet remains indebted to those early experiences and perhaps initial misconceptions.

In this book one of the key aims has been to extract grief from the internal, private, and personal to highlight the political and social shaping of grief, where grief is experienced not only in the individual psyche but factors into the political and economic running of society. By drawing out these links to the political and social this book can be seen as a response to the individualising and psychologising of grief, but equally it is a product of my perspective as a sociologist. The work of Lauren Berlant, Judith Butler and Sara Ahmed taught me a great deal about how emotions are central to social and cultural politics, from understanding the processes of nation building and who gets to count as a citizen, to what makes a life worth living. Inspired by this work and other feminist scholarship this book seeks to challenge the boundaries between the public and private.

In the process of producing the work in this book, I kept referring back to a passage written by Lauren Berlant in her blog *Supervalent Thought*: 'Most of the writing we do is actually a performance of stuckness. It is a record of where we got stuck on a question for long enough to do some research and write out the whole knot until the original passion and curiosity that made us want to try to say something about something got so detailed, buried, encrypted, and diluted that the energetic and risk-taking impulse became sealed and delivered in the form of a defence against thinking any more about it'.[1]

For me this statement expresses a great deal about the process of writing a Ph.D. thesis, the passion and curiosity it involves to keep a one-pointed focus for three years on a question that becomes so detailed, diluted, buried, encrypted, until it emerges as the thesis. It also expresses how grief too can be compared to a performance of stuckness, of being in liminality, of seeking out meaning or ways to manage one's emotions. And further how telling one's story of grief is commonly assumed as mode of individual healing, of recovery from grief, of not thinking any more about it.

This statement also underscores the end of the project, a knot that has been unravelled and sealed many times and is sealed again in the form of this book. Though my risk-taking impulses have indeed waned, I cannot say I will think no more about the questions raised within these pages. For as you will learn in this book, completion is an ongoing process.

* * *

I would like to acknowledge The Open University for funding the doctoral research on which this book is based. I am greatly indebted to my two wonderful Ph.D. supervisors Carol Komaromy and Sam Murphy in the completion of this project. Special thanks to Carol for consistently going above and beyond in terms of support, mentorship and invaluable advice. Thanks to Arnar Árnason, my Ph.D. examiner who suggested I turn the thesis into a book. A thanks to the multidisciplinary death studies community who have provided an intellectual home for me and for this book. Most important thanks to the participants whose accounts fill the pages of this book, for providing insight and sharing their experiences.

London, UK Caroline Pearce

Note

1. Berlant, Lauren. 2010. Sitting on an airplane, a mule. Supervalent Thought. https://supervalentthought.com/2010/09/18/sitting-on-an-airplane-a-mule/. Accessed on 27 December, 2018.

Contents

List of Tables

1

Introduction: Recovering Normal

What happens when people fail to recover from grief? Through a critical analysis of theory, policy, and practice, this book investigates how recovery is the prevailing discourse that measures and frames how people grieve, and how failures to recover are socially perceived and acted upon. Focusing on how people make sense of grief, how grief is managed, and the type of identities people come to inhabit following bereavement, this book draws on in-depth interviews with bereaved people and the professionals who help bereaved people to 'recover' from grief, to investigate how grief, commonly understood as a private issue, is increasingly framed as a public problem. The book begins by considering notions of normality and the changing constructions of what it means to successfully recover following bereavement. Mental health practice has a long history of defining and labelling normal and abnormal behaviours, and the influence of psychological theory on understandings of mental states once considered 'normal' reflects the general medicalization of everyday life. The defining and labelling of grief is a contested territory—a territory examined in this book—occupied by

C. Pearce, *The Public and Private Management of Grief*,
https://doi.org/10.1007/978-3-030-17662-4_1

prominent claims that posit scientific explanations for grief while experiencing repeated resistance from theories that emphasise the natural, human and 'normal' nature of grief.

Recovering Normal

In 2013, the fifth edition of the Diagnostic and Statistical Manual of Mental Disorders (DSM-5) (American Psychological Association 2013) was published, provoking a flurry of controversy in the field of grief and bereavement research. The DSM-5 included key changes that proposed a significant change in the understanding and treatment of grief. Bereaved people, if showing depression symptoms as little as two weeks following bereavement could be diagnosed with a major depressive disorder without any special consideration for their grieving state, and the manual proposed a new diagnostic category describing a persistent, complicated form of grief. The substantial criticism that arose from these changes centred on an objection to what was seen to be an increased 'medicalising' of grief. The critique of medicalization, which has a long history within the social sciences and the anti-psychiatry movement of the 1960s, garnered wide support from the pages of *The Lancet* (2012) and the *British Medical Journal* (2013) to *Psychology Today* whose regular columnist, psychiatrist Allen Frances, was one of the DSM-5's most ardent critics and who pleaded against what he argued was a medicalising of 'normal' grief (Frances 2012). The title of Frances' column 'Saving Normal' and his accompanying book of the same name (Frances 2013) set the tone for numerous critiques of the DSM-5, described as '[t]he war on grief' (Stolorow 2014). An editorial in *The Lancet* (2012) concluded: '[F]or those who are grieving, doctors would do better to offer time, compassion, remembrance, and empathy rather than pills' (589).

Within the responses to the DSM-5, grief was positioned as something under threat and to be protected, and psychiatric intervention as the dehumanising force intruding into the most human of emotions. While the dispute over the changes in the DSM-5 and the perceived attempt to 'medicalise' grief was a call to protect 'normal' grief, it was agreed 'abnormal' grief was something that required intervention (Bryant 2012). Even among those who most fervently opposed the idea that grief could be diagnosed as indiscriminately as depression, the belief in complicated or pathological forms of grief was widely accepted (Wakefield 2013a, b; Wakefield and First 2012; Walter 2006). Indeed, despite ongoing debates over the best means to categorise complicated forms of grief (Reynolds et al. 2017; Prigerson and Maciejewski 2017; Maciejewski and Prigerson 2017; Boelen and Smid 2017), the diagnosis of 'Prolonged Grief Disorder' proposed by Prigerson and colleagues (Prigerson et al. 2009) has been included in the World Health Organisation (WHO) 11th Edition of the International Classification of Diseases (ICD-11).

The debates surrounding the publication of the DSM-5 surfaced longstanding tensions in a field that strives to develop scientific means of theorising and treating grief. Dominant theories of grief, drawing from psychological studies, have presented 'normal' grief as a linear, staged process with a defined endpoint: often described as recovery. This is embedded within the familiar stage model of grief that suggests bereaved people move through five stages: denial, bargaining, depression, anger and acceptance (Kübler-Ross 1970). In recent decades, bereavement researchers have sought to dispute the validity of the five stages suggesting they should be 'relegated to the shelves of history' (Stroebe et al. 2017). Yet the lived experience of bereavement is still heavily embedded in enduring cultural logics of staged and time-limited grief (Kenny et al. 2017). This is evident in how 'complicated' or 'prolonged' grief is categorised, defined as a form of grief that has been 'derailed' from its agreed natural course (Shear 2012).

Specifically, the development towards establishing psychiatric categories of grief posed new questions for the notion of 'recovery' from grief, implying that in some cases people 'fail' to progress through grief to recovery. However, 'recovery' remains a contested term in grief and bereavement research and practice (Balk 2004, 2007). Recovery is a term that has connotations with illness and implies a return to prior functioning. Researchers and practitioners favour other terms such as 'resilience,' 'adapt,' 'deal with,' or 'adjust' (Paletti 2008; Tedeschi and Calhoun 2008). Yet, beyond the bereavement literature, there is a growing interest in recovery within United Kingdom national health care services, particularly mental health, where service users and providers are embracing a 'recovery model' of care (Department of Health 2001; Glyde 2014).

The role of government policy and psychiatric diagnostic categories are two of the types of social and political discourse analysed in this book, examining how different practices are popularised and how bereaved people are encouraged to make sense of and manage grief in certain ways. Yet theories of grief have tended to differentiate between 'private' and 'public' grief, demarcating an individual and natural course of grief and recovery as distinct from the cultural and political context. It is this distinction between public and private grief that I focus on next.

Public and Private Grief

Grief is commonly understood as a natural and inevitable part of human existence and yet academics, clinicians, psychologists, and psychiatrists have proposed numerous means of theorising, understanding, and treating grief. Grief has been described as a mode of detaching from the deceased person (Freud 1917), as a syndrome (Lindemann 1944), as a process (Parkes 1972), as containing a number of phases or stages (Kübler-Ross 1970), as well as a matter of reintegration, or reunion (Bowlby 1979; Klein 1940) and as an ongoing process of continuing bonds (Klass et al. 1996; Stroebe and Schut 2005). Grief is something of great territorial interest and has been viewed through various lenses: psychoanalytic, psychiatric, psychological, sociological, and increasingly as an object of neuroscientific study (O'Connor 2005).

Since the beginning of the twentieth century, the academic study of grief has grown, yet how bereaved people come to experience and express grief has been framed by the enduring belief in death as a 'taboo' in modern western societies; a thesis often attributed to the work of scholars such as Gorer (1965) and Ariès (1974) who claimed that western societies were 'death denying.' Robert and Tradii (2017; Tradii and Robert 2017) documented the origins and trajectory of this thesis highlighting how the belief in death as a societal taboo gained traction as a powerful ideology at the turn of modernity; a time where traditional rituals around death in westerns societies such as the UK were changing within the context of secularisation. The 'death denial' thesis served a purpose in stimulating the growth of organisations such as the Association for Death Education and Counselling (ADEC) in the United States and Cruse Bereavement Care in the UK, dedicated to promoting awareness of death and the support of bereaved people.

For sociologist Tony Walter this development of death awareness signalled a 'revival' of death that contested the notion of death and dying as a social 'taboo' (1994). This revival argued Walter, could be separated into the modern and postmodern period. Walter's theory claimed that in a postmodern era where the individual and their sense of identity is paramount, death and bereavement posed a threat in the absence of 'traditional' rituals that previously served to manage the uncertainty of death. This conflicted with a modern rationalism that saw medicine exert further control over death and which, as a result, formed a divide between 'public' and 'private' realms of grief where the public, in the form of medicalisation, was encroaching on the private nature of grief.

This distinction between modern and traditional forms of mourning, as described by Walter, is still commonly found in texts on grief and bereavement, as well as popular media, perpetuating the idea that the 'problem,' as it is considered, with grief today is due to an eradication and absence of rituals around death that previously provided the means of coping with grief. For example, a newspaper column by Owen Jones (2018) in *The Guardian* detailing the death of his father, described being faced with a culture that 'poorly equips us to deal with grief,' and that lacks the vocabulary to talk about death and to the bereaved. Offering Jewish customs as an example, Jones suggests that 'having some form of structure to process and manage grief collectively surely helps.' The support of this view was reflected in the hundreds of comments and letters sent in response to Jones' column (*The Guardian* 2018) sharing personal experiences and reiterating the taboo around death and expressions of grief.

In what follows I hope to blur the distinction between the private and public realms of grief and challenge the repeated claim that death is a social taboo against which people are poorly equipped to comprehend and manage. On the contrary, I demonstrate that there is a proliferation of guidance on how to manage grief; techniques that could be described as contemporary rituals. However, the idea that death is a societal taboo persists despite a growing number of public movements that seek to demystify death, such as the proliferation of 'Death Cafes,' and organisations like *Dying Matters* and *The Order of the Good Death*, that have managed to make death 'cool' (Meltzer 2018). In particular, the rising use of online spaces for memorialising those who die has been evidenced as a rejection of the 'taboo' around grief, where online platforms and new technologies are transforming the ways in which people both express grief and how they interact with and maintain relationships with the dead (Andrew 2014; Seligson 2014; Varga and Paulus 2013; Harnett 2016; Bassett 2017; Solon 2018). The 'unspeakably taboo' (Walter 1999) aspects of grief are now shared publicly on online platforms such as 'Modern Loss,' which encourages people to share their loss story and participate in 'candid conversation about grief.' Communities for bereaved people also exist online in less public settings in the numerous online discussion forums designed solely for the discussion of grief. In the setting of the private forum, arguably, the 'taboo' around grief is re-emphasised as the bereaved community is 'forced' to 'go underground,' making grief feel like a 'dirty secret' (Sidhu 2015).

In a year which witnessed the death of many popular entertainers, social media became an important medium in 2016 for the expression of public grief. A number of media commentators tried to make sense of the phenomenon arguing that the Internet and social media sites provided a platform upon which people could voice their 'natural' expressions of grief (Steinberg 2016; Penny 2016; Garber 2016; *The Guardian* 2016). In this view, digital technologies now provide an outlet for the chaotic feelings of grief that have long been repressed by the lack of traditional rituals to make sense of and organise death (*The Guardian* 2016). At the same time, the public performance of grief for those who lived their lives so publicly seems fitting, as emotional outpourings by the public punctuated the lives of these public figures. The mourning of Princess Diana demonstrates, with or without social media, the public mourning of celebrities and public figures. These public acts of grieving, online or offline, are presented as a contradictory mix of both a postmodern playful fashioning of selves and identity but also a claim to truth and the revelation of fundamental aspects of being human. Using social media to express grief is often considered only performative, as though grief expressed online is inauthentic compared with the management of grief through traditional rituals (Andrew 2014; Harnett 2016).

An art installation and performance *An Occupation of Loss* (2018) curated by Taryn Simon provides an illustrative example to consider how the authenticity of grief and ritual are judged. The installation gathered together professional mourners from around the world to simultaneously broadcast their lamentations in a fifty-minute performance, repeated several times a night daily for a three-week run. The performance took place in a dimly lit space under the streets of London that resembled a disused car park. The spectators were free to wander around the space, listen and walk close to the mourners, as they produced melodic songs, played instruments and wailed with tears. In the accompanying leaflet, Simon wrote that *An Occupation of Loss* was intended to underscore the tension between authentic and staged emotion. The task of the professional mourner is to guide the bereaved through the emotions of grief, through embodying and directing the emotions of others. The laments and emotions expressed initially appear and sound chaotic and yet the lament is precisely structured and ritualised.

In line with the aims of this book, *An Occupation of Loss* presents the performative nature of grief ritual, obscuring the distinction between authentic or inauthentic emotion and problematising common assumptions about the authenticity of 'traditional' rituals compared with modern forms of grieving. In this book, I focus on contemporary areas of concern that I contend seek to manage, make sense of and bring order to grief much like formal mortuary rites of the past. With the decline of religious narratives that traditionally furnished individuals with a world view within which to make sense of death and feelings of grief (Mellor and Shilling 1993), key academics have argued that psychology has grown in the western world as a means of providing counsel for the internal life of human beings (Howarth 2000, 2007; Rose 1985, 1989, 1998). Indeed, the debates around grief and recovery have largely been determined by the theory and practice of psychiatry and psychology.

Seale (1998) has described how modern rationality, of which medicalisation is one example, has a religious orientation: taking the place of religion in managing procedures around death and dying, but producing guidance and meaning that is equally powerful. Medical procedures have a ritual aspect that 'frame and box experience' (Seale 1998) and that are designed to reorient the living away from death and towards life. The classification of grief into normal and abnormal forms and the interventions carried out to enable people to recover from complicated grief can be understood, then, as a means of managing the boundaries between living and dead people that serves to contain the 'risk' the complicated griever poses (Howarth 2000). The complicated griever embodies the 'liminal' space between the living and the dead and so presents a danger by virtue of being matter 'out of place' (Douglas 1966).

Bloch and Parry (1982) defined mortuary practices as those that serve to reassert social order at death and further argued that social order is, itself, a product of rituals. These contemporary rituals, as I describe them, are not simply managing and organising grief but reshaping how grief is understood. In this understanding, rituals around death are productive sites that act to produce particular forms of subjects and are framed by the performing of certain emotions (Davies 2011). Ritual and emotion, rather than separate fields of experience are intricately intertwined, as I demonstrate by using Wetherell's (2012) concept of 'affective practices' and a detailed discussion of social theories of emotions in Chapter 5, to argue that grief cannot be understood apart from the rituals and practices that societies use to manage, express and make sense of grief. Yet mourning rituals also seek to reintegrate the bereaved person back into society (Turner 1969). In what follows I highlight different types of rituals bereaved people might engage in, including everyday informal rituals and practices, to navigate the liminal space of grief towards recovery or 'non-recovery,' a key concept I introduce next.

Framing Non-recovery

The acknowledgement of the broader cultural, political and economic concerns is central to the argument of this book which claims that the ways in which grief and recovery are understood and practised can be linked to permutations in contemporary neo-liberal governmentality; as Árnason's work has demonstrated (Árnason 2001, 2007; Árnason and Hafsteinsson 2003, 2018). Throughout this book I utilise the concept of 'governmentality,' originating in the work of Foucault (1973, 1975, 1984) and later employed in Rose's (1985, 1989) work on the 'psy' disciplines, to consider how diverse authorities, whether political, economic, medical, or from popular culture and media, seek to act upon the lives and conduct of the grieving person to achieve desirable states of health and happiness through 'régimes of truth.'

In Foucault's (2003) conceptualisation of modern power he described a shift from a sovereign power, which gained its power from the threat of taking life, and which was directly traceable to powerful figures, to the modern form of 'biopower,' which gains power from monitoring, managing and producing life through discourses which he called régimes of truth. For Foucault, biopower 'literally ignores death' (2003, 248). In what follows I explore how within the culture of recovery, where mental disorders and grief are framed as an economic burden, power is directed to managing the deterioration of life, emphasising human productivity and flourishing. I argue that what makes a happy life and what defines recovery are remarkably similar to the central tenets of neo-liberal values with the repeated emphasis on individual choice, rational agency and responsibility. The shaping of the neo-liberal subject thus sets the scene for how grief is valued and treated in contemporary UK society and demonstrates how the concept of recovery emerges to guide people away from grief and towards the happy life.

My analysis focuses on the question of what happens when people fail to recover. The question of what it means to not recover is what I asked myself when confronted with the variety of conflicting discourses around recovery. As I explore throughout the book, debates over how best to define recovery are divided between a deep attachment to recovery, and an equally strong aversion to not recovering. Within contemporary bereavement care practice, not recovering poses a threat to both ideas about grief and also the person who grieves. Failing to recover from grief reveals the difficulties people have in 'detaching' from deceased people, blurring the modern divide between life and death (Howarth 2000). Further, in a climate where mental distress is construed as a heavy 'burden,' not recovering from grief presents a problem to the political and economic running of society.

In exploring the possibility of not recovering, or rejecting dominant notions of recovery, I refer to an essay by Kauffman (2008) entitled: 'What is "no recovery"?' Kauffman's article draws on philosophical and clinical insight to suggest that following bereavement, no one recovers. Kauffman suggested 'no recovery' was not a transitional state but a condition of human existence. In such a state one might claim recovery if he or she finds that they can adapt to such conditions, but for Kauffman this was only a display of social adjustment, not a resolution of mourning. Often theories of grief seek to give grief a function whether enabling social cohesion or an opportunity for social transformation. Kauffman's state of no recovery suggests that no norms are sufficiently adequate to take care of the disruption caused by death, and so recovery becomes a moral or symbolic act, put simply: a socially framed performance.

Kauffman's essay provided a concept to explore: the question of no recovery, which I refer to in this book as 'non-recovery.' In exploring the possibility of non-recovery, recovery appears as only one way to respond to grief. Instead, it opens ways to explore how recovery might be a socially informed and constructed performance. To conceptualise the experience of 'non-recovery' I draw on van Gennep's (1960) and Turner's (1969) use of the concept 'liminality' to describe the experience of grief as one of inhabiting a liminal space. The word liminality derives from the Latin 'limen' meaning threshold or margin. Turner (1974, 1982) described a stage of liminality as one where the usual order of things is suspended, the past is momentarily negated, and the future has yet to begin. By comparing grief with liminality, I argue that, following bereavement, people may experience their sense of identity, and their sense of reality, has been suspended. I conceptualise grief as a virtual space of liminality that is experienced within the psyche but also in interaction with other people, organisations, and institutions. So, while a liminal space provides opportunities and possibilities to inhabit new identities, the space is also filled with various people and ideas to guide people in a particular direction.

The ways in which someone can negotiate this space are multiple and I highlight some key discourses that frame the contemporary experience of bereavement, and that influence how a person might make sense of their grief. I suggest that within this liminal space the bereaved person is searching to make sense of and manage grief, negotiating the ideas, norms and discourses around grief and recovery, following a trajectory of 'recovery' or 'non-recovery.' For example, the bereaved person negotiates various different powerful discourses from those groups and individuals with a vested interest in bereaved people recovering from grief. The growth of interest in the psychiatric categories of 'complicated grief' and 'prolonged grief disorder' provide clear classifications of what constitutes 'abnormal' or 'problematic' grieving in contemporary research and practice. As I discuss throughout, the emergence of the 'complicated griever' supplies an empirical example to examine the contested boundary between recovery and non-recovery.

Problematising Grief

Following bereavement people are encouraged either in some sense to return back to the life they had before, or to move on, as though grief is an experience that casts people outside of what is considered the normal realm of experience. In this book, I destablise the notion implicit in theories on grief that there is a normal mode of functioning and aim to show that grief provides an opportunity for normalising modes of address, and that recovery—if it can be described as anything—is best understood as a process of normalisation. In turn, the subtitle of this book—recovering normal—emphasises the way recovery from grief, has become a notion intertwined with particular visions of normality endorsed by neo-liberal governmentality.

In seeking to highlight the shortcomings of the way grief is currently theorised, and shed light on the possibility of 'non-recovery' and the person who 'fails' to recover, I turn to the work of Foucault (1970, 1971, 1973, 1975) who consistently critiqued the normative understandings of ideas, practices and subjectivities by highlighting how ideas about society and people are both socially and historically constructed through 'discourses,' and how identities are produced at the intersections between discourse and practice. Focusing on discourse involves analysing how certain ways of describing and practising ideas, people, or experiences, dominate in a particular historical context. Foucault analysed how ideas come to be governed by focusing on 'problematisations': how certain people, ideas and practices come to considered 'problematic' at key points in history in societies or cultures, and the strategies used to manage them. My aim was to analyse the bereaved person using this framework, to explore how grief had become a problem through the dominance of discourses of recovery, shaping grief and the bereaved person as something to be managed.

To focus on 'problematisations' is to question why certain ideas, practices or people might emerge as a 'problem' in a specific time and context. Foucault's *History of Sexuality* (1976) traced how sexuality had been viewed, repressed and liberated over time. In doing so, Foucault revealed that ideas or people become problematic not because of something inherent within that person or idea, but because of how it/they might pose concerns of a moral, political, economic, military or juridical nature. Therefore, analysing problematisations involves asking why something or someone comes to be identified as a problem at a certain point in time. It also involves acknowledging how problems emerge in relation to other sets of interests. Consequently, revealing that problems are contingent on their relation to a particular political, moral or economic context suggests that things could be otherwise. In this methodological approach, the aim is to destablise the present and it's taken-for-granted certainties, in such things as institutions (i.e. the prison system or similar orders), and ideas such as sexuality and its underpinning moral code.

Thus, destabilising the present can foreground alternate ways of conceptualising those ideas or persons that might be viewed as a 'problem.' In doing so, less dominant ideas come into view. Specifically, it allows for the exploration of the question: how does a story become hidden and how can it be made visible? The aim of this book is to bring alternatives to recovery into view, an aim demonstrated in Foucault's work through critiquing the 'figure of man' that western thoughts had relied upon. Foucault claimed that 'truth' was not absolute but multiple. Rather than seeing objects or identities as singular, they can comprise multiple 'truths'—often produced at the intersections of different discourses. Foucault disregarded any universal notion of truth because he argued that universal understandings are historicised, and examining the ways in which they are constructed and emerge out of a certain historical context reveals this 'truth' fallacy. In other words, truth is historically located and socially constructed.

This characterised Foucault's largely 'genealogical' approach to research, which involved building a 'critical history' of an object or phenomenon. In the 1961 Preface to *The History of Madness* (2009), Foucault wrote that his intention in the work was to write 'an archaeology of silence' that had been created by the language of psychiatry. The translation of madness into mental illness for Foucault meant there was no longer a common language in which the 'madman' could communicate with 'modern man.' In other words, the languages were incommensurable. This rupture in dialogue allowed psychiatry to emerge as the means to explain madness in terms of mental illness. Similarly, I argue the story of no recovery, the non-recovered, is a story hidden from view, its silencing limiting the possible alternatives and scope of recovery. In this book, I seek to bring to light the shape of the 'non-recovered' figure through revealing the ways in which current theories of grief and recovery were formulated around a vision of the bereaved person that had highlighted and obscured different aspects of grief and bereaved people's experiences.

Background to the Study

In bereavement research and practice, grief is understood as the subsequent natural, emotional response that emerges following bereavement. In this book, I use the term bereavement to refer to the event of losing someone from death. I refer to grief as the emotion or feelings that arise in response to bereavement. This distinction between the event of bereavement and the response of grief is important for I contend that though bereavement is an event which befalls many, grief as a response can be felt, expressed, and managed differently.

This book is based on fieldwork conducted in England, UK. The aims of the study were formulated from an interest in finding out how recovery and the failure to recover were negotiated: both in bereavement care practice and by those who experience bereavement. To address these aims I conducted interviews with; bereavement care practitioners working across England (see Table A1 in Appendix A) within the following organisations: the national bereavement charity Cruse Bereavement Care, a local bereavement counselling service, a South London based hospice and the non-profit organisation Grief Recovery UK (see Appendix B for detailed information on each organisation); people who had experienced bereavement (see Table A2); and current and former mental health service users (see Table A3). I also analysed a wide range of expert and lay literature including policy documents, reports, autobiographies and novels, to understand how grief and recovery are framed culturally and politically and reveal the ways in which the private experience of grief is inextricably linked with public discourses and practices.

Through carrying out the fieldwork, I discovered the provision and organisation of bereavement care services across England is dispersed in different sites, often situated within or between clinical mental health services and the charity and voluntary sector. Due to this lack of centrality in the provision of bereavement care services, bereavement care was often delivered by volunteers with varying levels of training and utilised a number of different approaches. As I have documented elsewhere (Pearce 2018), recent years have witnessed attempts to better integrate and control the quality of bereavement care services, while maintaining the belief that bereavement is something that should remain largely a matter for community and social networks rather than clinical services.

I spoke with people who had experienced a range of bereavement including the death of a spouse or partner, parent and sibling. This was because I did not want to accept the existence of a 'hierarchy' of grief and reaffirm it by choosing one type of bereavement over another and presume one form of bereavement would be more likely to 'predispose' a person to complicated grief. Rather I wanted to explore how any form of bereavement can become complicated depending on an array of factors: practical, psychological and sociological. For example, I did not want to claim the death of a child is the 'worst' form of bereavement. I wanted to give voice to those 'natural' bereavements too, of older people bereaved of their partner, which I suggest can pose just as much distress for the bereaved person.

The absence of a particular type of bereavement on which to focus my research posed a methodological problem in deciding who to recruit. It also meant that the findings gathered from the participants included in this study do not speak to a particular subfield of grief and bereavement research. However, I actively sought to avoid making general claims about grief, and further to avoid the segmenting of grief experiences found in bereavement research. The search for generalisability and 'validity' in grief research has encouraged a need for scientific accuracy in studies of grief. However, this search is reliant upon an unfounded assumption of the natural course of grief. The 'natural' course of grief has been inextricably intertwined with 'normal' societal expectations of grief. The elaboration of universal claims to grief and grouping grief into types, has not led to the 'truth' of the experience of grief but rather constructed further psychologically informed norms, epitomised in the psychological construction of 'complicated grief.' However, as the aim of this research was not to reflect a true reality but destabilise existing claims, it has been my task to point towards alternative modes of thinking about grief that can enable further research with scope for employing more and different methods.

Outline of the Book

This book is structured around three themes, that of meanings: how people make sense of grief; practices, how grief is managed; and identities, how people come to inhabit or resist identities following bereavement. The interwoven nature of meanings, practices and identities I describe are supported by a Foucauldian approach to study where the focus is on three areas: of how ideas come to be 'truth,' how practices and discourses establish objects in certain ways, and how people come to be identified as particular types of 'subjects.'

In the next chapter, I review the literature on grief and bereavement. I move chronologically beginning with Sigmund Freud's (1917) essay 'Mourning and Melancholia' up to present-day debates concerning 'complicated grief' and 'prolonged grief disorder.' I argue that the dominance of psychological studies into grief has transformed grief into a problem of the individual psyche, necessitating the creation of bereavement counselling and therapies. I explore the type of assumed subject on which the psychological view rests, questioning its validity. In Chapter 3, I focus on the first theme: meaning and how people make sense of grief. I explore a range of contemporary 'discourses' that I argue frame how grief is defined such as psychiatric diagnosis, literary narratives, economic policy on happiness and well-being and the growth of a 'recovery model' in mental health care. This chapter also presents how bereaved people make sense of their own feelings of grief and I discuss how people seek to find meaning from bereavement and the consequences of failing to make sense of grief. The existence of these at times contradictory discourses I discuss, reveals how making sense of and defining grief is an ongoing public and private endeavour. This sets the scene for Chapter 4 in which I describe the second theme: practices, and the ways in which both professionals and bereaved people seek to manage grief. I present the findings from the bereavement care practitioners, exploring what 'grief work' involves and how recovery is negotiated in practice. This formal form of 'grief work' is contrasted with the types of 'work' the bereaved participants described which focused on the everyday routines of the household and the role of material spaces and objects.

In Chapter 5, I critique the psychological notions of grief and the bereaved person by exploring other literature on grief, taking a different angle on Freud's understanding of mourning and melancholia. I outline the theory of liminality which underpins the conceptual basis of this book. I argue for the need for grief researchers to look beyond the psychology of grief into the study of emotions and affect to suggest an alternative multidisciplinary way of theorising grief. By drawing on literature on the body and practice I explore how grief can be theorised both as an individually felt and socially practised emotion. In Chapter 6, I explore the final theme, identity, and present the types of identities people come to inhabit in the liminal space of grief. Three key identities emerged: recovered, relational, and resistant identities. I describe how people come to move in and out of multiple identities, inhabiting and resisting categories. Chapter 7 concludes the book as I consider what the 'other side' of recovery could be by outlining the key conclusions as well as looking forward to the future of bereavement research and practice.

References

American Psychological Association. 2013. *Diagnostic and Statistical Manual of Mental Disorders*, 5th ed. Washington, DC: American Psychological Association.

Andrew, Joshua. 2014. "How We Grieve on Social Media." *The Atlantic*, April 25. https://www.theatlantic.com/health/archive/2014/04/grieving-in-public-tragedy-on-social-media/360788/.

Ariès, Philippe. 1974. *Western Attitudes Toward Death from the Middle Ages to the Present.* Baltimore: Johns Hopkins University Press.

Árnason, Arnar. 2001. "Experts of the Ordinary: Bereavement Counselling in Britain." *Journal of the Royal Anthropological Institute* 7 (2): 299–313.

———. 2007. "'Fall Apart and Put Yourself Together Again': The Anthropology of Death and Bereavement Counselling in Britain." *Mortality* 12 (1): 48–65.

Árnason, Arnar, and Sigurjón Baldur Hafsteinsson. 2003. "The Revival of Death: Expression, Expertise and Governmentality." *British Journal of Sociology* 54 (1): 43–62.

———. 2018. *Death and Governmentality in Iceland: Neo-Liberalism, Grief and the Nation-Form*. Reykjavík: University of Iceland Press.

Balk, David E. 2004. "Recovery Following Bereavement: An Examination of the Concept." *Death Studies* 28 (4): 361–374.

———. 2007. "A Modest Proposal About Bereavement and Recovery." *Death Studies* 32 (1): 84–93.

Bassett, Debra. 2017. "Shadows of the Dead: Social Media and Our Changing Relationship with the Departed." *Discover Society*, January 3. https://discoversociety.org/2017/01/03/shadows-of-the-dead-social-media-and-our-changing-relationship-with-the-departed/.

Bloch, Maurice, and Jonathan Parry. 1982. "Introduction: Death and the Regeneration of Life." In *Death and the Regeneration of Life*, edited by Maurice Bloch and Jonathan Parry, 1–44. Cambridge: Cambridge University Press.

British Medical Journal. 2013. "Medicalising and Medicating Unhappiness." *British Medical Journal* 347: 345–348.

Boelen, Paul A., and Geert E. Smid. 2017. "Disturbed Grief: Prolonged Grief Disorder and Persistent Complex Bereavement Disorder." *British Medical Journal* 357. https://doi.org/10.1136/bmj.j2016.

Bowlby, John. 1979. *The Making and Breaking of Affectional Bonds*. London: Tavistock.

Bryant, Richard A. 2012. "Grief as a Psychiatric Disorder." *British Journal of Psychiatry* 201 (1): 9–10.

Davies, Douglas J. 2011. *Emotion, Identity, and Religion: Hope, Reciprocity, and Otherness*. Oxford: Oxford University Press.

Department of Health. 2001. *The Journey to Recovery—The Government's Vision for Mental Health Care*. London: Department of Health.

Douglas, Mary. 1966. *Purity and Danger: An Analysis of Concepts of Pollution and Taboo*. London: Penguin.

Foucault, Michel. 1970. *The Archaeology of Knowledge*. New York: Pantheon.

———. 1971. "Nietzsche, Genealogy, History." In *The Foucault Reader: An Introduction to Foucault's Thought*, edited by Paul Rabinow, 76–100. London: Penguin.

———. 1973. *The Birth of the Clinic: An Archaeology of Medical Perception*. London: Routledge.

———. 1975. *Discipline and Punish: The Birth of the Prison*. New York: Random House.

———. 1976. *The History of Sexuality, Volume 1: The Will to Knowledge*. New York: Vintage.

———. 1984. "Polemics, Politics and Problematizations: An Interview with Michel Foucault." In *The Foucault Reader: An Introduction to Foucault's Thought*, edited by Paul Rabinow, 381–390. London: Penguin.

———. 2003. "1976." In *Society Must Be Defended: Lectures at the College de France 1975–1976*, 239–264. London: Allen Lane.

———. 2009. *History of Madness*. London: Routledge.

Frances, Allen. 2012. "DSM 5 Is Guide Not Bible—Ignore Its Ten Worst Changes." *Psychology Today*, December 2. https://www.psychologytoday.com/gb/blog/dsm5-in-distress/201212/dsm-5-is-guide-not-bible-ignore-its-ten-worst-changes.

———. 2013. *Saving Normal: An Insider's Revolt Against Out-of-Control Psychiatric Diagnosis, DSM-5, Big Pharma, and the Medicalization of Ordinary Life*. New York: William Morrow.

Freud, Sigmund. 1917. "Mourning and Melancholia." In *The Standard Edition of the Complete Psychological Works of Sigmund Freud*, edited by J. Strachey, 237–258. London: Hogarth Press.

Garber, Megan. 2016. "Enter the Grief Police." *The Atlantic*, January 20. http://www.theatlantic.com/entertainment/archive/2016/01/enter-the-grief-police/424746/.

Glyde, Tania. 2014. "The Recovery Position." *The Lancet Psychiatry* 1 (2): 119–120.

Gorer, Geoffrey. 1965. *Death, Grief and Mourning in Contemporary Britain*. London: Cresset Press.

Harnett, Emily. 2016. "Death and Emojis: How Grief Manifests on Social Media." *Broadly*, March 27. https://broadly.vice.com/en_us/article/xyebn3/death-and-emojis-how-grief-manifests-on-social-media.

Howarth, Glennys. 2000. "Dismantling the Boundaries Between Life and Death." *Mortality* 5 (2): 127–138.

———. 2007. *Death and Dying: A Sociological Introduction*. Cambridge: Polity.

Jones, Owen. 2018. "Grief Will Let Go Eventually: And Then I'll Remember Dad as He Was." *The Guardian*, May 12.

Kauffman, Jeffrey. 2008. "What Is 'No Recovery?'" *Death Studies* 32 (1): 74–83.

Klass, Dennis, Phyllis R. Silverman, and Steven L. Nickman (eds.). 1996. *Continuing Bonds: New Understandings of Grief*. London: Taylor & Francis.

Klein, Melanie. 1975 [1940]. "Mourning and Its Relation to Manic-Depressive States." In *Love, Guilt and Reparation and Other Works 1921–1945: The Writings of Melanie Klein Volume I*, 344–369. London: Hogarth Press.

Kübler-Ross, Elizabeth. 1970. *On Death and Dying*. London: Tavistock.
Lindemann, Eric. 1979 [1944]. *Beyond Grief: Studies in Crisis Intervention*. New York: Aronson.
Maciejewski, Paul K., and Holly G. Prigerson. 2017. "Prolonged, but Not Complicated, Grief Is a Mental Disorder." *The British Journal of Psychiatry* 211 (October): 189–191.
Mellor, P., and Shilling, C. 1993. "Modernity, Self-identity and the Sequestration of Death." *Sociology* 27 (3): 411–431.
Meltzer, Marisa. 2018. "How Death Got Cool." *The Guardian*, January 12.
O'Connor, Mary-Frances. 2005. "Bereavement and the Brain: Invitation to a Conversation Between Bereavement Researchers and Neuroscientists", *Death Studies* 29 (10): 905–922.
Paletti, Robin. 2008. "Recovery in Context: Bereavement, Culture, and the Transformation of the Therapeutic Self." *Death Studies* 32 (1): 17–26.
Parkes, Colin Murray. 1972. *Bereavement: Studies of Grief in Adult Life*. Harmondsworth: Penguin.
Pearce, Caroline. 2018. "Negotiating Recovery in Bereavement Care Practice in England: A Qualitative Study." *Bereavement Care* 37 (1): 6–16.
Penny, Laurie. 2016. "No More Heroes." *New Statesman*, December 28. https://www.newstatesman.com/2016/12/no-more-heroes.
Prigerson, Holly G., and Paul K. Maciejewski. 2017. "Rebuilding Consensus on Valid Criteria for Disordered Grief." *JAMA Psychiatry* 74 (5): 435.
Prigerson, Holly G., Mardi J. Horowitz, Selby C. Jacobs, Colin M. Parkes, Mihaela Aslan, Karl Goodkin, Beverley Raphael, Samuel J. Marwit, Camille Wortman, Robert A. Neimeyer, George Bonanno, Susan D. Block, David Kissane, Paul Boelen, Andreas Maercker, Brett T. Litz, Jeffrey G. Johnson, Michael B. First, and Paul K. Maciejewski. 2009. "Prolonged Grief Disorder: Psychometric Validation of Criteria Proposed for DSM-V and ICD-11." *PLoS Medicine* 6 (8): e1000121.
Reynolds, Charles F., Stephen J. Cozza, and Katherine Shear. 2017. "Clinically Relevant Diagnostic Criteria for a Persistent Impairing Grief Disorder: Putting Patients First." *JAMA Psychiatry* 74 (5): 433.
Robert, Martin, and Laura Tradii. 2017. "Do We Deny Death? I. A Genealogy of Death Denial." *Mortality*, online first.
Rose, Nikolas. 1985. *The Psychological Complex: Psychology, Politics and Society in England, 1869–1939*. London: Routledge & Kegan Paul.
———. 1989. *Governing the Soul: The Shaping of the Private Self*. London: Free Association Press.

———. 1998. *Inventing Our Selves: Psychology, Power and Personhood*. Cambridge: Cambridge University Press.

Seale, Clive. 1998. *Constructing Death: The Sociology of Dying and Bereavement*. New York: Cambridge University Press.

Seligson, Hannah. 2014. "An Online Generation Redefines Mourning." *The New York Times*, March 21.

Shear, M. Katherine. 2012. "Grief and Mourning Gone Awry: Pathway and Course of Complicated Grief." *Dialogues in Clinical Neuroscience* 14 (2): 119–128.

Sidhu, Kiran. 2015. 'A Dirty Secret Called Grief'. *The Guardian*, October 10.

Solon, Olivia. 2018. "How Close Are We to a Black Mirror-Style Digital Afterlife?" *The Guardian*, January 9.

Steinberg, Deborah Lynn. 2016. "Bowie, Diana, and Why We Mourn in Public." *The Conversation*, January 19. http://theconversation.com/bowie-diana-and-why-we-mourn-in-public-53396.

Stolorow, Robert D. 2014. "The War on Grief." *Psychology Today*, February 2. https://www.psychologytoday.com/gb/blog/feeling-relating-existing/201402/the-war-grief.

Stroebe, Margaret, and Henk Schut. 2005. "To Continue or Relinquish Bonds: A Review of Consequences for the Bereaved." *Death Studies* 29 (6): 477–494.

Stroebe, Margaret, Henk Schut, and Kathrin Boerner. 2017. "Cautioning Health-Care Professionals: Bereaved Persons Are Misguided Through the Stages of Grief". *Omega* 74 (4): 455–473.

Tedeschi, Richard G., and Lawrence G. Calhoun. 2008. "Beyond the Concept of Recovery: Growth and the Experience of Loss." *Death Studies* 32 (1): 27–39.

The Guardian. 2016. "The Guardian View on Celebrity Deaths: A Dramatic Meaning." *The Guardian*, December 27.

———. 2018. "Grief and the Importance of Listening to One Another." *The Guardian*, Letters, May 16.

The Lancet. 2012. "Living with Grief." *The Lancet* 379 (9816): 589.

Tradii, Laura, and Martin Robert. 2017. "Do We Deny Death? II. Critiques of the Death-Denial Thesis." *Mortality*, online first.

Turner, Victor. 1969. *The Ritual Process: Structure and Anti-structure*. Chicago: Aldine.

———. 1974. *Dramas, Fields, Metaphors: Symbolic Action in Human Society*. Ithaca and London: Cornell University Press.

———. 1982. *From Ritual to Theatre: The Human Seriousness of Play*. New York: Performing Arts Journal Publications.
Van Gennep, Arthur. 1960. *The Rites of Passage*. London: Routledge & Kegan Paul.
Varga, Mary Alice, and Trena M. Paulus. 2013. "Grieving Online: Newcomers' Constructions of Grief in an Online Support Group." *Death Studies* 38 (6): 443–449.
Wakefield, Jerome C. 2013a. "DSM-5 Grief Scorecard: Assessment and Outcomes of Proposals to Pathologize Grief." *World Psychiatry: Official Journal of the World Psychiatric Association* 12 (2): 171–173.
———. 2013b. "The DSM-5 Debate over the Bereavement Exclusion: Psychiatric Diagnosis and the Future of Empirically Supported Treatment." *Clinical Psychology Review* 33 (7): 825–845.
Wakefield, Jerome C., and Michael B. First. 2012. "Validity of the Bereavement Exclusion to Major Depression: Does the Empirical Evidence Support the Proposal to Eliminate the Exclusion in DSM-5?" *World Psychiatry: Official Journal of the World Psychiatric Association* 11 (1): 3–10.
Walter, Tony. 1994. *The Revival of Death*. London: Routledge.
———. 1999. *On Bereavement: The Culture of Grief*. Buckingham: Open University Press.
———. 2006. "What Is Complicated Grief? A Social Constructionist Perspective." *Omega: Journal of Death and Dying* 52 (1): 71–79.
Wetherell, Margaret. 2012. *Affect and Emotions: A New Social Science Understanding*. London: Sage.
World Health Organisation. 2018. *International Classification of Diseases, 11th Revision*. WHO.

2

Grief as a Psychological Object of Study

In this chapter, I review the key thinkers and theories that have populated the field of grief and bereavement research over the last century. This review begins chronologically to provide a brief history of the ideas that have sought to explain grief, from a largely western, psychological perspective, and their evolution into the expansive field of the study of grief and bereavement. I aim to show how some theories and models such as the work of Kübler-Ross (1970) and the five stages of grief remain popular to this day, while others either have lost favour or suffered from misinterpretation over time. The work of Freud (1917) is an exemplar of the latter case and is commonly where most literature reviews of grief and bereavement begin. However, I argue that the largely psychological field of contemporary grief research has inherited and reiterated overly simplistic renderings of Freud's writings in 'Mourning and Melancholia' where definitions of successful mourning are often still considered to be about 'letting go' and 'detaching' from the deceased. The dominance of psychological understandings of grief has, I demonstrate, led to particular ways of understanding grief as an individual intrinsic emotion. Crucially it configured recovery as a psychological process with various stages and tasks to 'work through.'

C. Pearce, *The Public and Private Management of Grief*,
https://doi.org/10.1007/978-3-030-17662-4_2

To contrast, I highlight the work of sociologists and anthropologists who critiqued this linear process view of grief and recovery by demonstrating the cultural variations in understandings and practices of grief and mourning, such as the 'continuing bonds' thesis of grief (Klass et al. 1996) and an interest in the stories of bereaved people, which its proponents argue is a more accurate means to capture how people experience and recover from grief (Walter 1996). I also discuss research into grief informed by the work of Foucault (Árnason and Hafsteinsson 2003, 2018; Foote and Frank 1999; Árnason 2001, 2007); to demonstrate the ways in which changes in theories of grief and recovery can be viewed alongside transformations in government rationality, where the aim of grief theories and practices is the production of autonomous and functional individuals. In closing, I consider the paradox that lies at the heart of grief theories and practices, that of the formation of a subject who is simultaneously autonomous and independent and yet liable to devastation at the death of another.

A Brief History of the Study of Grief

Freudian Beginnings

The academic study of grief is a relatively modern phenomenon with systematic research on death and dying only emerging in the aftermath of the Second World War (Small 2001). Grief study and its expression was previously the domain of the arts and literature (Archer 1999). The publication of Freud's essay 'Mourning and Melancholia' in 1917 is considered to be the first attempt at a 'scientific' understanding of grief, though Freud himself acknowledged his thoughts were not a claim to general validity and that the empirical material upon which his study was founded was 'insufficient' (Freud 1917, 243). In his essay, Freud sought to delineate the nature of the state of melancholia by comparing it to the condition of mourning. For Freud, the states of both mourning and melancholia shared the same causal influence: that of the loss of an object. The lost object was not only the loss of a person but could also be 'the loss of some abstraction which has taken the place of one, such as one's country, liberty, and ideal, and so on' (243). Melancholia was not strictly the consequence of failed mourning as it came to be understood in later research but rather this loss could be entirely abstract. Melancholia was characterised by:

> A profoundly painful dejection, cessation of interest in the outside world, loss of the capacity to love, inhibition of all activity, and a lowering of the self-regarding feelings to a degree that finds utterance in self-reproaches and self-revilings and culminates in a delusional expectation of punishment. (Freud 1917, 244)

The same traits were to be found in mourning aside from a disturbance in self-regard. What happened in melancholia was that the reproach one might feel towards a lost object was, in the absence of the object, turned inward appearing as a reproach against oneself, or in Freud's terms against one's ego. Freud viewed the psyche as structured into three parts: the 'ego,' the 'superego,' and the 'id.' The 'id' refers to the unconscious drives, composed of the life and death instincts. The life drive includes the 'libido,' which is often interpreted as referring to love or desire. The ego is the rational response between the id's unconscious urges and the societal norms and demands. The superego's function was to control the instincts of the id by incorporating the moral values of the society in which one is situated, learned from parents and others. The reproach one felt towards the other person that in their absence was turned against one's self, was an action of the 'libido.' The libido is always seeking out new connections. It is this belief that led Freud to suggest that the frustration of a desire caused by the absence of the object of desire turns back on to the person's ego, overwhelming it and causing a shadow of the object on the ego.

This understanding of how attachments and desire work framed the way Freud understood successful mourning. This was through a long and painful process of 'reality-testing' where 'each single one of the memories and expectations in which the libido is bound to the object is brought up and hyper-cathected' leading to a detachment of the libido so that the 'ego becomes free and inhibited again' (245). To understand the implications of this process there is a need to unpack some of the terms Freud used as well to put his ideas into the context of the rest of his work. First of all, 'reality-testing' involved recognising which aspects of the self were located in the dead person and retrieving them to better understand oneself. By contrast, in melancholia one does not know what she or he has lost: 'one cannot see clearly what it is that has been lost, and it is all the more reasonable to suppose that the patient cannot consciously perceive what he has lost either' (245). Melancholia is brought about by the inability to recognise not that someone has died but what she or he has lost in him or herself: 'he knows whom he has lost but not what he has lost in him' (245). The distinction then is that in melancholia what has been lost is withdrawn from consciousness, whereas in mourning the extent of loss is more or less apparent.

As I outline below, later theorists construed this to mean melancholia or the failure to mourn was largely caused by an inability to face the reality of the death. However, the question caused by the condition of melancholia: what it is that has been lost, also seeks the extent to which parts of the self, or ego, have been lost. Why this process is so difficult and prone to failure is because of the way in which objects of desire—a person or a perception of a person—become incorporated into oneself through a process Freud described as 'identification.' For Freud, all love relationships were fraught with ambivalence due to the way in which identification with an object meant the sustenance of one's existence was at least in part reliant upon the continuation and endurance of another object outside of oneself. The loss of the loved object thus brings that ambivalence, and the investment of one's expectations into another, out into the open, to be managed laboriously or experienced as a reproach towards oneself.

Klein (1940) in studies of child development and attachment prior to language further developed Freud's thoughts on mourning and melancholia, to understand mourning as the experience of losing one's internal 'good' objects. For Klein, the success of mourning in later life was dependent on how well the infant identified with a stable good object, which is in the form of the primary caregiver, and how these objects were internalised. The goal of development or recovery for Klein was the integration of good and bad recognising that they are located in the same person/object.

This process of identifying with an external object was crucial to the stability of the ego and its capacity to integrate experience. The loss of a loved person is one where the mourner feels he or she has lost their internal good objects as well. As Klein describes, '[h]e then feels that his internal "bad" objects predominate and his inner world is in danger of disruption' (353). Normal mourning seeks to reinstate the object as well as the internal objects that have been felt to be lost, therefore recovering what has been already attained in childhood. The splitting—as she called it—keeps the infant safe. Melancholia results when the experience of losing one's internal objects was not completed in childhood. The melancholic mourner fails to rebuild the disintegrated inner world and re-own the 'projective identification' that was lodged in the now deceased person.

For Klein and Freud, objects were mental images of a loved other that become internalised into the person's sense of self. Objects were not representative of the whole person but rather parts of the other that maintained and sustained the person's own self. Klein made the further distinction of recognising that objects can be 'good' and 'bad.' Furthermore, in Klein's theory it is possible to understand how objects go from good to bad in the event of bereavement. The melancholic figure is not then just holding on to lost objects but overwhelmed by bad objects, in part according to Klein because the first mourning as an infant was not completed.

In the theory of Freud and Klein, responses to bereavement, whether described as mourning or melancholia, seek to reconcile the same problem: the loss of a loved object. It is only that those expressions take different guises but are not inherently pathological. One reason why Freud might contend mourning is necessary is his explanation of the 'life drive.' In brief, the life drive is what impels the ego to preserve life—being alive—at all costs. Severing attachments to a dead object is thus more about the drive of the ego that is now faced with deciding 'whether it shall share this fate' (255). Mourning then is about the success of the life drive, of the ego, but this seems to leave unanswered why precisely the libido goes about directing its energies onto objects. The libido is formulated both as an energy independent of objects in which it can invest or divest itself whenever necessary and also as something that derives pleasure from, and is reconfigured by, the process of attaching to objects itself. So there's a contradiction in Freud but this is not Freud's contradiction alone. The paradox of why people form relationships only to have to mourn them is one that faces understandings of grief more generally, and one that, as will be demonstrated, has sought to be resolved through a variety of perspectives.

I return to Freud in Chapter 5 to discuss feminist interpretations of Freud that utilised his ideas quite differently. What remains important to mention here is that certain interpretations of Freud became the basis on which later work on grief was established, either affirming or rejecting his claims. Other academics have noted this disservice to Freud, as Small (2001, 25) argued, 'simply to talk about letting go and moving on … does not do justice to the idea of resolution presented by Freud.' Further, many have gone to pains to emphasise that Freud's intimation into what might be happening was not necessarily an invitation to do something about it (Granek 2013; Small and Hockey 2001). In fact, intervention into mourning was clearly opposed: 'We rely on its [mourning] being overcome after a certain lapse of time, and we look upon any interference with it as useless or even harmful' (Freud 1917, 244). The question I will seek to address in the rest of this chapter is why certain interpretations have survived and what or in whose interests they might serve.

Grief as a Syndrome

Whether influenced by Freud and the burgeoning community of psychoanalytic practitioners or as a consequence of the mass deaths suffered in the First and Second World Wars, the inter-war period saw an increase in research interest in grief that proposed categories of adjustment (Eliot 1932) and began to describe the process of grief, as well as focusing on recovery from war bereavement (Fulconer 1942). The psychiatrist Lindemann (1944) is commonly credited as carrying out the first systematic and empirical study of the symptoms of grief. In 1944 Lindemann published his article 'Symptomatology and management of acute grief' based upon 101 interviews he carried out largely on 'psychoneurotic' patients who were bereaved during their treatment, as well as relatives of hospital patients. Lindemann also spoke to survivors of the Coconut Grove nightclub fire in Boston in 1942. Lindemann's work is notable for the fact he described grief as a distinct syndrome with its own symptomology that needed to be worked through. Lindemann described grief as a universal syndrome that could be known and measured involving emotional and physical symptoms such as somatic distress, preoccupation with the image of the deceased, guilt, hostile reactions, and loss of patterns of conduct. What Lindemann's work sought to prove was a normal course of grief from which abnormal grief could be identified. Developing a universal symptomatology allowed grief to become a matter to be dealt with by psychiatry that could in turn aid people along the 'right' course. In fact, Lindemann was quite clear that grief was something only psychiatrists could assist with (Granek 2013, 59).

Establishing grief as a definite syndrome also had implications for what was considered a successful recovery. Grief required work and psychiatrists were encouraged to monitor whether people did the appropriate grief work, where grief work was understood as involving 'efforts at extricating himself (sic) from the bondage of the deceased and finding new patterns of rewarding interaction' (Lindemann 1944, 147). Echoes of Freud are clearly audible in this interpretation of grief work as implying a willing detachment from the deceased person, but Lindemann also emphasised the need to identify 'delayed' or 'absent' reactions to grief. Here Lindemann introduced the element of time into grief and its recovery, where grief was comprehensible as something that occurred and dissipated in a set time period. This also justified the need for intervention where the gaze of the psychiatrist could both identify and measure a person's movement along the now established normal course of grief.

Lindemann's research has since received criticism for the weakness of his methodology and lack of analysis. For example, Archer (1999) points out that Lindemann derived much of his argument from the Coconut Grove survivor accounts but they only made up 13 of the 101 participants. Methodological issues notwithstanding, Lindemann's work appeared to be driven by the ambitions of the psychiatric and psychological fields of practice at the time and the desire of both to establish themselves as scientific disciplines with procedures and classifications comparable to the rest of western medicine. Lindemann's work set forward an explanation of grief that subsequently became unquestioned: the idea of grief as distinct and measurable and involving a normal course from which any deviation was deemed to be abnormal. For some, grief becoming a matter for psychiatry and psychology provided new opportunities for research and practice, while in retrospect others, as Klass (2014) remarked, view Lindemann's study and its implications as contributing to a narrowing in understandings of grief in the twentieth century.

On the one hand, the expanding fields of psychology and psychiatry were changing the way grief was understood and managed, positioning grief as an object for psychiatric concern. On the other hand, influencing the management of grief was the declining significance of religion in the UK. This was the contention of Gorer's (1965) study first published in 1955. Gorer's research is notable by its absence in psychological reviews of the literature, though with his anthropological inclinations that may be unsurprising. Gorer carried out a survey of 359 people in the UK, 80 of whom took part in qualitative interviews. What was apparent from the survey and interview data was that there was a lack of religious belief and ritual in how people experienced or dealt with grief, leading Gorer to claim that people had lost the 'art' of grieving. Gorer, however, in line with his psychologist contemporaries still viewed grief as a psychological process. For Gorer, grief involved three stages: the initial stage of shock, followed by a period of intense mourning and withdrawal from the world, leading to a re-establishing of 'homeostasis.' Gorer also highlighted different 'styles of mourning' such as a 'denial' of mourning, 'hiding grief,' 'mummification,' and 'time-limited mourning.' For Gorer, religious and traditional rituals provided a time frame and activities for the mourning period, the absence of which led to 'unlimited mourning' or melancholia. As with Lindemann, time limits became an important measure of types of grief and Gorer suggested that time-limited mourning was the best means to achieving recovery or homeostasis. Gorer also viewed styles of mourning as subject to individual choice, drawing parallels with Lindemann's study where grief work became viewed as an individual action.

Gorer's work, like Lindemann's, received criticism for its clumsy and generalised analysis (Jalland 2010). However, what is evident from Gorer's study is the focus on individual patterns of mourning and time-limited mourning that resonated in later understandings of bereavement. The emphasis on establishing phases and time limits on acceptable and unacceptable grieving in turn served the interests of practitioners working within bereavement care. Having time limits and phases provides a rationale for intervention under the guise of assisting people along the healthy, normal course. Shortly after the publication of Gorer's study the first national bereavement charity Cruse Bereavement Care was established in the UK and the rise of the hospice movement witnessed the creation of the first modern hospice in 1967 at St Christopher's Hospice in South London. Bereavement care was growing into a profession in its own right, with its own designated institutions and organisations along with theories of bereavement, classifications and measures, and therapeutic interventions. Bereavement care practitioners, therefore, had a stake in perpetuating the relevance and demand for their services.

It is not without note that the research carried out into grief and bereavement over the twentieth century to the present day was, and is, overwhelmingly authored by psychologists and psychiatrists, and to a lesser extent, psychoanalysts. The growth of the field of bereavement care and research was situated within what Rose (1985, 1989) has described as the growth of the 'psy' disciplines: psychology, psychoanalysis and psychiatry. For Rose, the 'psy' disciplines were established in relation to organisational practices in many European states in the late nineteenth century that sought to organise people en masse according to particular objectives such as education, reform and cure. Later, the creation of the UK National Health Service necessitated the need to manage physical and mental health at the level of the population. The tools developed by psychology aided the institutionalisation of public health by constructing a psychological knowledge of the individual that through statistics and graphs showed 'normal' distribution and identified similarity and difference between individuals. The dominance of the field by a psychologically informed outlook, aimed to build an objective science of grief, shaping the concerns and the type of research that was produced.

Grief as a Process

The following two decades of grief research were marked by the pioneering work of Bowlby (1979, 1980), and further developed in the empirical studies carried out by the psychiatrist Parkes (1972, 2006; Parkes and Weiss 1983). Bowlby viewed grief as a biological reaction arising from natural selection. Bowlby's starting point was the idea already put forward by Darwin (1872) in his book *The Expression of the Emotions in Man and Animals* in which he sought to demonstrate how humans and animals both express emotions through similar facial expressions: these included grief. Grief was described as a universal emotion: one that was biologically programmed. Bowlby viewed grief as a separation response, a response that was first experienced in childhood. How people coped with bereavement in adulthood, Bowlby claimed, was largely determined by their experience of separation from their primary caregiver as a child. Bowlby described four phases of grief in adults: 'numbness,' 'yearning, searching and anger,' 'disorganisation and despair,' and 'reorganisation.' Bowlby provided the first successive phase model of grief setting a standard that soon became common practice. This was despite Bowlby's caveats that there should not be any time limits on grief nor were the phases to be considered discrete.

Parkes' work (1972), following from Bowlby, is often thought to have provided the beginning of a sound empirical basis for scientifically minded bereavement research (Archer 1999). Much of Parkes' initial research focused on the experience of widows, which led to the creation of a phase model that shared much similarity to Bowlby's original model. Parkes described grief as a process rather than a state, a process that involved a 'psychosocial transition.' This referred to the change in identity required in order to adjust to life without the significant other. Parkes also developed the concept of 'assumptive worlds' (1972) to describe how an individual's internal world ruptured in the face of loss. He argued that much of life is based on the security of what we can assume to be safely 'given.' Losing a significant partner results in the loss of that assumptive world. What is present in both Bowlby's and Parkes' work is an explanation of the relational nature of grief. The emphasis on the searching stage of grief, the separation anxiety caused by the other's absence, sought to bring to light a biological reasoning for the experience of grief. For Parkes (2006), grief was the 'cost of commitment.' Earlier in the chapter, I described how for Freud attachment to other people and objects was central to the drives of the libido. Bowlby's and Parkes' work provide further explanation for the role of attachment and its cost.

The legacy of Parkes' and Bowlby's research and writing however is that of supporting the development of a stage model of grief. The stage model soon became well-established in bereavement research and became a tool for researchers and practitioners alike to identify bereaved people along a linear course and recognise deviations. It therefore provided a basis for psychiatrists and psychologists on which to intervene. The stage model reached its pinnacle in Kübler-Ross' (1970) five stages of dying that were borrowed and applied to the grief process. It was perhaps the succinct nature of the five stages—'denial,' 'anger,' 'bargaining,' 'depression,' and 'acceptance'—which led to their popularity and prevalence not only within the field of bereavement care and research but in the popular imagination (Konisberg 2011). Davies (2005) noted how the popularity of Kübler-Ross' stages of dying coincided with a shift in palliative care where death was becoming increasingly professionalised and less domestic. From the 1960s onwards, Davies suggested, people were becoming less familiar with first-hand experience of death. The stages were of use in filling this 'experience gap' in people's lives. The early 1970s also witnessed the beginning of two of the key journals in the field: *Omega: The Journal of Death and Dying* and *Death Studies*. The study of death, dying and bereavement was growing in theory and practice with bereavement and the management of grief high on the research agenda. A recent overview of the history of publication trends in both *Death Studies* and *Omega* showed how research on grief and bereavement, largely quantitative, has overwhelmingly dominated the pages of both journals above other areas such as attitudes to death and dying and end-of-life care research (Wittkowski et al. 2015).

The next major contribution to the field came from Worden (1991). Worden developed a task model of bereavement in response to the stage model. Worden's task model set out four tasks the bereaved person was to accomplish in order to successfully resolve his or her grief. These tasks were: accepting the reality of a bereavement; experiencing the pain of grief or emotionally accepting the reality of the loss; adjusting to a new environment; withdrawing emotional energy from the deceased person and investing in new relationships. Worden (1991) later changed the last task to be concerned with relocating the dead person within one's life and finding ways to memorialise the person, pre-empting perhaps a move away from a model of detaching to one of 'continuing' bonds. The task model Worden described did not have to be completed in a set order and it allowed the bereaved person to become an active participant in their grief, whereas the phases implied passivity. However, the tasks also shifted responsibility for one's grief work onto the individual. Further, it provided bereavement practitioners with a set number of tasks to be accomplished before someone could be deemed 'recovered.' Worden's model shaped grief as something to be achieved and overcome individually yet accompanied by counsellors or other practitioners who could guide the individual to resolution. This emphasis on individual agency and responsibility for one's health and well-being, demonstrated through tasks and activities, echo early aspects of recent government policy on happiness, well-being and recovery, as discussed in Chapter 3.

Bowlby, Parkes and Worden's phases, stages and tasks remain influential in contemporary bereavement research and practice. All three figures and the results of their work emerged repeatedly in my interviews with bereavement counsellors, which it could be claimed is proof of their accuracy in describing grief. Alternatively, it could simply highlight how well suited such a phase or task-orientated model is to the counselling profession that requires both an assumed normal course from which to identify pathology and justify therapeutic intervention, and also a time-limited model of grief to suit the demands of the counselling endeavour.

The Need for Expert Help

The growth of psychology as a discipline and the tools and measures it developed provide an explanation of why grief, as it became an object of study for psychology, found its means of cure through psychological counselling interventions. Although the position of bereavement care across different settings and sectors is still undergoing clarification, the purpose of bereavement care is well supported, with bereavement viewed as an experience that has a detrimental impact on individual health. As Stroebe et al. (2007) argued, bereavement has been associated with excess risk of mortality and morbidity. Bereavement is often related to a host of mental and physical disorders from cancer and cardiovascular disease (Richardson et al. 2015) to attachment issues and depression (Harrison and Harrington 2001; Sbarra and Hazan 2008). The risks are not only to individual health but also to the national economy and society. A report (Stephen et al. 2014; SECOB Project Research Group 2013) sought to estimate the socioeconomic costs of bereavement in Scotland. Drawing on three secondary data sets, the researchers concluded that supporting spousal bereavement alone cost approximately £20 million annually, while bereavement has other detrimental economic costs in the number of people who drop out of employment and take bereavement leave. The National Council for Palliative Care, in partnership with the National Bereavement Alliance, published a paper in 2014 highlighting the need to address bereavement as a major public policy issue (National Council for Palliative Care 2014). The report entitled *Life After Death* cited the report from Scotland, estimating that England's annual costs to the economy were much higher, at around £150–190 million. With deaths predicted to rise 15% by 2035, the paper proposed six steps of action including a national review of the impact of financial, administrative and economic changes on those who have been bereaved and clear and organised rather than 'patchy' bereavement support.

The findings of these reports serve to reaffirm the belief in bereavement as both an individual and public health concern. The conventional response to this concern has been an increase in provision of bereavement counselling support. However, there is considerable debate and questioning among researchers over the empirical value of grief counselling and whether 'grief work' actually works (Jordan and Neimeyer 2003; Larson and Hoyt 2009; Schut 2010; Stroebe and Stroebe 1991). A number of reviews have claimed that grief counselling is ineffective and potentially harmful, finding that the 'scientifically demonstrated efficacy' of formal interventions for bereaved people is 'distressingly low': far below other types of psychotherapeutic intervention (Jordan and Neimeyer 2003). A more recent systematic review concurred with these findings, describing the overall quality of studies of bereavement intervention as 'poor' with results showing 'mixed effectiveness' (Waller et al. 2016). Counselling has become a standard response to all forms of traumatic event, yet as Groopman (2004) discussed, the benefits of the common procedure of 'debriefing' after traumatic events lacks scientific evidence.

However, the need for bereavement counselling and support is portrayed by bereavement organisations, not as politically or economically directed, but as driven by those experiencing bereavement themselves. This belief is supported to an extent by empirical evidence such as the nationwide survey conducted by organisation *Dying Matters* that polled 2058 adults in the UK and which revealed that one in five (21%) bereaved people reported wanting to talk about their grief but could not find anyone to listen (Dying Matters 2014). These findings highlight at least some need for listeners in the event of bereavement, albeit not a universal need and, indeed, not necessarily listeners with expertise. This concurs with the common understanding in counselling work, repeated by the bereavement counsellors interviewed for this book, that maintains that the client has to be willing to talk and do the work, otherwise the role of the counsellor is redundant.

An alternative way of thinking about this 'need' to receive counsel, or be listened to, could be construed as the result of an increasing reliance on the psychological sciences to provide remedy to the troubles of daily existence. For Rose (1998), the authority of psychology is justified through its claims to the truth of persons and their mental states. Rose argued the 'techne' of the confessional was employed by psychology and created the emphasis on talking therapies in overcoming mental distress.

A new relationship between psychological experts and those who consult them was thus formed, what Rose (1998) described as a kind of 'discipleship.' Bereavement counselling is thus another extension of the 'psychologisation' of everyday life. The need for a therapeutic response to grief becomes self-explanatory once those who have been bereaved come to understand and relate to themselves and their grief as matters of the psyche to be resolved via a working through of the emotions.

The early and mid-twentieth century had already laid down some solid foundations in bereavement research that configured grief as a concern for the 'psy' disciplines. This was achieved by identifying a normal course of grief, initiated by Freud and elaborated by Lindemann, that allowed for the demarcation of abnormal forms of grief. Detecting and classifying abnormal forms of grief provided psychologists and psychiatrists with a basis for therapeutic interventions, the shape of which was defined by the clarification of the grief process into phases, stages and tasks. Next, I describe how this established 'risk factors' for certain types of bereavement as well as the formation of certain types of grief as a psychiatric disorder. Within the creation of multiple models of grief, recovery emerged as something prescribed whether through tasks or monitored on a linear process of phases, and as something to be achieved within a given time period. All the while though grief was assumed as a universal phenomenon, a natural response to death. Yet at the same time grief required work whether from the bereaved individual alone or accompanied by a counsellor or expert. This paradox sits uneasily through the psychological accounts described so far as well as in the research that followed it, as I discuss now.

A 'New Dawn' of Bereavement Research?

Towards the end of the twentieth-century, researchers and practitioners influenced by sociological and anthropological studies of grief and bereavement began to question the orthodoxy of the stage model of grief. The stage theories of grief were criticised for being too rigid and not capturing the complexity and diversity of the grief experience. What followed was a 'new dawn' of bereavement research (Hall

2014; Rothaupt and Becker 2007) that proposed non-linear models of grief, and where psychologists sought to emphasise how people construct meaning from loss and how people continue rather than relinquish bonds with the deceased. This 'revolutionary phase' (Walter 1999) emerged in light of several critiques of the stage models that put the notion of a 'normal' process of grief into question.

Rosenblatt et al. (1976) in their book *Grief and Mourning in Cross-Cultural Perspective* sought to demonstrate how grief was dealt with in different cultures. Their efforts went some way to destabilising the idea that grief had a universal process of recovery, however, they still assumed that grief itself was a universal emotion, which consisted of a set number of symptoms. Wortman and Silver (1989) went further to undermine the assumptions that had already become ingrained in bereavement research and practice, by outlining some of the 'myths' about grief such as the assumption that every person bereaved will feel distress or that the absence of reactions is pathological. They also criticised the idea of 'grief work,' as did Stroebe and Stroebe (1991) who argued that the need to do grief work was a 'truism' rather than empirically founded. Stroebe and Stroebe discovered in a study of 60 widows and widowers that avoiding the loss can actually be more beneficial for long-term outcomes. Furthermore, Rodgers and Cowles (1991) highlighted that the growing lack of consensus concerning the parameters of 'normal' grief, seriously jeopardised any attempts to discuss aberrations from the expected response.

Later, in 1999 Stroebe and Schut set out their 'dual process model of coping with bereavement' (Stroebe and Schut 1999) which intended to critique the 'grief work hypothesis' that formed part of the stage theories of grief. The dual process model suggested that people oscillate in their grief from a 'restoration-orientation' to 'loss-orientated' activities. A loss orientation would be characterised with facing the loss and focusing on emotions. The restoration-orientation would be where the person would focus on new activities, distractions from their grief and build new roles and identity. The aim of the model was to counteract the idea that grief had to progress, and Stroebe and Schut argued that people experienced grief as an oscillation between two different modes. Further, the dual process model aimed to highlight how people continued bonds with the deceased person, an idea proposed by another highly influential new theory of grief: the continuing bonds thesis.

Continuing Bonds

Klass et al. (1996) in their edited collection, *Continuing Bonds: New Understandings of Grief*, argued that psychological theories of grief had thus far emphasised the importance of detaching from the deceased person as the means to successful recovery. In the introduction to the book Klass et al. (1996) instead proposed 'that it is normative for mourners to maintain a presence and connection with the deceased, and that this presence is not static' (17). Their argument was in direct reference to the work of Freud, Bowlby and Parkes, which they viewed as stating that severing ties was the only way to resolve grief. These models, Klass et al. (1996) claimed, were based on a view of the self and the world that saw people as separate from each other. They promoted a modern western world view that prized autonomy and independence and judged dependence as 'bad' (14). Silverman and Klass called for recovery to be replaced with 'accommodation,' a term that captured how people incorporated past relationships into their ongoing lives.

The idea of continuing bonds certainly had an impact on how grief was theorised, yet I suggest that Klass et al.'s argument was not as revolutionary as it was made to appear. Throughout the work of Freud, and also that of Bowlby and Parkes, are attempts to articulate the problem that loss poses to human attachments. Grief emerges precisely because it is believed that human attachment is a vital, if not a biological, imperative. So while the stage theories of grief came to be interpreted in a way that emphasised 'separateness,' the models were based around the belief that humans were already inherently dependent on others. Furthermore, the continuing bonds theory itself does not overcome this problem, as Árnason (2012) has noted, to continue bonds still assumes a prior separation. The starting point of the continuing bonds theory is the grieving person who experiences the presence of the deceased, which suggests that what gets continued is a matter of choice by the bereaved person. However, the very question of what precisely is continued and what is relinquished remains a matter of debate (Field and Filanosky 2009; Stroebe and Schut 2005). After all, continued bonds in the form of being haunted by the deceased might be quite unpleasant and somewhat problematic in finding the means to safely accommodate the deceased into one's life. Continuing bonds thus became about how living people can make choices about the ways in which they might incorporate dead person, whether through keeping photographs on display in the home or carrying out rituals that celebrate and honour the dead. The continuing bonds theory, then, was not necessarily one with the notion of human interdependence at its centre, as it shaped presence only as an inner relationship with the deceased, one that the individual has a level of control over. In this way, the work of Klass et al. served to affirm the western values of the autonomous agency and individual choice they originally sought to critique.

Meaning-Making and Stories

Finding a way to continue a relationship with the deceased person might be one way to make the experience of grief meaningful. Neimeyer (2005; Neimeyer et al. 2010) has claimed that finding meaning from loss is the principal task in coping with grief. His work is grounded in the belief that humans are by nature meaning-making beings who need to make sense of their world and build a coherent narrative. Bereavement is an instance, Neimeyer has argued, that challenges established beliefs about the world and people struggle to assimilate the loss into their existing self-narratives. Neimeyer (2005) recommends that successful recovery from loss is achieved by reconstructing new narratives through techniques of 'narrative retelling' and 'therapeutic writing.' Meaning reconstruction is about 'benefit finding,' so that loss can actually serve to strengthen meaning. The failure to reconstruct meaning is associated with chronic and complicated forms of grief. This method thus lends itself well to therapeutic intervention as counsellors can aid the bereaved person to reconstruct meaning through retelling the story of the death and finding new narratives. What remains unclear in Neimeyer's work is what types of meaning are to be constructed.

Meaning is assumed as a neutral good, but of course having a purpose in life can be directed to many different things, not all that might be beneficial. Meaning is also posited as a thing to be found rather than, as the event of a meaningless death suggests, one constructed story of events, a story that is unstable and always in flux. At the heart of the meaning-making endeavour then, is the belief in universal meanings and values, where narratives are tools to find the 'truth.'

Walter (1996), in the first volume of the interdisciplinary journal of death, dying and bereavement *Mortality*, claimed to have found a 'new model of grief' that went against the 'clinical lore' of past bereavement research. Walter's model shared many parallels with new approaches to grief in psychology and the emphasis on continuing bonds and constructing meaning, in that he described how the work of grief should be about constructing a 'durable biography' of the deceased. The aim was to create a true and accurate picture of the deceased in order to integrate the deceased into one's life. This was in contrast to dealing with or expressing emotions. For Walter, healing was achieved not through emotion work but through talking about the deceased with others. Walter's model received criticism from others (Footman 1998; Mclaren 1998; Stroebe 1997) who argued that the ideas of talking about the deceased in order to integrate their memory was already part of common counselling practice.

Furthermore, Walter's model, in striving to build an 'accurate' picture of the deceased, suffered the same shortcomings as the meaning-making approach in that both relied upon the idea that talking about the deceased can construct a 'true' biography or retelling of the deceased. Árnason (2000) pointed out that what is being constructed is not a biography but stories about the deceased, and that these stories are a creative achievement rather than reflecting reality. The stories people tell about the deceased are as much about the bereaved storyteller as they are the person who died. People use devices such as emplotment and build characters to convey their stories. Within stories then, different truths about grief are to be found and these are constantly changing with each retelling. As Valentine (2008) also demonstrated, narratives are socially constructed; people draw on cultural scripts to express their meanings. Narratives and stories thus reveal a complex interplay between the private experience of grief and cultural discourses about grief. Telling one's story is a strategy to preserve the personhood of the dead but it is also a mode of reaffirming the personhood of the living. Walter drew on the work of sociologist Giddens (1991) who argued that late modern western society has witnessed the rise of individualism where individual identity has become a reflexive project no longer tied to traditions of the past but freed to be shaped by individual choice and agency. The imperative to individually story one's experience of grief, as well to memorialise individuals is part of this reflexive project of the self, where identity becomes something to be constantly worked upon, and preserving individual legacy becomes paramount.

A Medical Model of Grief

While the focus on continuing bonds and narrating meaning remains strong in current bereavement counselling practice, the dominant research agenda reaffirms psychologists' originating desire to establish a scientifically measurable definition of the normal and abnormal course of grief. As mentioned in the introductory chapter, research seeking to define the categories of 'complicated grief' and 'prolonged grief disorder' has dominated psychiatric and psychological research into grief and bereavement over the past two decades (Horowitz et al. 1997; Prigerson et al. 1995, 1996; Zisook and Shear 2009). In an edited volume dedicated to complicated grief, Stroebe et al. (2013) remarked that: 'In our view complicated grief is perhaps the most important contemporary topic of concern both for the scientific community of bereavement researchers and for health care professionals supporting bereaved people' (3). With the inclusion of the category 'prolonged grief disorder' (PGD) in the 11th edition of the International Classification of Diseases (ICD-11) and 'persistent complex bereavement disorder' (PCBD) featured in the DSM-5 for further research, abnormal forms of grief are becoming not only theories but also recognisable psychiatric diagnoses to be implemented in practice. In the studies, successful mourning is described in much the same terms: to be re-engaged in daily life, reconnected to others, to experience hope for a future, for grief to be transformed and integrated. Equally, symptoms of complicated grief mirror those of 'normal grief' such as: intense yearning, intrusive and preoccupying thoughts, loss of meaning in life, incessant questioning and ruminating, caught up in counterfactual thinking rather than reflecting on the reality of death. Yet the emphasis is on the length of time the 'symptoms' are shown and the 'level of impairment' to social functioning (Stroebe et al. 2013).

Arguably, the ambitions Lindemann first set out in his study in 1944 have now reached fulfilment. Previous research that sought to uncover the normal process of grief has enabled the discovery of complicated or prolonged grief. By continuing in the assumption of the existence of a normal course of grief, the identification of abnormal forms was made possible. Furthermore, the normal course of grief is described as an instinctive psychological mechanism that humans possess in order to heal after loss (Shear 2012). Complicated grief emerges specifically when there is difficulty in progressing through the natural healing process (Zisook and Shear 2009). The normal course of grief is time-bound to six months, persisting in grief longer is an instance of grief becoming 'derailed.' Intervention is thus warranted as a means to get people 'back on track.' After all, states Shear (2012), it would be 'inhumane to leave such anguish untreated.' Shear further describes how bereavement is analogous to an injury where grief is the 'inflammatory response' and complicated grief the 'superimposed infection.'

Debates continue over what complicated grief involves; one might expect that if normal grief were instinctive and measurable, complicated grief also would be self-evident. Yet whatever constitutes 'normal grief' remains just as contested. However, even those that seek to critique the empirical validity of the diagnostic category of complicated grief (Wakefield 2013; Walter 2006) agree that it does exist. In addition, bereavement has now become a focus of neuroscientific research which claims that complicated grief patterns can be identified in the brain (O'Connor 2005, 2012; Gündel et al. 2003). A study by O'Connor et al. (2008) asserted that in people with complicated grief the part of the brain associated with rewards was activated when viewing a picture of their dead loved one, leading researchers to argue that complicated grief is prolonged partly because people find pleasure in reveries over the deceased.

Biological explanations for successful recovery from grief are present too in the growing research interest in resilience. Bonnano and colleagues (Bonanno 2004, 2009, 2016; Bonanno and Keltner 1997) have argued that the majority of people who experience grief have a brief period of distress and then return to functioning at the same level as before. This, claims Bonnano, is due to the fact that most people are naturally resilient to difficult conditions including bereavement. Bonnano's claims have disputed the idea that people go through stages and phases. In a study that analysed facial expressions, Bonnano and Keltner (1997) questioned the need to carry out grief work and concluded that avoiding emotions in grief leads to better adjustment.

Interestingly, while talk of recovery has lost favour in bereavement research, resilience is growing in popularity (Sandler et al. 2008). Balk (2007) described his confusion over this, as resilience implies an even speedier return to normal than recovery. Further, Balk questioned where the element of personal growth was in resilience. However, Balk viewed grief and recovery as a moral endeavour, whereas the discourse of resilience seeks scientific reasoning for how people respond differently to bereavement. To claim people are naturally resilient makes sense when grief is a natural and instinctual process. Yet if this were so, then there would be little requirement for bereavement counselling and models of grief. Hence complicated forms of grief provide pathology for the 'psy' disciplines to focus on and justify interventions. The prominence of research on resilience might be less about instinctual reactions and more about a social context that commends the type of traits resilience involves. In either case, increasing reference is made to the brain and biology to provide the explanation for why people succeed or fail in their recovery from grief. This is quite a different notion to thinking about constructing stories and narratives and finding meaning. What remains from this 'new dawn' of bereavement research is a combination of both a broadening in perspective on how grief is conceptualised and a move away from the grief process, yet an increasing medicalisation of grief that relies upon the presumed normal course of grief that many others have rejected. Subsequently, there has been a polarisation of certain forms of grief as abnormal, justifying the need for psychiatric intervention.

The Social Construction of Grief

In this section, I turn away from psychology and psychiatry to explore ideas that have questioned the belief that grief is a natural process by emphasising the ways in which grief is shaped and policed by different societal influences. As outlined in the previous sections, the psychological canon of grief research made it appear as though Freud was the culprit for promoting a particular definition of grief, yet research from the historical, sociological and anthropological disciplines presents a different picture.

Historical perspectives on grief and grieving culture have illuminated how grief might be considered as at least to some extent culturally constructed. Stearns and Knapp (1996) present how a rich Victorian grief culture was in various ways unseated by modernity. Stearns and Knapp, and the historical work of Jalland (2010), have demonstrated that the changing attitudes towards grief and the management of grief over the nineteenth to twentieth century were not quite the simple narrative proposed in some work. Rather the shift in emotional culture emerged as a reaction against Victorian sentimental grief practices which Stearns and Knapp illustrated through an 'anti-grief' campaign that featured in middle-class popular commentary in newspapers and magazines. The shift was also framed by Enlightenment ideals that regarded excessive grief as unnecessary, as well as religious beliefs in the survival of the soul, which outpourings of grief appeared to contradict. This increasingly modernist and pragmatic outlook on emotions was reinforced by the ubiquity of death that occurred during the First World War that called for people to maintain self-control over their grief.

Yet as Stearns, Knapp and Jalland all emphasise, how grief was experienced did not change, however, the changes in societal norms did foster a disjuncture between the private experience of grief and the changing social prescriptions. In this view, there still remained some belief in the reality of the experience of grief apart from its social norms. Indeed, work that explored the social construction of grief tends to either retain the assumption that grief is natural while granting its cultural differentiation (Klass et al. 1996; Rosenblatt et al. 1976) or alternatively view grief as something that is produced by cultural norms to the extent that it is not possible to speak of grief as a purely or inherently 'natural' experience (Foote and Frank 1999). A Durkheimian perspective takes the latter view to the extreme, as for Durkheim all emotions were socially produced: 'Mourning is not the spontaneous expression of individual emotions … it is a duty imposed by the group' (Durkheim 1915, 397). Durkheim's work on suicide was highly significant in presenting how society produced behaviours, by arguing that a state of 'anomie' is caused by alienation from society not a dysfunctional pathology in the individual psyche. Yet, because for Durkheim human behaviours were socially produced and to be understood by reference to the social group of which people belong, the biological individuality of human beings was downplayed, overlooking why people require interdependence in the first place that leads to a state of anomie.

However, sociological perspectives on grief have tended to rest their analysis on the belief that grief is a universal human emotion. Jakoby's (2012) notable proposal for understanding grief as a social emotion highlighted how grief is framed by cultural rules and affected by social structures, yet her theory still depended on the belief that grief is an 'elementary human experience' and integral to human life. Jakoby's contention was concerned with the argument that grief involves a higher order of cognitive processes than simply a reaction to biological separation. Grief is a social emotion because it 'emerges from relationships, attachments, expectations, and obligations' (Jakoby 2012, 680). The work of Klass and Rosenblatt (Klass 2014; Rosenblatt 2008) has provided many rich examples of the way in which different cultures manage grief in diverse ways. In their research, the focus is on the diversity of the grief responses and rituals but there is no question that the feeling and emotion of grief is the same. Interestingly, Rosenblatt's perspective on grief shifted in his later works. In his remarks here, it is possible to see how Rosenblatt was beginning to see how whatever individual grief was, it could not be separated from the cultural context: 'Culture is such a crucial part of the context of bereavement that it is often impossible to separate an individual's grief from culturally required mourning' (Rosenblatt 1993, 104). More recently in an interview in *Bereavement Care* Rosenblatt (Rosenblatt and Bowman 2013) spoke openly about how when he first began publishing work on grief he thought he had a clear understanding of grief but now critiques research that assumes grief as an identifiable 'thing.' Grief is not a discrete object, he argues, but a 'sociolinguistic construction.' In Rosenblatt's view, much contemporary work features a great deal of assertiveness and definiteness about what grief is that implies there is an underlying commonality across grieving.

The Policing of Grief

Rosenblatt's change of perspective highlights how grief is often taken as self-evident even in work that seeks to emphasise the cultural and social influences on grief. Sociological perspectives on grief have striven to relocate grief in a social context by focusing on the social norms around types of death, the 'hierarchy' of grief and how grief responses are managed (Charmaz and Milligan 2006; Lofland 1985; Robson and Walter 2013; Walter 2007, 2010). Lofland's (1985) article, for example, questioned the universality of grief by emphasising the social shaping of grief, yet as important as her argument is, grief was still positioned as a 'thing' upon which social structures or cultural norms have a lesser or greater level of influence. Because of this, studies that look at the social construction of grief tend to view the social as an additional factor that explains variability in how grief is done, but not of what grief is.

This work is certainly not without its value, often emerging in response to the dominant 'clinical lore' of the psychological definition of grief (Walter 1999). Walter (1999) described the ways in which grieving was policed in modern and postmodern Western societies, adopting a broadly Durkheimian view that emotions, namely grief, are disruptive to modern rational industrial society and so require policing or managing. The 'anomie' that can result from feeling alienated from one's social group is underlined in modern societies where there is an absence or decline in traditional mourning rituals to help the grieving person through grief. Instead, postmodern society encourages a mode of self-policing one's grief as part of the individual reflexive project of self of which the maintenance of a coherent self-narrative is part.

There is a large body of work that has described a condition of 'disenfranchised grief' that is seen to occur when someone's grief is not socially acceptable or recognised (Doka 1989). Proponents of disenfranchised grief theory propose that all grief should be considered in equal terms and that restrictive social norms around grief should be eradicated. As Fowlkes (1990) described, different types of losses are assigned differential social merit. Some losses are conferred a socially legitimate right to grieve while others are not. For Fowlkes, these normative criteria have implications for how people experience grief and what role they are assigned, thus forming a hierarchy of grief. Walter and Robson (2013) argued against the very concept of disenfranchised grief itself by stating that a person can undergo a 'process of disenfranchisement' but grief itself cannot be 'disenfranchised.' Walter and Robson (2013) instead argued that norms are essential to grieving and that all losses are not equal and thus hierarchies of grief are required to determine appropriate responses to grief.

It seems that at the centre of discussions of disenfranchised grief is the need for social recognition and the consequences of failing to be recognised. This suggests that dealing with grief is an interdependent and socially informed activity. A hierarchy of types of loss expects different modes of behaviour and emotional expression appropriate to each loss. The hierarchy is thus constructed and maintained through an understanding of what lives are considered 'grievable.' To be considered grievable one has to have been recognised as living a 'life worth living' while they were alive (Butler 2004). As Walter and Robson comment, to grieve too little or too much might require careful presentation of the self to appear to be grieving appropriately and thus elicit the appropriate responses from those around them. The grieving individual therefore might be recognised via the hierarchy yet might also still feel a sense of disenfranchisement due to the gap in felt emotion and the emotions they present to others.

The Disciplining of Grief

I now go on to discuss work that sought to question the 'truth claims' of the psychological and psychiatric theories of grief. Curiously, psychologists tend to be blind to the effects of their own theories on the concept of grief, so much so that when they seek to outline the social and cultural nature of grief and how cultural contexts 'oppress' or 'police' expressions of grief they neglect to identify how counselling or therapeutic interventions contribute new regulatory norms and perpetuate existing ones (Harris 2010; Neimeyer et al. 2014). It is apparent in this lack of reflexivity that psychologically informed theories of grief are understood not in the same terms as cultural discourses about grief but as revealing a fundamental 'truth' about grief.

Wambach's study (1985) presented what happens when the construct that was supposed to reflect reality becomes more real than the actual reality that it purported to demonstrate. In her study of widow support groups, she found that the grief process, composed of stages, was taken as a factual account of the experience of grief. When Wambach herself sought to challenge the order of the process she was dismissed by the participants who retorted: 'You can tell you've never been through it' (204). Often the women's experience would contradict the stages, which caused distress and yet the process was so naturalised most widows did not realise the grief process had an origin and was a social creation. Instead, the process was a means to monitor themselves against a timetable and to judge their progress.

Foote and Frank (1999) adopted a Foucauldian approach in their analysis of bereavement counselling and theory. They argued that grief was a 'site of disciplinary power' upon which claims about the truth of grief were made. These claims, they argued, were productive in Foucault's sense of the word, in that certain claims on the truth of grief, such as the grief process, create bereaved people as 'docile' subjects. This was demonstrated in Wambach's (1985) study where the women began to monitor their own progress against a timetable they assumed was true. For Foote and Frank, the bereaved become objects of knowledge to be known by therapy and shaped by therapeutic knowledge. This, they claim, reiterating sentiments expressed earlier in this chapter, was possible because of an assumption of normal grief upon which the clinical criteria of abnormality could be established, criteria that continue to expand until the normal is defined out of existence. The normal thus remains less a reality than a therapeutic ideal. Yet the normal is required to support the technology that relies upon it. As discussed in this chapter, therapeutic intervention in bereavement has been based on the premise that there are normal and abnormal responses to death and loss. This division, argue Foote and Frank, must exist in order to demarcate the abnormal as the legitimate object of therapeutic intervention: 'Abnormal is what can be brought back to normal by means of therapeutic fixing' (164). Further, Foote and Frank suggest complicated grief could be interpreted as an 'embodied refusal' to adhere to the norms of bereavement.

Árnason's work (2001, 2007; Árnason and Hafsteinsson 2003, 2018) also employed a Foucauldian perspective in his ethnographic research of the bereavement counselling organisation Cruse Bereavement Care carried out in the late 1990s. Árnason explored how bereavement counselling produced certain ideas and 'truths' about grief and served to produce bereaved clients as individual autonomous beings 'encouraged to govern themselves, as befits a liberal and democratic regime' (2007, 49). What Árnason demonstrated was the notion of personhood implicated in bereavement counsellors' understanding of grief and emotions. It is a paradoxical personhood that is both individual and autonomous yet liable to devastation at the death of another. Árnason's study linked together the management of grief in Cruse and the theories it used with the discourse of neo-liberal governmentality. Bereavement counselling was viewed as a technology through which individuals learned to govern themselves and their emotions in accordance with political processes of subjectification. Contrary to theories and practices of grief that assumed an idea of personhood as individual and autonomous with a need to express emotions, Árnason argued this was an idea of the self that was produced through techniques such as bereavement counselling. In response to Walter's claim of the postmodern 'revival of death' that emphasised choice, individuality and a liberation from previous restrictive norms, Árnason and Hafsteinsson (2003) highlighted how, to describe the postmodern revival of death as the efforts of ordinary people to express their emotions freely, 'is not only to naturalise the need for emotional expression but misses sight of the effects of neo-liberal governmentality' (59). Bereavement counselling was a device for meaning production, one that naturalised the notion of the self and its emotional expression, as individuals with an 'inner' emotional life. This links to an earlier point referring to the rising interest in narrating stories as a means to recovery. The belief that stories can liberate someone from trauma depends upon the assumption of this particular notion of personhood that needs to tell one's story and will find autonomy and freedom in doing so, an idea I return to in Chapter 3.

In this section, I have presented how the psychological notions of grief have been criticised and relocated to a social context to highlight how grief is shaped, regulated and policed. Throughout much of this work however, grief is still positioned as a 'thing' upon which the social has its influence to varying degrees. Grief is universal, but its recovery is context-dependent. Complicated grief is then a consequence of a missing, inadequate or twisted larger cultural response (Klass 2014). However, as elucidated by Árnason, the ethos of bereavement counselling produces a certain type of personhood, a personhood that coincides with neo-liberal governmentality.

Conclusion

In this chapter, I have traced the growth of research into grief and bereavement to unpack how grief has been theorised and the implications this has had for notions of recovery. Throughout there has been an assumption of a certain type of person who has a natural, instinctive capacity to grieve. Árnason's work mentioned above has critiqued this type of personhood through the example of bereavement counselling to explore how an autonomous, individual subjectivity is produced and naturalised. Throughout the psychological theories of grief was an absence of critical reflection on both what type of person is being assumed in the models and further what type of person might be produced through therapeutic interventions. What emerged was a paradoxical figure, first highlighted in Freud, who seeks attachment as a means of survival but in the event of losing the loved object, must regain autonomy in order to recover successfully. This is an autonomy that appears to prefigure the bereavement and yet to feel grief it would imply that one must have already relinquished one's autonomy by entering into relationality.

It would seem from much of the work reviewed in this chapter that this paradox is a biological one. Yet from an evolutionary perspective grief poses a puzzle. Grief can be construed as a by-product of natural selection, which, as Bowlby sought to demonstrate, was an important reaction to separation. Anxiety and distress at the separation of a primary caregiver was an adaptive response, as their absence poses a threat to survival. However, it is clear that grief is not considered to have any adaptive function. Rather grief is widely viewed as maladaptive, hence the wealth of studies outlined in this chapter that have sought to remedy its negative effects on the morbidity of the population. Thus the puzzle grief poses might explain why some have viewed grief as a disease or pathology (Engel 1961). Archer (1999) concluded that grief is a 'trade-off,' and, like Parkes, viewed grief as the cost incurred 'in pursuit of something which has an important adaptive consequence' (250).

Grief is a response, suggests Archer, 'an alarm reaction set of by a deficit signal in the behavioural system underlying attachment' (153). This alarm reaction involves a link between evolutionary principles and a behavioural mechanism that is characterised by the strength of the attachment. As Darwin claimed, it is not only humans who show signs of grieving. Studies have sought to explain that animals grieve in similar ways to humans (King 2013). This appears to suggest that there is a common evolutionary response to absence. However, it is also clear that the forms grief and its recovery takes are strongly culturally determined. It is pertinent to ask then, how and why 'prolonged' or maladaptive forms of grief occur. For, if grief is a natural response, why does grief require 'work,' and why does its recovery take 'unnatural' forms?

References

Archer, John. 1999. *The Nature of Grief: The Evolution and Psychology of Reactions to Loss*. New York: Routledge.

Árnason, Arnar. 2000. "Biography, Bereavement, Story." *Mortality* 5 (2): 189–204.

———. 2001. "Experts of the Ordinary: Bereavement Counselling in Britain." *Journal of the Royal Anthropological Institute* 7 (2): 299–313.

———. 2007. "'Fall Apart and Put Yourself Together Again': The Anthropology of Death and Bereavement Counselling in Britain." *Mortality* 12 (1): 48–65.

———. 2012. "Individuals and Relationships: On the Possibilities and Impossibilities of Presence." In *Emotion, Identity and Death*, edited by Douglas Davies and Chang-Won Park, 59–70. Surrey: Ashgate.

Árnason, Arnar, and Sigurjón Baldur Hafsteinsson. 2003. "The Revival of Death: Expression, Expertise and Governmentality." *British Journal of Sociology* 54 (1): 43–62.

———. 2018. *Death and Governmentality in Iceland: Neo-Liberalism, Grief and the Nation-Form*. Reykjavík: University of Iceland Press.

Balk, David E. 2007. "A Modest Proposal About Bereavement and Recovery." *Death Studies* 32 (1): 84–93.

Bonanno, George A. 2004. "Loss, Trauma, and Human Resilience: Have We Underestimated the Human Capacity to Thrive After Extremely Aversive Events?" *American Psychologist* 59 (1): 20–28.

———. 2009. *The Other Side of Sadness: What the New Science of Bereavement Tells Us About Life After Loss*. New York, NY: Basic Books.

———. 2016. "Resilience in the Face of Potential Trauma." *Current Directions in Psychological Science* 14 (3): 135–138.

Bonanno, George A., and Dacher Keltner. 1997. "Facial Expressions of Emotion and the Course of Conjugal Bereavement." *Journal of Abnormal Psychology* 106 (1): 126–137.

Bowlby, John. 1979. *The Making and Breaking of Affectional Bonds*. London: Tavistock.

———. 1980. *Attachment and Loss Volume III: Loss, Sadness and Depression*. London: Hogarth Press.

Butler, Judith. 2004. *Precarious Life: The Powers of Mourning and Violence*. London: Verso.

Charmaz, Kathy, and Melinda J. Milligan. 2006. "Grief." In *The Handbook of the Sociology of Emotions*, edited by Jan Stets and Jonathan H. Turner, 516–538. New York: Springer.

Darwin, Charles. 1872. *The Expression of the Emotions in Man and Animals*. London: John Murray.

Davies, Douglas J. 2005. *A Brief History of Death*. Oxford: Blackwell.

Doka, Ken J. (ed.). 1989. *Disenfranchised Grief: Recognising Hidden Sorrow*. Lexington, MA: Lexington Books.

Durkheim, Emile. 1915. *The Elementary Forms of the Religious Life*. London: George Allen & Unwin.

Dying Matters. 2014. *Public Attitudes to Bereavement Survey*. London: ComRes.

Eliot, Thomas D. 1932. "The Bereaved Family." *Annals of the American Academy of Political and Social Science* 160: 184–190.

Engel, George. 1961. "Is Grief a Disease?" *Psychosomatic Medicine* 23: 18–22.

Field, Nigel P., and Charles Filanosky. 2009. "Continuing Bonds, Risk Factors for Complicated Grief, and Adjustment to Bereavement." *Death Studies* 34 (1): 1–29.

Foote, Catherine E., and Arthur W. Frank. 1999. "Foucault and Therapy: The Disciplining of Grief." In *Reading Foucault for Social Work*, edited by Adrienne Chambon, Allan Irving, and Laura Epstein, 157–188. New York: Columbia University Press.

Footman, Els Ballhausen. 1998. "The Loss Adjusters." *Mortality* 3 (3): 291–295.

Fowlkes, Martha R. 1990. "The Social Regulation of Grief." *Sociological Forum* 5 (4): 635–652.

Freud, Sigmund. 1917. "Mourning and Melancholia." In *The Penguin Freud Reader*, edited by Adam Philips, 310–326. London: Penguin.

Fulconer, D. 1942. *The Adjustive Behavior of Some Recently Bereaved Spouses*. Unpublished Doctoral Thesis, Northwestern University, Evanston, IL.

Giddens, Anthony. 1991. *Modernity and Self-Identity: Self and Society in the Late Modern Age*. Cambridge: Polity Press.

Gorer, Geoffrey. 1965. *Death, Grief and Mourning in Contemporary Britain*. London: Cresset Press.

Granek, Leeat. 2013. "Disciplinary Wounds: Has Grief Become the Identified Patient for a Field Gone Awry?" *Journal of Loss and Trauma* 18 (3): 275–288.

Groopman, Jerome. 2004. "The Grief Industry." *The New Yorker*, January.

Gündel, Harald, Mary-Frances O'Connor, Lindsey Littrell, Carolyn Fort, and Richard D. Lane. 2003. "Functional Neuroanatomy of Grief: An fMRI Study." *The American Journal of Psychiatry* 160 (11): 1946–1953.

Hall, Christopher. 2014. "Bereavement Theory: Recent Developments in Our Understanding of Grief and Bereavement." *Bereavement Care* 33 (1): 7–12.

Harris, Darcy. 2010. "Oppression of the Bereaved: A Critical Analysis of Grief in Western Society." *Omega* 60 (3): 241–253.

Harrison, Lucy, and Richard Harrington. 2001. "Adolescents' Bereavement Experiences: Prevalence, Association with Depressive Symptoms, and Use of Services." *Journal of Adolescence* 24 (2): 159–169.

Horowitz, Mardi J., Bryna Siegel, Are Holen, George A. Bonanno, Constance Milbrath, and Charles H. Stinson. 1997. "Diagnostic Criteria for Complicated Grief Disorder." *The American Journal of Psychiatry* 154 (7): 904–910.

Jakoby, Nina R. 2012. "Grief as a Social Emotion: Theoretical Perspectives." *Death Studies* 36 (8): 679–711.

Jalland, Pat. 2010. *Death in War and Peace: Loss and Grief in England 1914–1970.* Oxford: Oxford University Press.

Jordan, John R., and Robert A. Neimeyer. 2003. "Does Grief Counseling Work?" *Death Studies* 27 (9): 765–786.

King, Barbara J. 2013. *How Animals Grieve.* Chicago: University of Chicago Press.

Klass, Dennis. 2014. "Grief, Consolation, and Religions: A Conceptual Framework." *Omega* 69 (1): 1–18.

Klass, Dennis, Phyllis R. Silverman, and Steven L. Nickman (eds.). 1996. *Continuing Bonds: New Understandings of Grief.* London: Taylor & Francis.

Klein, Melanie. 1975 [1940]. "Mourning and Its Relation to Manic-Depressive States." In *Love, Guilt and Reparation and Other Works 1921–1945: The Writings of Melanie Klein Volume I*, 344–369. London: Hogarth Press.

Konisberg, R. D. 2011. *The Truth About Grief: The Myth of Its Five Stages and the New Science of Loss.* New York: Simon & Schuster.

Kübler-Ross, Elizabeth. 1970. *On Death and Dying.* London: Tavistock.

Larson, Dale G., and William T. Hoyt. 2009. "Grief Counselling Efficacy: What Have We Learned?" *Bereavement Care* 28 (3): 14–19.

Lindemann, Eric. 1944. *Beyond Grief: Studies in Crisis Intervention.* New York: Aronson.

Lofland, Lyn H. 1985. "The Social Shaping of Emotion: The Case of Grief." *Symbolic Interaction* 8 (2): 171–190.

Mclaren, Jan. 1998. "A New Understanding of Grief: A Counsellor's Perspective." *Mortality* 3 (3): 275–290.

National Council for Palliative Care. 2014. *Life After Death*. London: NCPC.

Neimeyer, Robert A. 2005. "Grief, Loss, and the Quest for Meaning: Narrative Contributions to Bereavement Care." *Bereavement Care* 24 (2): 27–30.

Neimeyer, Robert A., Laurie A. Burke, Michael M. Mackay, and Jessica G. van Dyke Stringer. 2010. "Grief Therapy and the Reconstruction of Meaning: From Principles to Practice." *Journal of Contemporary Psychotherapy* 40 (2): 73–83.

Neimeyer, Robert A., Dennis Klass, and Michael Robert. 2014. "A Social Constructionist Account of Grief: Loss and the Narration of Meaning." *Death Studies* 38 (8): 485–498.

O'Connor, Mary-Frances. 2005. "Bereavement and the Brain: Invitation to a Conversation Between Bereavement Researchers and Neuroscientists." *Death Studies* 29 (10): 905–922.

———. 2012. "Immunological and Neuroimaging Biomarkers of Complicated Grief." *Dialogues in Clinical Neuroscience* 14 (2): 141–148.

O'Connor, Mary-Frances, David K. Wellisch, Annette L. Stanton, Naomi I. Eisenberger, Michael R. Irwin, and Matthew D. Lieberman. 2008. "Craving Love? Enduring Grief Activates Brain's Reward Center." *NeuroImage* 42 (2): 969–972.

Parkes, Colin Murray. 1972. *Bereavement: Studies of Grief in Adult Life*. Harmondsworth: Penguin.

———. 2006. *Love and Loss: The Roots of Grief and Its Complications*. Hove: East.

Parkes, Colin Murray, and Robert S. Weiss. 1983. *Recovery from Bereavement*. New York: Basic Books.

Prigerson, Holly G., E. Frank, S. V. Kasl, C. F. Reynolds, B. Anderson, G. S. Zubenko, and D. J. Kupfer. 1995. "Complicated Grief and Bereavement-Related Depression as Distinct Disorders: Preliminary Empirical Validation in Elderly Bereaved Spouses." *The American Journal of Psychiatry* 152 (1): 22–30.

Prigerson, Holly G., A. J. Bierhals, S. V. Kasl, C. F. Reynolds, Katherine Shear, J. T. Newsom, and S. Jacobs. 1996. "Complicated Grief as a Disorder Distinct from Bereavement-Related Depression and Anxiety: A Replication Study." *The American Journal of Psychiatry* 153 (11): 1484–1486.

Richardson, Virginia E., Kate M. Bennett, Deborah Carr, Stephen Gallagher, Jinhyun Kim, and Noelle Fields. 2015. "How Does Bereavement Get Under the Skin? The Effects of Late-Life Spousal Loss on Cortisol Levels." *The Journals of Gerontology: Series B, Psychological Sciences and Social Sciences* 70 (3): 341–347.

Robson, Patricia, and Tony Walter. 2013. "Hierarchies of Loss: A Critique of Disenfranchised Grief." *Omega* 66 (2): 97–119.

Rodgers, Beth L., and Kathleen V. Cowles. 1991. "The Concept of Grief: An Analysis of Classical and Contemporary Thought." *Death Studies* 15: 443–458.

Rose, Nikolas. 1985. *The Psychological Complex: Psychology, Politics and Society in England, 1869–1939*. London: Routledge & Kegan Paul.

———. 1989. *Governing the Soul: The Shaping of the Private Self*. London: Free Association Press.

———. 1998. *Inventing Our Selves: Psychology, Power and Personhood*. Cambridge: Cambridge University Press.

Rosenblatt, Paul C. 1993. "Grief: The Social Context of Private Feelings." In *Handbook of Bereavement: Theory, Research, and Intervention*, edited by Margaret S. Stroebe, Wolfgang Stroebe, and Robert O. Hansson, 102–111. Washington: American Psychological Association.

———. 2008. "Grief Across Cultures: A Review and Research Agenda." In *Handbook of Bereavement Research and Practice: Advances in Theory and Intervention*, edited by Margaret S. Stroebe, Wolfgang Stroebe, and Robert O. Hansson, 207–222. Washington: American Psychological Association.

Rosenblatt, Paul C., and Ted Bowman. 2013. "Alternative Approaches to Conceptualizing Grief: A Conversation." *Bereavement Care* 32 (2): 82–85.

Rosenblatt, Paul C., R. Patricia Walsh, and Douglas A. Jackson. 1976. *Grief and Mourning in Cross-Cultural Perspective*. New York: Human Relations Area Files.

Rothaupt, Jeanne W., and Kent Becker. 2007. "A Literature Review of Western Bereavement Theory: From Decathecting to Continuing Bonds." *The Family Journal* 15 (1): 6–15.

Sandler, Irwin N., Sharlene A. Wolchik, and Tim S. Ayers. 2008. "Resilience Rather Than Recovery: A Contextual Framework on Adaptation Following Bereavement." *Death Studies* 32 (1): 59–73.

Sbarra, David A., and Cindy Hazan. 2008. "Coregulation, Dysregulation, Self-Regulation: An Integrative Analysis and Empirical Agenda for

Understanding Adult Attachment, Separation, Loss, and Recovery." *Personality and Social Psychology Review* 12 (2): 141–167.

Schut, Henk. 2010. "Grief Counselling Efficacy: Have We Learned Enough?" *Bereavement Care* 29 (1): 8–9.

SECOB Project Research Group. 2013. *Socio-Economic Costs of Bereavement in Scotland: Main Study Report*. March, Aberdeen: SECOB.

Shear, M. Katherine. 2012 "Grief and Mourning Gone Awry: Pathway and Course of Complicated Grief", *Dialogues in Clinical Neuroscience*, 14 (2): 119–128.

Small, Neil. 2001. "Theories of Grief: A Critical Review." In *Grief, Mourning and Death Ritual*, edited by Jenny Hockey, Jeanne Katz, and Neil Small, 19–48. Buckingham: Open University Press.

Small, Neil, and Jenny Hockey. 2001. "Discourse into Practice: The Production of Bereavement Care." In *Grief, Mourning and Death Ritual*, edited by Jenny Hockey, Jeanne Katz, and Neil Small, 97–124. Buckingham: Open University Press.

Stearns, Peter N., and Mark Knapp. 1996. "Historical Perspectives on Grief." In *The Emotions: Social, Cultural and Biological Dimensions*, edited by Ron Harre and W. Gerrod Parrott, 132–150. London: Sage.

Stephen, Audrey I., Colin Macduff, Dennis J. Petrie, Fu-Min Tseng, Henk Schut, Silje Skår, Anne Corden, John Birrell, Shaolin Wang, Cate Newsom, and Stewart Wilson. 2014. "The Economic Cost of Bereavement in Scotland." *Death Studies* 39 (1–5): 151–157.

Stroebe, Margaret. 1997. "From Mourning and Melancholia to Bereavement and Biography: An Assessment of Walter's New Model of Grief." *Mortality* 2 (3): 255–262.

Stroebe, Margaret, and Henk Schut. 1999. "The Dual Process Model of Coping with Bereavement: Rationale and Description." *Death Studies* 23 (3): 197–224.

———. 2005. "To Continue or Relinquish Bonds: A Review of Consequences for the Bereaved." *Death Studies* 29 (6): 477–494.

Stroebe, Margaret, and Wolfgang Stroebe. 1991. "Does 'grief work' work?" *Journal of Consulting and Clinical Psychology* 59 (3): 479–482.

Stroebe, Margaret, Henk Schut, and Wolfgang Stroebe. 2007. "Health Outcomes of Bereavement." *Lancet* 370 (9603): 1960–1973.

Stroebe, Margaret, Henk Schut, and Jan van den Bout (eds.). 2013. *Complicated Grief: Scientific Foundations for Health Care Professionals*. Hove: East.

Valentine, Christine. 2008. *Bereavement Narratives: Continuing Bonds in the 21st Century*. London: Routledge.

Wakefield, Jerome C. 2013. "The DSM-5 Debate over the Bereavement Exclusion: Psychiatric Diagnosis and the Future of Empirically Supported Treatment." *Clinical Psychology Review* 33 (7): 825–845.

Waller, Amy, Heidi Turon, Elise Mansfield, Katherine Clark, Bree Hobden, and Rob Sanson-Fisher. 2016. "Assisting the Bereaved: A Systematic Review of the Evidence for Grief Counselling." *Palliative Medicine* 30 (2): 132–148.

Walter, Tony. 1996. "A New Model of Grief: Bereavement and Biography." *Mortality* 1 (1): 7–25.

———. 1999. *On Bereavement: The Culture of Grief*. Buckingham: Open University Press.

———. 2006. "What Is Complicated Grief? A Social Constructionist Perspective." *Omega* 52 (1): 71–79.

———. 2007. "Modern Grief, Postmodern Grief." *International Review of Sociology* 17 (1): 123–134.

———. 2010. "Grief and Culture: A Checklist." *Bereavement Care* 29 (2): 5–9.

Wambach, Julie Ann. 1985. "The Grief Process as a Social Construct." *Omega* 16 (3): 201–211.

Wittkowski, Joachim, Ken J. Doka, Robert A. Neimeyer, and Michael Vallerga. 2015. "Publication Trends in Thanatology: An Analysis of Leading Journals." *Death Studies* 39 (8): 453–462.

Worden, J. William. 1991. *Grief Counselling and Grief Therapy: A Handbook for the Mental Health Practitioner*, 2nd ed. London: Routledge.

Wortman, Camille B., and Roxane Cohen Silver. 1989. "The Myths of Coping with Loss." *Journal of Consulting and Clinical Psychology* 57 (3): 349–357.

Zisook, Sidney, and Katherine Shear. 2009. "Grief and Bereavement: What Psychiatrists Need to Know." *World Psychiatry* 8 (2): 67–74.

3

Making Sense of Grief

How people make sense of grief has salience in contemporary cultures with conflicting understandings of the meaning, role and value of grief. In the opening chapter, I stated my concern with the contradiction between the increasingly public face of grief and the persistent belief in grief as a social taboo. In this chapter, I discuss the psychological, political, and cultural framing of grief and recovery, resisting the idea popular in literature on death that with the decline of religion people are left with no resources with which to make sense of grief. Instead, I explore the discourses that continue to shape grief, albeit in different forms, where competing definitions of grief and recovery reflect the ambiguity over what constitutes the normal course of grief and recovery. Howarth (2000) has described how, with the destabilisation of religious narratives and a diminished belief in the afterlife, life and death have become separated so that death is no longer a continuation of life, but a threat to life. Grief too in its expression of loss and death is out of place in a society oriented towards life rather than death. It is thus unsurprising that the concept of recovery with its allusions to rebirth and revival of the individual has been embraced by mental health care, and in models of grief, where recovery serves to rescue the individual from the polluted

C. Pearce, *The Public and Private Management of Grief*,
https://doi.org/10.1007/978-3-030-17662-4_3

boundaries of death and depression. How grief is made meaningful, whether drawing on medical, rational, ritualistic, or symbolic explanations, provide justifications that enable grief to become governable or calculable. The existence of these, at times, contradictory discourses, reveals how making sense of and defining grief is an ongoing public and private endeavour.

The chapter begins with the ongoing debate concerning the establishment of psychiatric diagnostic categories of grief, to discuss how certain forms of grief have come to be considered problematic. Following on from the previous chapter, I explore the ways grief has become a psychological object of study through detailing political reforms in mental health that have encouraged a contemporary political and economic climate focused on individual happiness and well-being. Through government-driven initiatives, improving one's well-being and recovering from mental illness are understood as a matter of individual choice and responsibility, as continues to be the trend in public health. A thriving economy is key to many mental health reforms due to the huge financial costs of mental health within the National Health Service (NHS) budget, estimated in 2016 at an annual cost of £105 billion: the biggest item of expenditure. In such a climate, focus on improving happiness and human flourishing, 'negative' emotions like grief, and mental disorders like depression, became not part of life and something to be accommodated but something to overcome, not only in the name of individual health but also for the economic stability of the nation. Put simply, unlimited grief is constructed as a 'burden' in a society that favours happy emotions, time-efficient mental health services and continued productivity through employment.

While the acts of government and psychologists certainly have consequential effects, in literature and the arts grief is prized with a special human value. In the second section of this chapter, I consider the portrayal and presentation of grief, in texts such as memoirs, novels and poetry. I contrast the ways in which grief appears, on the one hand, to be increasingly a matter of medical concern with, on the other, the literary uses of grief, in memoirs, fiction and poetry. The grief memoir or narrative is set within a broader growth in non-fiction writing, specifically autobiographical writing or writing that narrates personal experiences. The emergence of what has been described as the 'autobiographical novel,' epitomised by contemporary writers such as Karl Ove Knausgaard and Rachel Cusk, has served to blur the boundaries between what is considered fiction or non-fiction. While it can be argued that it certainly is not new for authors to depict their own lives in their work, the autobiographical novel poses new questions over not only how narratives are constructed, but how they come to be categorised and consumed, and further how work comes to be judged as fiction or not. In terms of the grief memoir, the blurring of boundaries between fiction and non-fiction suggests a fluidity in the 'truth claims' made about grief. The grief memoir is viewed as an acceptable medium within which to make experiences of bereavement public and as such blurs simple distinctions between the 'public' and 'private' expressions of grief.

In the third section of this chapter, I present findings from the bereaved participants I interviewed and discuss the different discourses participants drew upon to narrate their experiences. These discourses were both rational and traditional ones, offering symbolic meaning in pain and bereavement through signs, superstitions, and metaphors but also reliant on more established ideas such as grief models and bereavement counselling to make sense of grief. This suggests that for the bereaved participants drawing on rational and symbolic types of explanations was not necessarily contradictory, though could appear ambiguous in trying to make sense of the event of bereavement. How people utilised these different discourses problematised not only the understanding of individual choice within policy on recovery but also the ways in which the personal or private modes of explaining grief can adhere to and reject dominant narratives in ways that are not clear cut. In closing, I explore and challenge the understanding that grief needs to be made sense of or found meaningful in order for people to successfully 'recover.' I reflect on what happens when there is a failure to make sense of grief, drawing on the understanding within counselling and therapy that being unable to find meaning from grief causes a lack of recovery from grief.

Public Narratives of Grief and Recovery

Grief as a Disorder

In 2013, the publication of the DSM-5 (American Psychological Association) caused considerable debate across the field of grief and bereavement research, in particular the proposal of a new diagnostic category 'Persistent Complex Bereavement Disorder' (PCBD) to be considered for inclusion in future editions of the manual. Controversy over the proposed diagnosis of PCBD was centred on internal disputes between two well-researched categories of abnormal grief: 'prolonged grief disorder' (PGD) proposed by Prigerson and colleagues (Prigerson et al. 2009; Boelen and Prigerson 2012) and 'complicated grief' (CG), the category described by Shear and colleagues (Shear 2010, 2012; Zisook and Shear 2009). PCBD was in effect a faulty compromise, a product of criticisms of over-medicalisation in the preparation stages of DSM-5. The two respective research groups continue to disagree over which category—prolonged grief disorder or complicated grief—is the most robust, leading to a back and forth commentary in the pages of medical journals including the *British Medical Journal* and *JAMA Psychiatry*, highlighting the shortcomings of the others research and claiming the superior scientific validity of their own (Maciejewski and Prigerson 2017; Reynolds et al. 2017; Prigerson and Maciejewski 2017).

The scientific rigour of the work on prolonged and complicated grief is much flaunted, however, not enough criticism has been directed to the inconsistencies of each diagnostic category. Boelen and Prigerson (2012) provide a comparison of the symptoms of PGD, CG and PCBD highlighting both the similarities and marked differences between diagnostic categories. The most notable difference is the length of time a person is expected to demonstrate symptoms before diagnosis. For example, PGD requires symptoms to be present for six months before intervention, while a diagnosis of PCBD is recommended only if symptoms are present at least 12 months following bereavement. There are also varying opinions on how many people are affected by these disorders; from seven to ten per cent of bereaved people claimed by Shear

(2010, 2012) to a much higher 15% of all bereaved people by Bryant (2012) who remarked 'there are over a million new cases of prolonged grief in the USA each year, representing a public health issue' (10). Although the use of the categories of prolonged or complicated grief is currently less prevalent in bereavement care and practice in the UK, as I detail in Chapter 4, initiatives such as the 'Early Intervention Project,' run by Cruse Bereavement Care and funded by the Department of Health, reveal how complicated grief is becoming a prominent focus of concern.

While proponents of complicated grief argue that the growth of research into the area is merely the recognition of a disorder that already existed and experienced by bereaved individuals, there appears to be some ambiguity around why complicated grief develops in some people and not others. The ICD-11 defines PGD as a:

> [P]ersistent and pervasive grief response characterised by longing for the deceased person or persistent preoccupation with the deceased accompanied by intense emotional pain.

The grief response is defined as prolonged if it has persisted for:

> (…) an atypically long period of time following the loss (more than six months at a minimum) and clearly exceeds expected social, cultural or religious norms for the individual's culture and context.

It is the 'atypically long' time period, which most clearly demarcates complicated from normal grief, and yet as I argued in Chapter 2, the meaning of 'normal' grief, is still under considerable debate. Despite this lack of clarity, this has not prevented the creation of diagnostic categories based on the assumption of a normal course of grief.

Brown (1995) suggests there is a need to ask of medical diagnosis: why is it that conditions get identified at certain times? And why is action taken—for whose benefit and at what cost? Indeed, receiving a diagnosis has direct practical implications for the person's social status and standing. A diagnosis can help people to access treatment; it can legitimise contested conditions and provide coherence and a narrative to its sufferers. As Hacking (1986, 1999) has argued, psychiatric diagnosis is not merely the recognition of an illness already present but one that is socially produced. In other words, mental illness and disorder are made 'visible' in an individual body through the clinician's 'gaze,' using labels, diagnostic categories, and other tools of psychiatry. These tools, that emerged with the birth of modern medical practice as Foucault (1973) and Rose (1985) have described, sought to localise illness in the body, or more specifically in this case, in the mind or brain. As I describe further in the following sections, the locating of illness inside the mind meant both the cause and management of mental disorder became largely a responsibility of the individual.

The way in which such medical rituals are used suggests the danger a complicated griever might pose to what are considered to be normal, healthy emotions and behaviours. Therefore, to understand why prolonged grieving poses a risk and has become problematic for many requires a wider analysis in the realm of political, economic and societal concerns. While a time limit is important in distinguishing complicated from normal grief and time-limited mourning is present in a number of mourning rituals, it takes on new relevance when considering time limits in the treatment and recovery of mental disorders. Further, these time limits, established in the creation of a psychiatric diagnosis of complicated or prolonged grief, might be considered as a 'technology of temporalisation' (Foucault 1975) that serve to contain mental distress or unhappiness. As I will discuss below, such time limits on grief take on renewed relevance in a political and economic climate where maintaining happiness and well-being and being a productive worker are primary markers of the good citizen.

No Health Without Mental Health

The second half of the twentieth century witnessed a shift away from disease prevention located at the level of public health to an emphasis on individual responsibility. This trend was captured in policy such as the White Paper *Choosing Health: Making Healthy Choices Easier*, published in 2004 by Blair's Labour government, which set the tone for policy decisions that followed with an emphasis on individual choice and responsibility over one's well-being. This was also followed in David Cameron's 'Big Society,' the ethos of which was to give people more control over their lives, in the belief that when people are made to feel as if they are the 'authors of their own destiny' their sense of self-worth and well-being increases. More recently the Health Secretary Matt Hancock has encouraged people to take more responsibility for their own health and make better health choices, reaffirming the government policy on public health (*BBC News* 2018).

In *No Health Without Mental Health* (Department of Health 2011a) the Conservative-Liberal Democrat coalition government set forth an improved policy to tackle mental illness. While the principles underpinning the report were individual 'freedom,' 'fairness,' and 'responsibility,' there was also a great deal of focus on the economic impact of mental illness. Commonly described as the 'burden' of mental health (Department of Health 2011a; Wittchen et al. 2011), the report quantified the cost of poor mental health in 2011 as £105 billion, accounting for 23% of the total illness burden in the UK. The same figures were featured in a government-commissioned report published in February 2016 by the NHS England independent mental health task force (chaired by the MIND charity CEO), which proposed a five year forward plan for mental health care (The Mental Health Taskforce 2016). The report coincided with Prime Minister Cameron's announcement of nearly a billion-pound investment in mental health care, adding to the estimated 34 billion pounds spent on mental health each year (Department of Health 2016).

Wittchen et al. (2011), in their review of statistics across the European Union (EU) countries, concluded that one-third of the EU population suffers from mental disorders: a finding that revealed a much greater burden of disease than previously considered. Disorders of the brain, they stated, are the core global health challenge of the twenty-first century. *No Health Without Mental Health* was preceded by a number of other government-directed reports such as the Foresight Report (Jenkins et al. 2008) that focused on ways to create 'positive mental capital.' The report described the 'important societal value' of positive mental health as:

> (I)ncluding overall productivity. It is an important resource for individuals, families, communities and nations, contributing to human, social and economic capital. (Jenkins et al. 2008, 15)

The ways in which 'positive' mental health and mental disorders were positioned was clear: mental illness is a costly burden, and well-being is productive, most crucially in economic terms. The way to remedy the burden called for the introduction of accessible psychological therapies. Lord Layard's report, entitled *The Depression Report* (The Centre for Economic Performance's Mental Health Policy Group 2006), provided an in-depth proposal of a psychological service that would reduce the costs of absenteeism and incapacity benefits caused by mental ill health by aiding people to recover more quickly and return to work. The Improving Access to Psychological Therapies service (IAPT) was thus born, with the 2011 government mental health policy including many of Layard's proposals. The IAPT service was set up to provide nationwide access to evidence-based therapies in accordance with the National Institute for Clinical Excellence (NICE) guidelines, including therapies of different 'intensity' levels. The therapy of choice in IAPT was cognitive behavioural therapy (CBT) approved by NICE for its evidence-based success rate, and favoured for its brief treatment time. IAPT was thus targeted largely at mild depressive and anxiety disorders where the delivery was lightweight with a maximum of six sessions of CBT and, in some instances, merely referral to other services or provision of leaflets.

Addressing mental health in 2011 was particularly poignant in what might be considered the lowest point in the economic recession. In the supplementary document to *No Health Without Mental Health* which focused on the introduction of talking therapies, Paul Burstow, then Minister of State for Care Services, made explicit this connection when he wrote: 'Following the recession, it is clear we need to heal emotional wounds, which means we are looking for a psychological recovery outside our economic recovery' (Department of Health 2011b, 2).

The therapy IAPT provided was seen to benefit not only the individual 'but also the nation by helping people come off sick pay and benefits and stay in or return to work' (5). Ehrenreich (2010) in her book *Smile or Die*, attacked the 'Pollyannaism' of a political agenda focused on individual well-being, arguing it was the delusion of positive thinking that caused the financial crash to occur in the first place. Halting economic progress was not in question, even if it had been the cause of misery for many. The answer to the economic recovery was not a restructuring of the type of neoliberal economics that arguably created the problem but a psychological recovery of the citizens bearing the brunt of its aftermath.

A Happiness Agenda

It was not only those considered to be mentally ill who required assistance. In late 2010 Prime Minister David Cameron announced that the coalition government would begin measuring the nation's happiness (Cabinet Office 2010). The Office for National Statistics (ONS) was directed to include a set number of questions in their Household Survey that sought to gauge the happiness levels of the population. The establishment of a 'happiness index' emerged out of a series of events both in the UK and internationally; the central one being the revelation that more money and increased gross domestic profit (GDP) did not make people happier. What became known as the 'Easterlin paradox' derived from a number of studies by Easterlin (Easterlin and Angelescu 2009), revealed that in developed countries after reaching a certain level of wealth, happiness and well-being plateaued. The identification of an inverse relationship between money and happiness led economists and politicians to seek out new measures of progress alongside GDP. Cameron's announcement marked the beginning of the peak of political and economic interest in happiness and well-being. It also tapped into what had become an established sub-field of psychology that focused on the fostering of positive emotions. The new field of positive psychology, stemming from the former chair of the American Psychological Association Seligman's (2002) seminal text *Authentic Happiness* provoked a wave of interest in happiness, an emotion Seligman claimed had been historically neglected in psychology with the discipline's over-emphasis on the melancholy. The goal of positive psychology was not only to stop people being ill but help them 'be well' by building the 'enabling' conditions of life. As Seligman (2002) described, it was about getting people from zero to 'plus five.'

While some thought the plans for a happiness index 'woolly' and 'impractical' (Duncan 2010; The Midlands Psychology Group 2007), Cameron's announcement was met with considerable support. The organisation 'Action for Happiness' founded by Layard, Geoff Mulgan (formerly Director of Policy in Blair's Labour government) and Anthony Seldon (the historian known for his biographies of British prime ministers) was re-launched with the goal to make a happier society. Meanwhile, the New Economics Foundation (NEF) created well-being as one of its key themes, formulating a Happy Planet Index (HPI) which aimed to show where the happiest and healthiest place was to live, and instructing people of the 'five ways to well-being'.[1] The media interest in Cameron's announcement sparked what Davies (2015) has described as a 'happiness industry.' From the BBC's 'Happiness Challenge,' to laughter coaches and happiness phone apps, happiness was at its peak.

The ability to measure happiness provided the tools to define happiness in objective terms, but as a consequence of the discovery of the 'Easterlin paradox' happiness has been defined not as something dependent on the structures of society but on individual thoughts and feelings. Happiness has thus come to be framed as something within the individual's reach, if only he or she could learn to make the right choices about their health and well-being. Yet the research into happiness had revealed that, even when presented with accurate information, people did not always make the 'right' choices about their health. In order to address these 'toxic biases' a government policy unit called the 'Behavioural Insights Team' (BIT) was formed. The BIT was quickly dubbed the 'nudge unit' referencing Thaler and Sunstein's (2009) book *Nudge* that put forward the idea that people would make better choices for themselves if only their behaviour was 'nudged' the right way. While standard economic analysis had been based on the assumption that humans are rational and behave in their own self-interest, behavioural economics rested on the belief that people repeatedly make mistakes about what brings them well-being (Cromby and Willis 2013). The happiness agenda and behavioural economics appeared to be utilising different types of subjectivities: one that was resilient, self-motivated and in control of their well-being, and one that was simultaneously at the whim of unconscious drives and government nudges. Mol described how this contemporary 'logic of choice' within health care services in western societies promises a level of mastery over one's life but hides what it costs to reshape the world in a way that 'situations of choice' are created (2008). Along the same lines Borgstrom (2015; Borgstrom and Walter 2015) illustrated the limits of the choice agenda within end-of-life care where choices over a 'good death' are not always possible.

The political and economic agendas within the happiness agenda were, I suggest, hidden within a discourse that revitalised an Aristotelian view that happiness is what all people desire. From how it is thus defined, happiness is perceived as a neutral term, flexible to the subjective views of the individual. Yet Ahmed (2010) identified how the idea of happiness that has evolved is a limited and restrictive one, specifically critiquing the way in which the rise and emphasis on happiness is at the exclusion of certain individuals, groups and ideas. The history of happiness, Ahmed argues, is not one of inclusivity; the criteria for happiness has discounted certain individual and groups and affected how 'negative' emotions are socially perceived and acted upon.

The move towards classifying complicated forms of grief can be considered as part of this broader political and economic imperative to alleviate the 'burden' of mental disorder and create happier more productive citizens. Within the happiness agenda, happiness is an object, both individual and collective which all are encouraged to obtain. When happiness and positive emotions are viewed as the endpoint of all endeavours, unhappiness registers as something that gets in the way. Instead, Ahmed posed the argument that unhappiness should be treated as more than something to overcome. Yet, as I will go on to discuss, recovery from unhappiness and mental distress is precisely the goal that individuals, governments and health care services are orientating themselves towards.

The Journey to Recovery

Alongside the proliferation of government policy, psychological research and public interest in happiness and well-being, was the popularising of a 'recovery model' in mental health care. The move towards recovery sought to bring acceptance to living with a mental illness and to broaden the notion of recovery outside of medical requirements in an attempt to remedy what was considered the 'epistemic injustice' at the heart of the way health care services have been administered (Carel and Kidd 2014). It is not an understatement to note that recovery is one of the most significant transformations in mental health care policy in recent times. NHS mental health services now declare themselves as 'recovery-orientated' or 'recovery-focused'; 'recovery colleges' have been set up around the UK, numbering 76[2] at the time of writing, and recovery is a central focus in psychiatric research (Roberts and Wolfson 2004; Slade et al. 2012, 2014; Summerfield 2002). In this section I shed light on what recovery means for mental health care policy and suggest why recovery has captured the imagination of policymakers and service users alike.

Establishing what recovery means is no straightforward task and most policy, articles or books on the topic will begin with the preface that no one definition of recovery exists. This is in part an intentional consequence as mental health service users and survivors first embraced the term recovery as a way to describe ways of living fulfilling and meaningful lives with their mental illness. Oft-cited definitions of recovery include that of Anthony (1993), who described recovery thus:

> [Recovery is] a deeply personal, unique process of changing one's attitudes, values, feelings, goals, skills and/or roles. It is a way of living a satisfying, hopeful, and contributing life even with limitations caused by the illness. Recovery involves the development of new meaning and purpose in one's life as one grows beyond the catastrophic effects of mental illness.

> Recovery from mental illness involves much more than recovery from the illness itself. (1993, 11)

Another popular definition is provided by Deegan (1996) who, in her book *Recovery as a Journey of the Heart*, described that the goal of the recovery process:

> (…) is not to become normal. The goal is to embrace our human vocation of becoming more deeply, more fully human. (1996, 92)

Policy and research papers such as *No Health Without Mental Health* detailed above frequently cite these two definitions. In these definitions of recovery, the unique and self-defined nature of recovery is emphasised. This reflects the radical beginnings of the recovery movement made possible by the anti-psychiatry of the 1970s and the rise of a psychiatric survivors' radical movement that demanded change to the paternalistic and often oppressive mental health care of the past. Recovery thus began as a liberatory message of resistance against the medical model of understanding mental illness and what were considered the normative goals of psychiatric care, yet has since permeated mainstream mental health services. The official introduction of recovery into NHS mental health services was heralded with the New Labour government's 'vision' for mental health care in 2001 entitled *The Journey to Recovery* (Department of Health 2001). In this document, the government laid out their plans for modernising the 'defective' and 'chaotic' mental health care services of the past, where it was claimed people with mental illness were not expected to recover. In the 'services of the future' recovery will be spoken about as much as illness, after all 'the vast majority have real prospects of recovery' (Department of Health 2001, 24). The contemporary model of recovery, however, has also incorporated the consumer movement in health care as well as applying the insights of positive psychology where choice, hope, and responsibility are terms commonly found in descriptions of recovery. This theme was illustrated in the emphasis on enabling and empowering citizenship as closely tied to recovery, acknowledging a need to aid service users into engaging with 'ordinary social activities' and finding a 'meaningful occupation' (25).

By 2010 recovery had been well-established in mental health care policy as demonstrated by *No Health Without Mental Health*, where one of its six main objectives was that 'more people with mental health problems will recover' (Department of Health 2011a). In many respects, the New Labour vision could be considered a noble one, wanting to 'foster the understanding that mental illness is no more to be frowned at than breaking a leg' (25). Yet the 'mainstreaming of recovery' (Rose 2014) was not without its problems. Service users began to express their dissatisfaction with a notion of recovery that had come to be shaped by government-directed outcomes rather than being individually defined. Recovery came to be defined by policymakers and service users in two ways: clinical and personal recovery. What was being established were two dividing notions of recovery, one that could be decided from a clinical perspective, and that had to be proved to have universal application; and one that was defined individually and that could reaffirm, resist or be completely detached from normative beliefs around recovery.

This distinction, argue Harper and Speed (2012, 13), 'functions to effectively locate "personal recovery" as an adjunct to clinical recovery, and this complementarity avoids recovery being seen as inherently contested.' This somewhat distorted the definitions of those like Anthony and Deegan, which policymakers and NHS services were themselves referencing. Recovery then was provided with outcomes, such as the 'recovery star'[3] rather than being a unique self-defined exercise. Arguably, as recovery began to be co-opted and incorporated into mainstream practices, radical demands coincided with, or indeed were diluted by, a government agenda of autonomy and individual responsibility (Braslow 2013). This was perhaps a result of the 'plastic' nature of recovery that was designed to be inclusionary unlike the exclusionary nature of the health care of the past. However, neither of these definitions of recovery incorporated a socially informed model of recovery, for instance one that emphasised how recovery was achieved by being in relation to certain ideas, people, organisations, rather than simply being a matter of individual choice and will.

A Culture of Trauma

The state intervention into recovery approaches to mental health is a recent development but one that can be traced to a longer history of 'moral treatment' (Rose 1985). Accounts of the rise of the recovery model often highlight the description of the York Retreat written by Tuke in 1813 as a turning point towards the humane treatment of mental disorder (see, for example, Carson et al. 2010) away from the Victorian asylums, now written about with much disdain as 'overcrowded,' 'awful' and 'appalling' places (Department of Health 2001). More significant, perhaps, was the development of thinking about the causes of mental illness that allowed for the changes in the provision for and care of people with mental distress. Rose (1985) has documented the rise of psychology as a discipline and its incorporation from the fringes of experimental pseudo-science to a domain of knowledge that increasingly came to influence and govern different populations from the military to children and families. The First and Second World Wars seem to have provided a catalyst for change over the twentieth century in the shifting perceptions of the cause and treatment of mental disorders. The emergence of the shell-shocked soldier has become a poignant figure that signalled this shift from understanding the causes of mental distress as moral and hereditary to a physical phenomenon (Leese 2002; Shepard 2002). Shell shock was remarkable in its indiscriminate reach, presenting as a cluster of symptoms previously viewed as specific to female hysteria (Appignanesi 2008; Leys 1994). The sheer quantity of cases of this non-physical trauma of war posed an interesting problem to the medical profession, which arguably paved the way for the first wide-scale intervention into the mental health of the population.

The treatment of shell shock was a key instance of mental illness becoming a matter of 'social hygiene' (Rose 1989). Mental disturbance produced from the experience of war rather than an inherited trauma based in family history, stimulated the experimentation with new behavioural therapies at places such as the Maudsley hospital (Marks 2012) that dispensed with Freudian heavy psychoanalytical approaches. With a strong need to get soldiers fit enough to return to the front line, behavioural therapies emerged amid an interest in treating the symptoms instead of the mind, an approach that had a more materialistic understanding of mental distress. During and following the First World War, society witnessed the creation of specialist hospitals such as those at Maghull, the Maudsley, and Craiglockhart (Jones and Wessley 2005), the latter made famous by the Regeneration Trilogy by Pat Barker. Other notable developments included the opening of 'recovery homes' by the Ministry of Pensions and the formation of a national network of psychotherapy clinics in 1919–1920 (Leese 2002). Many of the doctors who treated shell shock during the war worked across the UK afterwards, so the new ideas in the relatively new specialism of psychiatry spread. It also cemented a new relationship between psychology and the military, where recruits had to undergo psychological screening for vulnerability (Jones and Wessley 2005; Shepard 2002). As Shepard (2002) has documented, this was rediscovered during the Vietnam War, giving rise to the establishment of Post-Traumatic Stress Disorder (PTSD) as a psychiatric disorder in the DSM III in 1980.

By the end of the twentieth century, through the impact of war and the growth of psychological expertise, understandings of mental distress had undergone a process of re-categorisation, witnessing the creation of legitimised categories of mental disorder. While there were obvious advantages to the recognition of PTSD, for Shepard, from this 'rediscovery' of trauma emerged a whole 'culture of trauma' that saw for example debriefing by counsellors after traumatic events as common practice (Seeley 2015) and a rising interest in real-life trauma stories as a form of media entertainment. This culture of trauma involved not only a reconfiguration in clinical and academic understandings of mental distress but also promoted particular modes of recovery, significantly that of talking therapies, setting the appropriate environment for notions of psychological recovery that proliferate today.

Glyde (2014) described the 'recovery industrial complex' embodied in the powerful ethos of Alcoholics Anonymous (AA), established by recovering alcoholic Bill Wilson in 1935 originally with an evangelical Christian and overtly masculine overtone, where the solution was for religion to replace addiction. Central to the recovery industrial complex is the telling of individual stories of trauma, underlined by the therapeutic belief that the narration of stories enables one to heal and recover from trauma. Trauma has been described as marking the disjunction between the event and a belated incomplete understanding of the event (Caruth 1995). It is implied that the cause, or perpetuation of, mental trauma is not having a coherent story and so cures of mental distress are often directed at enabling people to find a story (for example in the treatment of PTSD). This is demonstrated in psychodynamic treatment where the construction of case histories is used to provide meaning and comprehension of events and thus recovery (Goody 2006). This ethos of psychological recovery, a recovery made possible through the telling of trauma, is evident from self-help recovery groups such as AA to the industrial complex that is Oprah Winfrey promoting her own brand of self-help and empowerment through her talk show and various books (Travis 2009). Psychological notions of mental distress and recovery in turn permeated popular culture influencing the way people publicly expressed and managed emotions such as grief, as I describe next.

A Private Vocabulary for Grief

Narratives of Grief

A culture of trauma encouraged the expression of individual stories and developed a captive audience for accounts of traumatic experiences such as grief. In this section, I juxtapose the modern rationality of medicalisation with the burgeoning creative use of grief in literature, a mode of making sense of grief that embraces a sentiment more reminiscent of the Romantic period. Hockey et al. (2001) have documented the influence of romantic ideology on mourning practices, where responses to death were increasingly understood through an emotional paradigm. If the modern 'rationalisation' of grief, which has given rise to psychiatric classifications, can be understood as a product of enlightenment thought, the popularity of the grief memoir might be viewed as a continuation of the romantic individual and emotional expression through literature.

In 2015, several of the most prestigious book awards were won by autobiographical accounts of grief and bereavement. *The Iceberg* written by Coutts (2014) who won the 2015 Wellcome book prize and Macdonald (2014) who won both the 2015 Samuel Johnson prize and the Costa book award for *H is for Hawk*, received critical acclaim for their depictions of grief over the loss of a husband and father, respectively. The success of these titles evidences the continuing popularity of grief as a theme for literature. These titles are not anomalies; the bereavement memoir remains a consistent bestseller. Lewis's (1961) *A Grief Observed*, first published in 1961 was republished in 2016 as a new edition and has been adapted for film and theatre. Other popular titles include Didion's (2006) *The Year of Magical Thinking*, *Wild* (2012) by Strayed (and accompanying film) and *The Long Goodbye* (O'Rourke 2011). As well as fictional work like *Grief is the Thing with Feathers* (Porter 2015), the post 9/11 grief of *Extremely Loud and Incredibly Close* (Foer 2005) and classic depictions of grief in Shakespeare's *Hamlet* and Bronte's *Wuthering Heights*, and even the place of grief in J. K. Rowling's *Harry Potter* series. Not to mention the great canon of elegiac poetry which serves to provide consolation from grief through its accurate expression of the emotions.

Why might people be drawn to writing about grief? In her memoir describing the death of her mother, O'Rourke (2011) wrote her 'pervasive loneliness' was the result of 'the privatisation of grief.' To write about the experience of grief is both to find a way to express the 'unsayable' of death (Watkin 2004), and to make public what is felt to be private. Arguably, the popularity of such written accounts of grief fills the gap left between the modern divide of life and death, a gap that the authors such as O'Rourke (2011) claims are not adequately fulfilled by professional grief literature. When the understanding that grief is a 'taboo' persists, then writing openly about an experience like bereavement enables people to connect to otherwise hidden and silenced stories: they offer guidelines to recovery. Dennis (2008) in his analysis of contemporary bereavement memoirs described how grief accounts become 'vehicles of information and instruction for fellow citizens in the community of grieving' (802). The autobiographical account thus acts to provide a map for others in their navigation through the liminal space of grief, arguably offering some form of consolation in learning that someone else has also endured a similar sense of pain. Dennis outlines six narrative dimensions of the grief memoir: restitution (trying to fix things), evaluative (positive reappraisal), interpretive (making sense of it), affirmation (of deceased, of continued relationship), affective (emotional disclosure) and transformation. The well-established narrative outline provides a ready format for the reader to make sense of their loss.

Grievers also turn to language, metaphor and the imagination to find expression for their emotions. Metaphors are often utilised in writing about grief, for example Porter (2015) in his short novel *Grief is the Thing with Feathers* conjures the image of the Crow, famously the talisman of choice for the poet Ted Hughes. In his story of a bereaved partner and father and his two young sons Porter draws on the idea of the crow as 'stronger than death' and the echoes of Hughes' 'Crow,' who becomes the healing force in the story. A bird also plays the healer, in this case a literal bird, in McDonald's memoir of grief in which she decides to train a Goshawk. In explaining her actions, she remarked: 'You can't tame grief, but you can tame hawks' (Willoughby 2015). In both books, the birds, whether fictional or real, become symbolic of the grief which they cannot express but also provide a model of being; McDonald explained: 'The hawk was everything I wanted to be: solitary, self-possessed, free from grief, and numb to the hurts of human life' (Macdonald 2014, 85).

In the grief memoir, the author and their feelings are made prominent, and so rather than a 'death' of the author (Barthes 1967), the biographical details of the author are especially relevant. The grief memoir plays a cathartic role for its author. The drive to write about one's grief is not always made explicit, more often it is assumed that writing and claiming one's narrative is automatically healing. Finding the words to tell one's story has a central role in the politics of, and recovery from, trauma. Grief is widely believed to be an event that disrupts an individual's 'self-narrative' (Neimeyer 2005). This is a belief that rests on a further assumption: that each individual possesses his or her own 'narrative-identity.' Creating a story about illness or grief, remedies the disruption of personal self-identity caused by traumatic experiences.

Coutts described the process of producing *The Iceberg* as one of 'writing against annihilation' (Law 2014).

What has been described as a 'narrative turn' in the social sciences sought to acknowledge how telling stories is 'universal' and that human beings understand and make sense of their lives in narrative (Bury 2001; Clandinin and Connelly 2000; Frank 2010; Squire 2005). Gilbert (2002) states that humans are 'naturally orientated' to storytelling and use narrative and stories to organise, bring order and structure experience. Constructing narratives is considered to be a 'characteristically human' process; the 'narrative parsing and organisation of experience are rooted in our biology,' claim Neimeyer et al. (2014, 487–489). The healing properties of narrative have been especially highlighted in studies of illness, and increasingly in grief and bereavement, where constructing a narrative is believed to repair disrupted identities and enable people to reconstruct their biographies (Bury 2001; Frank 2006). The emerging field of 'narrative medicine' (Charon 2006) has embraced the importance of narrative to understanding illness, placing emphasis on listening to the story of the patient as a means of producing a more humane and ethical medical practice.

Within the excitement about narratives there is a tendency to overstate the power of narration. Frank (2010), for example, enthusiastically describes the 'exceptional' nature of narratives, listing the functions of narrative: narratives connect people and enable membership of social groups; narrative is the means through which humans learn who they are and learn between good and bad actions. For 'without stories, there would be no sense of action as ethical' (Frank 2010, 665). Neimeyer et al. (2014) make a further leap inferring from a rather preliminary study using fMRI scans on people who had been bereaved (O'Connor 2005) to suggest that: '[t]he human penchant for "storying" events, to organise temporal experience in terms of plot structures with meaningful beginnings, middles, and ends, appears to be anchored in brain structures' (Neimeyer et al. 2014, 487). Similar claims exist in support of the healing act of writing, where it is contended that 'unresolved' trauma can 'easily spill over … into our emotions and into the very way our immune system interacts with disease' (Watts 2011, 8).

However, in his essay on oral and written storytelling, Goody (2006) demonstrated how narrative is not a predominant characteristic of adult intercourse in purely oral (non-literate) cultures. Contrary to beliefs that narrative is a universal form of expression, Goody argued narrative is less a universal human trait and more something promoted by literacy and the advent of printing, which introduced the fictional novel as a narrative form. In his essay 'The blob' Bloch (2011) described how humans possess a 'narrative level.' This narrative level is not an inherent mode of cognition as some psychologists might claim, but a form of learnt expression. Tilly argued that westerners (1999) acquired standard story packaging, causing individuals to organise experience in standard story form. He described a standard story structure as composed of a limited number of interacting, independent and self-motivated characters that make deliberate actions and possess specific motives, with the story located in time and place. Tilly and Goody both point out life histories do not just emerge automatically but are heavily constructed by the culture in which they are situated. The proliferation of narratives of grief is not merely the freeing of the truth about grief but the production of particular types of stories about grief. Moreover, it naturalises a type of self that demands personal and emotional expression.

The resistance of a standard story structure is also, then, a resistance to an easily classifiable identity. Ramazani (1994) has described how modern forms of elegy diverge from the late romantic tradition of death poetry as one of self-definition to an 'unmasking' of the poet. The modern elegist attacks the dead or themselves and refuses orthodox consolation in God or rebirth. Modern elegies tend not to achieve but to resist consolation, not to heal but to reopen wounds of loss. This melancholic form of elegy provides no answers or solace but is purposely resistant and recalcitrant. For example, Ramazani drew on a variety of poets including Seamus Heaney and Wilfred Owen who both refused to see any consolation in the deaths in the many victims of war, or indeed place faith in the recuperative effect of poetry. For Ramazani modern elegies are 'a compromise-formation in response to the privatisation of grief' (1994, 15–16). However, it would seem that in the act of refusing consolation, the modern elegy provides a different form of 'refuge from the social denial of grief.' The popularity of grief memoirs could be seen in a similar fashion in that even if written in the act of refusing recovery the act of writing provides its own refuge from the 'impact of the thing' itself, as Lewis (1961) described. Yet for writers or poets to find consolation in the act of writing is hardly surprising. The question remains as to how accessible such a vocabulary is and what ways people might use such vocabularies to make sense of their grief.

Telling stories and giving voice to one's pain is a commonly accepted tool to provide liberation from suffering and oppression (Charmaz 1999; Charon 2006; Smith and Sparkes 2008). Yet, not all stories get to be heard and the act of storytelling reduces the forms of expression into 'standard' narratives, excluding those unable to articulate their stories. Creative writing and literature potentially provide a privileged site where grief and different expressions of grief are accepted, though access to this site is not available to all. Furthermore, the expression of grief through literature can be used not only as a source of consolation but as a form of 'resistance' to assumed notions of appropriate grieving.

Rational and Symbolic Explanations

Science and literature within modern society are divided along the lines of the public and the private and the two realms have served to reflect a divided face of grief. While science utilises psychiatric manuals and literature uses metaphor, I suggest that neither one should be seen to be filling a gap left by the other. Rather they both produce explanations about the same thing: grief. In this section, I present excerpts from interviews with bereaved people to address how people often draw on both rational and symbolic explanations, and at times inconsistent ideas, to make sense of their own feelings of grief.

I begin by exploring how participants retold the story of the death of their partner or family member and what explanations—both rational and symbolic—they drew on to make sense of their experiences. In their accounts, participants included descriptions of events and activities and also emotions and metaphors. The participants strove to narrate a chronological and comprehensive story of the death and the character of their partner or family member, including fine details of dates and events. On the one hand, there was a need to confirm the truth of what happened when the person died, and yet on the other hand participants referred to signs and metaphors to help them make sense of the death and their feelings of grief. While most of the participants competently narrated their stories to me by drawing on narrative features such as plot, characters and metaphor, finding meaning in their experiences was a different activity to telling a story about it.

Many of the participants in their interview accounts addressed three key areas: the process of a partner or family member dying, the event of the death and the subsequent response to the death and feelings of grief. Following the setting up of the scene of death, participants continued to describe events that happened after the death and which were interspersed with their own feelings and often biographical information about themselves, their partner or family member that died and even other family members and friends. In line with Árnason's (2000) discovery, I argue the participants were constructing not so much a 'durable biography' of the deceased person, argued by Walter (1996), but a story of themselves and their relationship with their deceased partner or family member.

Most participants narrated their experiences using this structure with little prompting from me, the interviewer. Typically, I would begin the interview with a question that referred to a detail the participants had shared with me prior to the interview, such as, 'You mentioned your husband died four years ago?'. This led in the majority of cases to a description of the death; for example, Laura relayed to me how her husband died in this way:

> He needed his medication so the two paramedics took him into the ambulance ... when I came down the ambulance was closed up and rocking and it was at that point he'd collapsed and he had, it turned out, a ruptured aorta ... Very traumatic. Massive shock. Went into shock for I would say six months. I functioned, I went, I was back at work, because we buried him, well cremated him on 6th January and he died on 22nd December.

The participants followed a largely chronological order starting with the story of the death and for some, the illness that may have preceded it. Rose, for example, wrote me a timeline of her life with her husband, that she emailed to me prior to our interview. 'A compressed history' she described it, which presented a chronology from when they met up to the year of his death. This sense of a need to be thorough in their accounts was common. At the close of the interview, Anne reached for some notes she had written beforehand to ensure she had told me all the details. For Anne, the death of her husband became a matter for a police investigation, of which she spoke at length. The question over the cause of her husband's death propelled Anne into a search for the true sequence of events, as she explained:

> He fell out of an office window. It was an accident. That's what happened. He was closing it, and he fell four floors … Now in fact what happened was he had fallen out of window, at his work, at quarter to seven at night. ... Your head—in the absence of information your head grabs at anything it possibly can to make it work, to make sense.

Following the death of her husband, Anne described the task of reconciling what she thought to be true about her husband with the alternative options suggested by the police investigation. In this excerpt from Anne's account, it is possible to see how important it was for Anne to locate the story in time and place, as well to clarify the truth of what 'in fact' happened. In both Anne and Laura's accounts, there was a reliance on—or need for—the 'truth' where the emphasis was on the maintaining the accuracy of the date, time and sequence of events. However, participants also readily drew on more symbolic means of making sense of death. For example, Rose, whose husband died 26 years prior to the interview, narrated the account of his death by drawing on signs and symbolic references:

> 37, both of us were 37. He was born on a Saturday, died on a Saturday. Born on third of the month, died on the third of the month. Born at

> 4.30, died at 4.30. And I even added to that, he was breech birth and the first thing I saw when I was coming down the stairs was his feet … [W]hen we swapped the house and when we moved in, there was this vase of flowers on the table, now I don't know if you know of the, there's a superstition do not have lilac in the house because they'll be a death in the family, but there was lilac in this arrangement and I remember saying oh we shouldn't have, but I adore lilac so I left it and we got home and he died, there's a death in the family. It's not logical but you can't help but sort of go, it's weird.

Like Anne and Laura, Rose focused on the details surrounding the death, which she recalled even 26 years later. Yet this emphasis on the factual detail was given a symbolic meaning, so that in her narration Rose's husband's death appeared somewhat fated. In her description, Rose highlighted details such as the lilac in the house and endowed the superstition with meaning, even as she acknowledged, 'it's not logical.' 'Signs' from Rose's husband were present too after his death, and as I discuss in Chapter 6, her husband's presence remained very much alive in Rose's life.

While understanding and knowing the 'truth' of what happened was one part of the process of being able to narrate the story of bereavement and grief, it appeared that describing the internal experience of grief within a rational framework posed difficulties. Participants remarked that they found it hard to describe the feeling of loss, saying how 'complex,' 'ethereal' and difficult to 'quantify' grief was. Participants, therefore, often drew on metaphors to describe their feelings. Grief was described as a place of darkness where the 'light had gone out,' feelings felt 'dark' and 'black' and it was a place that people would move 'down' into. Spatial metaphors were present as Laura described widowhood as a 'very strange land' with 'no map.' Anne too explained her experience of navigating grief as being lost at sea:

> I needed to try something, to catch at some sort of straw because I did feel like a little rubber duck in the most amazing storm at sea, no land, no light, just waves and lightning and thunder and no shore.

While grief was described as a place in which the participants had unwillingly entered, the individual bodily effects of grief were described as physical pain. For example, the pain of grief was described using physical descriptors such as 'spiky' and 'stabbing' and 'raw.' Anne detailed in visual terms the experience of grief and how she once thought it was just a 'metaphor' but discovered the bodily 'affects' of grief:

> I always thought that was a metaphor, it's not, it's physical. My whole body cavity just screamed in pain and even now, when I'm stressed, my sternum feels like all my tendons are pulling off it physically. I just had to this view of the inside of my body being this black and splattered cavity where my heart and soul had just splattered into a million soggy pieces. And there's an awful lot of, trying to stick pieces back together, and it's still a right old mess.

The almost violent imagery conjured up by Anne portrayed a vivid picture of the embodied experience of grief. In the interview Anne drew on metaphors quite often to describe her feelings, acknowledging that she liked to use metaphors. However, I suspected that not all participants were as able to convey the embodied experience of grief through language, moreover in an interview setting. In Chapter 4, I describe the importance of safety the bereavement counsellors and support workers emphasised in the counselling setting, where the client was made to feel they were in a relationship that could hold the 'unbearable' pain of grief. When participants would state things such as: 'It's just awful' or 'the worst experience of my life' I imagined they were referencing this 'unbearable' pain that was hard to quantify and articulate. Further, this was a pain the participants described as embodied, evidenced in a physical impact on the body causing symptoms such as sleeplessness, difficulty eating or as Anne described, a pain located around the sternum.

Therefore, the use of metaphors was one strategy that enabled participants to convey the experience of grief, yet there could be a limit to how much meaning could be made from the experience of grief. In Chapter 6, I discuss further the limits of language (and my chosen method of interviews) in expressing the 'unbearable' physical and emotional pain of grief. While the participants would narrate what had happened, they also remarked how they had not quite understood what had happened. As John remarked over his wife's death:

> Still can't understand why it's all happened, I still don't. I find it difficult to accept it, you know, when I'm daydreaming in a way. It's only when I think to myself, come out, snap out of it.

Speaking about the sudden death of her husband Tania told me:

> Yeah it's a bit strange. I sometimes think now did all that actually really happen?

Listening to the participants' accounts of grief it was as though the rational—or at least those explanations that were available—had reached their limit when it came to explain the event of bereavement. Therefore, participants would use rational and symbolic explanations interchangeably, as demonstrated by Rose's statement above 'it's not logical but.' For Anne it was the nature of her husband's death for which she struggled to find any meaning:

> It just doesn't make sense and, it shouldn't happen. We're in a first world country, we can do all sorts of things and yet we can't keep people safe in office buildings … I never imagined that he wouldn't make it out the front door of the office.

As Anne highlighted, the death of her husband felt nonsensical in a 'first world country' where she felt accustomed to the idea that she and the people around her were relatively safe from immediate threats to life (at least in office buildings). The experience of her husband's death thus challenged Anne's whole belief system, her sense of ontological security. Anne went on to explain how she had lost her faith as a result, unable to 'compute' the death of her husband:

> The thing is through this process, well, I lost all my faith. The point is whether you suddenly start seeing signs in everything that drops from

> the clouds or every rainbow, you either go one way or the other. You either talk about people looking down from heaven and meeting you again or you say no-one could allow that to happen it can't be ... And there is, even four years later I can say to myself what? How on earth? That can't be right, that does not compute.

Anne's 'assumptive world' (Parkes 1972) following the death of her husband, had been transformed. Anne was then left to search for a new sense of meaning. In doing so, she referenced the use of signs and heaven that she acknowledged other people might use to make sense of death but found them unsatisfactory. Yet Anne still relied on some wider meaning to the universe even as she described she no longer believed in the idea of God. Instead she found some meaning in the idea of 'multiverses,' which enabled her to believe the energy and soul of her husband was not destroyed but potentially existing in another dimension.

Despite the individuality of grief, it was interesting to see how the narration of the experience of grief was situated in relatively few 'domains.' Rosenblatt (2000) in his study of parents' narratives of grief found that what the parents talked about fell within a limited number of domains including the moment of death and events following the death and finding meaning and managing feelings. Participants did find various meanings, some of which I have described above, for example, Rose's signs and superstitions and Anne finding comfort in science and multiverses. As I described earlier, the growing medicalisation of grief that seeks to provide a scientific rationale for grief has left individual expressions of grief the preserve of literature and autobiographical accounts. Bennett and Bennett's (2000) study of bereaved participants who experience the presence of deceased people found that the participants interpreted their experience of the presence of a deceased person through both a scientific and supernaturalist interpretive framework, opting for a different discourse depending on the circumstance in which they provided their account. These accounts of bereavement suggest a disjuncture in the public narration and private experiences of grief.

In this section, I have discussed how bereaved people used a mixture of both rational and symbolic explanations to describe their experiences of bereavement and feelings of grief. For instance, Rose described the signs that suggested her husband's pending death, signs not of a medical nature but of a vase of lilac and how it symbolised death in the family. Anne made reference to the story of Harry Potter by J. K. Rowling to symbolise the transition of her husband to another world. Further, Anne told me that although her original religious faith had diminished following bereavement, she believed in multiverses, and that her husband's spirit lived on in a different dimension. For some, the grief theories resonated, others found comfort in spiritual ideas. So, while the public narrative of grief appears to give a clear outline of stages and tasks, in the daily experience of grief people used a variety of discourses to make sense of grief. This creative exploration of meaning-making reaches its limit however when one fails to make sense of grief. In the next section I want to draw further attention to this struggle to piece together a satisfactory story through the account of John, to consider the effects of being unable to find the right story.

Failing to Make Sense of Grief

As alluded to earlier, telling stories and giving voice to one's pain is a commonly accepted tool to provide liberation from suffering and oppression (Charmaz 1999; Charon 2006; Smith and Sparkes 2008). Yet, not all stories get to be heard and the act of storytelling reduces the forms of expression into 'standard' narratives, excluding those unable to articulate their stories. Creative writing and literature potentially provide a privileged site where grief and different expressions of grief are accepted, though access to this site is not available to all. Furthermore, the expression of grief through literature can be used not only as a source of consolation but as a form of 'resistance' to assumed notions of appropriate grieving.

What struck me about John's account was his need to find coherence in what happened and the struggle he encountered in living in the face of incoherence. Rather than viewing this necessarily as a biological need to narrate, I suggest the dominance of certain narrative forms in western cultures can serve to isolate experiences and events that lack a resolution and cannot be easily assimilated into a linear pattern, as anomalous or problematic. Here I present John's search for coherence and his need to find a satisfactory line of reasoning for his wife's death. John's wife died after a short period of illness of terminal cancer. Due to the speed of events, John found it was six months after her death, at the point of interview, that he was going over the details of the death and questioning things:

> I'm finding it harder to accept that than I did straightaway. But it was very quick, it was literally from October, 30th October to the 5th March so it was, barely four months … and I just feel that it's hard that someone who's looked after herself so well, she didn't smoke, hardly drank, kept herself fit, ate the right things and wallop done completely, completely wiped out in four months.

John highlighted details about his wife's lifestyle such as being fit, eating well and being a non-smoker that did not fit with the broader narrative of dying of cancer. John reflected on the things his wife could have done differently saying he felt 'let down' that, as a nurse, she failed to look after herself like her patients. In retrospect, John could see the signs of his wife's stomach pain and how they 'missed' them. He described how now he had the urge to go over the details of his wife's death to solve the puzzle of why she died:

> I keep on looking at it from the point of view that we should've been able to see it coming you know. There should have been some indication that, what did we miss, what did I miss, what did my wife miss … And I kept everything at home, I've kept all the paperwork and we tried to make notes about what people were telling us. … I did think about trying to write it all down and try to do some sort of putting it all in chronological order and try to make some sense of it all … At other times I think to myself well would that do me any good in a way, would it just all bring it, bring it up again and then I'd be left with, what would I do with it then you know. So, it's a bit of a conundrum really.

John appeared to oscillate between the two plans of action: to sit down and make sense of it or to accept he could not do anything about it. It was clear though, evidenced by his wrestling over this conundrum that living with uncertainty was not a comfortable place to be. I asked John how it felt to potentially live with and accept things might not be resolved, he replied:

> Well, I'd rather be clear in my mind where things stood, well you know what the problem was, how it came to be, all those issues. But I just think they're all, well a lot of them are beyond, beyond resolving in effect. You can't do that now. So, I'm just, it's something that I'm pretty certain that I'm just going to have to live with really. Have to sort of say well that's it I just can't take that any further and sort of try and get on with life.

Without an acceptable story of what happened John found he was lacking a resolution that had forced him into what I have called a (liminal) space where it was not clear where 'things stood.' In this liminal space, as John ruminated on his recent past, he was unable to go forward and 'get on with life.' He explained how without this resolution about what had happened he could not make sense of the present or the future:

> It's when you start looking back isn't it, when you, you can put some sort of picture to it all and I think that's probably one of the problems at that moment is that I can't do that. Because my life has changed so much with my wife passing away that until I've got a little bit of history that I can look back on and sort of judge where I am at that, whatever, time. Whereas at the moment I can't do that.

I argue that the absence of a 'little bit of history' meant John could not locate himself in the present and make sense of his life without his wife. Living with unanswered questions John was left with a tenuous attachment to the present where, on the one hand, he recognised he had to just accept and live with it and yet, on the other, the desire to know and make sense remained strong. This sense of ambivalence however was not easy to overcome. John acknowledged the only resolution was then to settle for the absence of an answer:

> And I suppose I'll have to get over that because there's no way round it, I can't, I don't, it'll never be solved that question. I'm never going to resolve it, it's just a feeling I've got and I'm going to have to live with it. Can't, I can't, no-one's going to say, no-one's going to come up with an answer to that problem, I'm just going to have to accept that it's happened and just get on with it really. Hard. Very hard.

It seemed that not having a coherent story placed John outside linear time where he could not rely on a past and a history that made sense from which to locate himself in the present. Instead, John was in a cyclical mode of time, taking each day as it came. This was the only way to manage living on where the past was unclear, and the future was uncertain. Without a story, settling for uncertainty and liminality was the only option. Crafting a clear story about the death was one mode of bringing coherence and understanding to an incomprehensible event. However, the focus on narratives hides the struggle to find a story as described through the account of John, and disadvantages those that lack the language, ability or desire to construct a narrative and allow it to be heard. Living outside of this linear narrative structure meant the need to build familiar structures in daily life through routine and physical activities became increasingly important, as I describe in the next chapter.

Public and Private Narratives of Grief

This chapter has covered a variety of cultural, political and personal factors that frame the meanings of grief and recovery. The space of grief and recovery is a terrain mapped by changing guidance and discourse, from the role of psychiatric diagnosis of mental disorders, the politics of happiness and the transformation of mental health policy, to autobiographies and individual narratives. In this enquiry I have sought to delineate two themes shaping notions around recovery, emotions, and grief. The first is the appearance of an increasing medicalisation of mental distress and an unprecedented intervention of the government into the private and emotional lives of the population. The second is the acknowledgment that alongside this there is a celebration of the individuality and diversity of grief experiences through the proliferation and consumption of individual stories and narratives.

Making sense of grief is a public enterprise, and grief is framed within a modern post-enlightenment discourse that values scientific understandings of health and the emotions. The need for a meaningful story relies on an understanding of the world and the self that is always coherent and comprehensible. In this view, people need to find meaning or be assisted to find meaning; there is no option to decide that grief and death are without meaning. Not finding meaning in grief thus becomes problematic to the public narrative of grief where there is little space for unhappy emotions or stories without a resolution. Further, while making sense of grief is both a formalised activity and increasingly about individual choice and creativity, not all stories are permitted in the public narrative. Grief stories are then categorised into genres where those who fail to recover, or otherwise grieve in a way that could be described as complicated, become worthy of features in newspapers that highlight how certain stories of grief are disagreeable (McQuire 2015; The Mirror 2017; Moore 2014; Parris 2009).

The complicated griever, the wealthy but unhappy, the traumatised soldier, are some of the figures discussed in the first section of this chapter. These figures, through the discourse of recovery have found themselves bound to new authorities in the name of freedom, a relationship all the more subjectifying because the guidance offered appears to emanate from their individual desires (Rose 1989, 17). There is, however, the echo of resistance against this 'obligation to be free,' a resistance often voiced through stories and narratives. However, this is a resistance that embraces the forms of individuality and self-expression produced by the type of governmentality against which it is reacting. The privileged site of literature provides a platform for a variety of grief expression but arguably, it is a platform gained by learning how to tell the right stories.

Taking into account Frank's (2010) argument that narration is a moral impulse, not having a narrative or story about oneself and one's experience apparently has a high price. In this line of argument, the refusal to narrate one's experience of suffering is a refusal of the moral implications of what counts as 'fundamentally' human. Within the recovery model of mental health, the experiences of service users are increasingly presented by mental health services as stories of recovery (Carson et al. 2010; Central and North West London NHS Foundation Trust 2014). However, a growing number of service users have argued that their stories have been sanitised of elements of resistance and incorporated into a neoliberal agenda (Costa et al. 2012; Rose 2014). For these mental health service users, the truly radical move now is to remain silent about one's 'story' and refuse to narrate one's life and experiences (Costa et al. 2012).

This resistance to storytelling has resulted from the realisation that telling one's story can have limited reach in producing change. I argue too that for the bereaved participants the ability to narrate their experiences of bereavement was different to finding meaning and resolution, or to producing tangible changes, either internally or externally. Grief posed a problem that could not be resolved, offering only an ongoing and never-ending process of adjustment. Grief was an experience and feeling particularly resistant to the format of the linear narrative, even as the bereaved participants worked within those structures in their attempt to provide an account of their experience in the interviews.

This need to make sense of grief in order to recover was presented in John's account, where the obligation to make sense was somehow at odds with his desire to remain mulling over the events of his wife's death. John felt the need to write down the timeline of his wife's illness and death in the hope that in doing so he would have a clearer understanding of, and perhaps an answer to, what had happened. Similar sentiments appeared in bereaved participants' accounts; disbelief at the death and dissatisfaction with the medical or other authorities to effectively manage, prevent and make sense of the death. As they described it, it was the apparent failure of such external authorities that hindered their ability to make sense of the death. The authorities that people might turn to in order to make sense of death, such as medical professionals, had failed to provide a satisfactory discourse that enabled the participants to make sense of death. In a modern culture where death cannot be left without a medical cause, the failure to find meaning in grief, and resistance to fitting experience into a meaningful narrative, produces the same outcome of 'non-recovery.'

Notes

1. The five ways to wellbeing: connect, be active, take notice, keep learning, give. Further details available at: https://neweconomics.org/2011/07/five-ways-well-new-applications-new-ways-thinking.
2. List of Recovery College providers available at Mind Recovery Net: http://mindrecoverynet.org.uk/providers/.
3. Triangle Consulting Social Enterprise Limited. 2008. "Recovery Star: The Outcomes Star for adults managing their mental Health." Further details available at: http://www.outcomesstar.org.uk/using-the-star/see-the-stars/recovery-star/.

References

Ahmed, Sara. 2010. *The Promise of Happiness*. Durham and London: Duke University Press.

American Psychological Association. 2013. *Diagnostic and Statistical Manual of Mental Disorders*. 5th ed. Washington: American Psychological Association.

Anthony, William A. 1993. "Recovery from Mental Illness: The Guiding Vision of the Mental Health Service System in the 1990s." *Psychosocial Rehabilitation Journal* 16 (4): 11–23.

Appignanesi, Lisa. 2008. *Mad, Bad and Sad: A History of Women and the Mind Doctors from 1800 to the Present*. London: Virago.

Árnason, Arnar. 2000. "Biography, Bereavement, Story." *Mortality* 5 (2): 189–204.

Barthes, Roland. 1967. "The Death of the Author." In *Art and Interpretation: An Anthology of Readings in Aesthetics and the Philosophy of Art*, edited by Eric Dayton, 383–386. Peterborough, ON: Broadview.

BBC News. 2018. "NHS Prevention Plan Aims to Boost Healthy Life Expectancy." November 5. https://www.bbc.co.uk/news/health-46093750.

Bennett, Gillian, and Kate Mary Bennett. 2000. "The Presence of the Dead: An Empirical Study." *Mortality* 5 (2): 139–157.

Bloch, Maurice. 2011. "The Blob." *Anthropology of This Century*, May 1.

Boelen, Paul A., and Holly G. Prigerson. 2012. "Commentary on the Inclusion of Persistent Complex Bereavement-Related Disorder in DSM-5." *Death Studies* 36 (9): 771–794.

Borgstrom, Erica. 2015. "Planning for an (Un)Certain Future: Choice Within English End-of-Life Care." *Current Sociology* 63 (5): 700–713.

Borgstrom, Erica, and Tony Walter. 2015. "Choice and Compassion at the End of Life: A Critical Analysis of Recent English Policy Discourse." *Social Science & Medicine* 136 (137): 99–105.

Braslow, Joel Tupper. 2013. "The Manufacture of Recovery." *Annual Review of Clinical Psychology* 9: 781–809.

Brown, Phil. 1995. "Naming and Framing: The Social Construction of Diagnosis and Illness." *Journal of Health and Social Behavior*, Extra Issue: 34–52.

Bryant, Richard A. 2012. "Grief as a Psychiatric Disorder." *British Journal of Psychiatry* 201 (1): 9–10.

Bury, Mike. 2001. "Illness Narratives: Fact or Fiction?" *Sociology of Health & Illness* 23 (3): 263–285.

Cabinet Office. 2010. "PM Speech on Wellbeing." November 25, 2010. https://www.gov.uk/government/speeches/pm-speech-on-wellbeing.

Carel, Havi, and Ian James Kidd. 2014. "Epistemic Injustice in Healthcare: A Philosophical Analysis." *Medicine, Health Care and Philosophy* 17 (4): 529–540.

Carson, Jerome, Frank Holloway, Paul Wolfson, and Michelle McNary. 2010. *Recovery Journeys: Stories of Coping with Mental Health Problems*. London: South London and Maudsley NHS Foundation Trust.

Caruth, Cathy. 1995. *Trauma: Explorations in Memory*. Baltimore: John Hopkins University Press.

Central and North West London NHS Foundation Trust. 2014. *Recovery Stories*. London: Central and North West London NHS Trust.

Charmaz, Kathy. 1999. "Stories of Suffering: Subjective Tales and Research Narratives." *Qualitative Health Research* 9 (3): 362–382.

Charon, Rita. 2006. *Narrative Medicine: Honoring the Stories of Illness*. Oxford: Oxford University Press.

Clandinin, D. Jean, and F. Michael Connelly. 2000. *Narrative Inquiry: Experience and Story in Qualitative Research*. San Francisco: Jossey-Bass.

Costa, Lucy, Jijian Voronka, Danielle Landry, Jenna Reid, Becky Mcfarlane, David Reville, and Kathryn Church. 2012. "Recovering Our Stories: A Small Act of Resistance." *Studies in Social Justice* 6 (1): 85–101.

Coutts, Marion. 2014. *The Iceberg: A Memoir*. London: Atlantic Books.
Cromby, John, and Martin E. H. Willis. 2013. "Nudging into Subjectification: Governmentality and Psychometrics." *Critical Social Policy* 34 (2): 241–259.
Davies, William. 2015. *The Happiness Industry: How the Government and Big Business Sold Us Well-Being*. London: Verso.
Deegan, Patricia. 1996. "Recovery as a Journey of the Heart." *Psychiatric Rehabilitation Journal* 19 (3): 91–97.
Dennis, Michael Robert. 2008. "The Grief Account: Dimensions of a Contemporary Bereavement Genre." *Death Studies* 32 (9): 801–836.
Department of Health. 2001. *The Journey to Recovery—The Government's Vision for Mental Health Care*. London: Department of Health.
———. 2011a. *No Health Without Mental Health: A Cross-Government Mental Health Outcomes Strategy for Mental Health*. London: Department of Health.
———. 2011b. *Talking Therapies: A Four-Year Plan of Action—A Supporting Document to No Health Without Mental Health: A Cross-Government Mental Health Outcomes Strategy for Mental Health*. London: Department of Health.
———. 2016. "Prime Minister Pledges a Revolution in Mental Health Treatment." Januaury 11, 2016. https://www.gov.uk/government/news/prime-minister-pledges-a-revolution-in-mental-health-treatment.
Didion, Joan. 2006. *The Year of Magical Thinking*. London: Harper Perennial.
Duncan, Grant. 2010. "Should Happiness-Maximization Be the Goal of Government?" *Journal of Happiness Studies* 11 (2): 163–178.
Easterlin, Richard A., and Laura Angelescu. 2009. "Happiness and Growth the World over: Time Series Evidence on the Happiness-Income Paradox." Discussion Paper No. 4060, March. Bonn: The Institute for the Study of Labor.
Ehrenreich, Barbara. 2010. *Smile or Die: How Positive Thinking Fooled America & the World*. London: Granta.
Foer, Jonathan Safran. 2005. *Extremely Loud & Incredibly Close*. Boston, MA: Mariner Books.
Foucault, Michel. 1973. *The Birth of the Clinic: An Archaeology of Medical Perception*. London: Routledge.
———. 1975. *Discipline and Punish: The Birth of the Prison*. New York: Random House.
Frank, Arthur W. 2006. "Health Stories as Connectors and Subjectifiers." *Health* 10 (4): 421–440.

———. 2010. "In Defence of Narrative Exceptionalism." *Sociology of Health & Illness* 32 (4): 665–667.
Gilbert, Katherine R. 2002. "Taking a Narrative Approach to Grief Research: Finding Meaning in Stories." *Death Studies* 26 (3): 223–239.
Glyde, Tania. 2014. "The Recovery Position." *The Lancet Psychiatry* 1 (2): 119–120.
Goody, Jack. 2006. "From Oral to Written: An Anthropological Breakthrough in Storytelling." In *The Novel Volume 1,* edited by Franco Moretti, 3–36. Princeton, NJ: Princeton University Press.
Hacking, Ian. 1986. "Making up People." In *The Science Studies Reader*, edited by Mario Bagioli, 161–171. London: Routledge.
———. 1999. *The Social Construction of What?* Cambridge, MA: Havard University Press.
Harper, David, and Ewen Speed. 2012. "Uncovering Recovery: The Resistible Rise of Recovery and Resilience." *Studies in Social Justice* 6 (1): 9–25.
Hockey, Jenny, Jeanne Katz, and Neil Small, eds. 2001. *Grief, Mourning and Death Ritual.* Buckingham: Open University Press.
Howarth, Glennys. 2000. "Dismantling the Boundaries Between Life and Death." *Mortality* 5 (2): 127–138.
Jenkins, Rachel, Howard Meltzer, Peter B. Jones, Terry Brugha, Paul Bebbington, Michael Farrell, David Crepaz-Keay, and Martin Knapp. 2008. *Foresight Mental Capital and Wellbeing Project. Mental Health: Future Challenges*. London: The Government Office for Science.
Jones, Edgar, and Simon Wessley. 2005. *Shell Shock to PTSD: Military Psychiatry from 1900 to the Gulf War.* Hove: Psychology Press.
Law, K. 2014. "It Was My Duty to Stop Tom Being Destroyed Before His Death—And Eugene by It", *The Evening Standard,* June 30.
Layard, Richard. 2011. *Happiness: Lessons from a New Science.* London: Penguin.
Leese, Peter. 2002. *Shell Shock: Traumatic Neurosis and the British Soldiers of the First World War.* Basingstoke, Hampshire: Palgrave Macmillan.
Lewis, C. S. 1961. *A Grief Observed.* London: Faber and Faber.
Leys, Ruth. 1994. "Traumatic Cures: Shell Shock, Janet, and the Question of Memory." *Critical Inquiry* 20 (4): 623–662.
Macdonald, Helen. 2014. *H Is for Hawk.* London: Jonathan Cape.
Maciejewski, Paul K., and Holly G. Prigerson. 2017. "Prolonged, but Not Complicated, Grief Is a Mental Disorder." *The British Journal of Psychiatry* 211: 189–191.

Marks, Sarah. 2012. "Cognitive Behavioural Therapies in Britain: The Historical Context and Present Situation." *Cognitive Behaviour Therapies*, 1–24.

McQuire, Caroline. 2015. "Grieving Mother Defends Decision to Buy Her Stillborn Baby Presents Three Years after His Death: 'Placing Toys in His Room Gives Me the Strength to Carry On.'" *The Daily Mail*, January 7.

Mol, Annemarie. 2008. *The Logic of Care: Health and the Problem of Patient Choice*. Oxon: Routledge.

Moore, Anne. 2014. "Tragedy in Thailand: It's Taken 10 Years to Accept that My Sister Died in the Tsunami." *The Guardian*, December 6.

Neimeyer, Robert A. 2005. "Grief, Loss, and the Quest for Meaning: Narrative Contributions to Bereavement Care." *Bereavement Care* 24 (2): 27–30.

Neimeyer, Robert A., Dennis Klass, and Michael Robert Dennis. 2014. "A Social Constructionist Account of Grief: Loss and the Narration of Meaning." *Death Studies* 38 (8): 485–498.

O'Connor, Mary-Frances. 2005. "Bereavement and the Brain: Invitation to a Conversation Between Bereavement Researchers and Neuroscientists." *Death Studies* 29 (10): 905–922.

O'Rourke, Meghan. 2011. *The Long Goodbye: A Year of Grieving*. London: Virago.

Parkes, Colin Murray. 1972. *Bereavement: Studies of Grief in Adult Life*. Harmondsworth: Penguin.

Parris, Matthew. 2009. "I Don't Want to 'Get over' My Father's Death." *The Spectator*, August 12.

Porter, Max. 2015. *Grief Is the Thing with Feathers*. London: Faber and Faber.

Prigerson, Holly G., Mardi J. Horowitz, Selby C. Jacobs, Colin M. Parkes, Mihaela Aslan, Karl Goodkin, Beverley Raphael, Samuel J. Marwit, Camille Wortman, Robert A. Neimeyer, George Bonanno, Susan D. Block, David Kissane, Paul Boelen, Andreas Maercker, Brett T. Litz, Jeffrey G. Johnson, Michael B. First, and Paul K. Maciejewski. 2009. "Prolonged Grief Disorder: Psychometric Validation of Criteria Proposed for DSM-V and ICD-11." *PLoS Medicine* 6 (8): e1000121.

Prigerson, Holly G., and Paul K. Maciejewski. 2017. "Rebuilding Consensus on Valid Criteria for Disordered Grief." *JAMA Psychiatry* 74 (5): 435.

Ramazani, Jahan. 1994. *Poetry of Mourning: The Modern Elegy from Hardy to Heaney*. Chicago: University of Chicago Press.

Reynolds, Charles F., Stephen J. Cozza, and M. Katherine Shear. 2017. "Clinically Relevant Diagnostic Criteria for a Persistent Impairing Grief Disorder: Putting Patients First." *JAMA Psychiatry* 74 (5): 433.

Roberts, Glenn, and Paul Wolfson. 2004. "The Rediscovery of Recovery: Open to All." *Advances in Psychiatric Treatment* 10 (1): 37–49.

Rose, Diana. 2014. "The Mainstreaming of Recovery." *Journal of Mental Health* 23 (5): 217–218.

Rose, Nikolas. 1985. *The Psychological Complex: Psychology, Politics and Society in England, 1869–1939*. London: Routledge & Kegan Paul.

———. 1989. *Governing the Soul: The Shaping of the Private Self.* London: Free Association Press.

Rosenblatt, Paul. 2000. *Parent Grief: Narratives of Loss and Relationship*. Philadelphia: Brunner/Mazel.

Seeley, K. 2015. *Therapy After Terror: 9/11, Psychotherapists and Mental Health*. Cambridge: Cambridge University Press.

Seligman, Martin. 2002. *Authentic Happiness: Using the New Positive Psychology to Realise Your Potential for Lasting Fulfilment*. New York: Simon & Schuster.

Shear, Katherine. 2010. "Complicated Grief Treatment: The Theory, Practice and Outcomes." *Bereavement Care* 29 (3): 10–14.

———. 2012. "Grief and Mourning Gone Awry: Pathway and Course of Complicated Grief." *Dialogues in Clinical Neuroscience* 14 (2): 119–128.

Shepard, Ben. 2002. *A War of Nerves*. London: Pimlico.

Slade, Mike, Neal Adams, and Mary O'Hagan. 2012. "Recovery: Past Progress and Future Challenges." *International Review of Psychiatry* 24 (1): 1–4.

Slade, Mike, Michaela Amering, Marianne Farkas, Bridget Hamilton, Mary O'Hagan, Graham Panther, Rachel Perkins, Geoff Shepard, Samson Tse and Rob Whitley. 2014. "Uses and Abuses of Recovery: Implementing Recovery-Oriented Practices in Mental Health Systems." *World Psychiatry* 13 (1): 12–20.

Smith, Brett, and Andrew C. Sparkes. 2008. "Changing Bodies, Changing Narratives and the Consequences of Tellability: A Case Study of Becoming Disabled Through Sport." *Sociology of Health & Illness* 30 (2): 217–236.

Squire, Corinne. 2005. "Reading Narratives." *Group Analysis* 38 (1): 91–107.

Strayed, Cheryl. 2012. *Wild: From Lost to Found on the Pacific Crest Trail.* New York: Alfred A. Knopf.

Summerfield, Derek. 2002. "Effects of War: Moral Knowledge, Revenge, Reconciliation, and Medicalised Concepts of 'Recovery'." *British Medical Journal* 325: 1105–1107.

Thaler, Richard H., and Cass R. Sunstein. 2009. *Nudge: Improving Decisions About Health, Wealth and Happiness*. London: Penguin.

The Centre for Economic Performance's Mental Health Policy Group. 2006. "The Depression Report: A New Deal for Depression and Anxiety Disorders." London School of Economics and Political Science, Centre for Economic Performance Special Papers.

The Mental Health Taskforce. 2016. *The Five Year Forward View for Mental Health*. London: NHS England and Department of Health.

The Midlands Psychology Group. 2007. "Questioning the Science and Politics of Happiness." *The Psychologist* 20 (7): 422–425.

The Mirror. 2017. "'I Will Eat Mum'—Grieving Daughter to Sprinkle Ashes on Christmas Dinner." *The Mirror*. http://www.mirror.co.uk/news/uk-news/i-eat-mum-christmas-day-11706456.

Tilly, Charles. 1999. "The Trouble with Stories." In *The Social Worlds of Higher Education: Handbook for Teaching in a New Century*, edited by Bernice A. Pescosolido and Ronald Aminzade, 256–270. London: Sage.

Travis, Trysh. 2009. *The Language of the Heart: A Cultural History of the Recovery Movement from Alcoholics Anonymous to Oprah Winfrey*. Chapel Hill, NC: The University of North Carolina Press.

Walter, Tony. 1996. "A New Model of Grief: Bereavement and Biography." *Mortality* 1 (1): 7–25.

Watkin, William. 2004. *On Mourning: Theories of Loss in Modern Literature*. Edinburgh: Edinburgh University Press.

Watts, David. 2011. "The Healing Art of Writing." In *The Healing Art of Writing*, edited by Joan Baranow, Brian Dolan, and David Watts. San Francisco: University of California Press.

Willoughby, Nick. 2015. "'You Can't Tame Grief': Helen Macdonald on Her Bestselling Memoir 'H Is for Hawk.'" *Salon*, March 10. http://www.salon.com/2015/03/09/you_can%E2%80%99t_tame_grief_helen_macdonald_on_her_bestselling_memoir_h_is_for_hawk/.

Wittchen, H. U., F. Jacobi, J. Rehm, A. Gustavsson, M. Svensson, B. Jönsson, and H.-C. Steinhausen. 2011. "The Size and Burden of Mental Disorders and Other Disorders of the Brain in Europe 2010." *European Neuropsychopharmacology* 21 (9): 655–679.

Zisook, Sidney, and Katherine Shear. 2009. "Grief and Bereavement: What Psychiatrists Need to Know." *World Psychiatry* 8 (2): 67–74.

4

Affective Practices: Managing Grief

This chapter explores the different practices that seek to manage grief. I adopt Wetherell's (2012) term 'affective practices' to express the ways grief is embodied, situated and performed. The 'affective practices' I detail reflect a mixture of both 'formal' rituals such as funerals or professional counselling, and everyday mundane activities that took on a new purpose in grief. In the first section of this chapter, I present accounts from my study which highlight a distinction between the rituals concerning the management of the disposal of the body, which were already prescribed by the cultural tradition, and the management of grief, which had a less clear route to follow. Following bereavement, the people I interviewed described a changed world where the time and space they inhabited had been transformed. As discussed in the previous chapter, in such a liminal space the boundaries between appropriate and inappropriate behaviours dissolved and the bereaved participants described feeling as if they were in a world where everything was 'black,' without a map or guide to help them through. Planning a daily routine emerged as particularly important in giving meaning to an existence lacking in sense, a meaning that was upheld by a person that had now gone. Participants described the interaction with space and objects,

C. Pearce, *The Public and Private Management of Grief*,
https://doi.org/10.1007/978-3-030-17662-4_4

as well as the ritualisation of the everyday events, as strategies that enabled them to carry on living. In this liminal space, being busy in the present helped to locate a self where the past was difficult to narrate, and the future had been lost.

While such activities were described by the bereaved person as crucial to their ability to get on with daily life, within the framework of productive work the bereavement practitioners viewed these ordinary activities as 'distractions' from grief work or 'short-term' fixes. In the second section of this chapter, I highlight some of the components of bereavement support, largely in the format of bereavement counselling, and how such support seeks to aid recovery from grief. In all of the bereavement practitioners' accounts there was an emphasis on 'grief work.' Describing grief as 'work' is not an accidental metaphor, for the process involves a meticulous labour both within the psyche and in the social relational life of the person. Even in times of grief the bereaved person is encouraged to be productive and do one's homework; the effects of discipline showing their traces in conceptualising grief as work. I argue grief work is a 'technology of the self,' which as Foucault (1988) claimed, people undertake in the hope it will bring them a positive value such as happiness. The technology of grief work both expects and produces active subjects, willing to follow the method and overcome their grief. Further, bereaved people are also managing themselves; doing the work of surveillance on behalf of the 'authorities.' In this way, grief work becomes a collaborative project. In turn, the relationship people have with their own grief also changes, from a subjective feeling to something that can be objectively measured and classified and worked upon. Drawing on interview findings I reveal the nuances, conflicts and ambiguities in bereavement counselling, and how the therapeutic response is not merely disciplinary but a productive encounter. As elucidated in the work of Árnason (1998, 2001, 2007), bereavement counselling occurs within a productive rather than repressive setting, where identities are crafted as a co-production. Finally, I consider the failure to perform grief, or deviant forms of grieving practices that reveal the social norms that constrain the seemingly 'natural' expression of grief.

Rituals

Distractions

From the interviews I noted how following bereavement, it was not just a person who had been lost but also a motivating force in people's lives, and the routine and structure that had been created by living with and being in partnership with another person. Household work became significant for some participants, particularly John and Paul, who were in retirement. The shift in daily routine was also amplified for those who had been long-term carers for their partners or parent before they had died. Paul and Saadhia had both left their employment to take over caring responsibilities. They both described how their daily routine was intimately entwined with another person. The absence of that person highlighted how much space had been occupied by the work of caring and how the days were timetabled with activities, as Paul described following the death of his wife:

> [Y]ou get a closer bond so it was even more, probably even more painful because it, the routine you had, getting up and doing things and looking after them and making sure this and doing some washing every day and washing her and cleaning up and making sure she's okay and using the commode, clearing that up multiple times a day and doing this and doing that you know it's (sighs). And then when that's not there …

In a similar way following the death of her mother Saadhia explained:

> … when you get yourself into this routine and timetable, and then you hear the voices. I hear her calling me, she used to always say: 'Saadhia, Saadhia!'

For both Paul and Saadhia being a carer provided a centre around which their life had revolved. The loss of the person they cared for daily made the absence all the more acute. However, for all participants, including those who were not carers, there was still a feeling that the centre of their life was lost and with it the 'incentive' or 'motivation' to carry on living. Paul described how walking his dogs created a routine, where he felt following the death of his wife he had nothing to do:

> Even now I haven't got an awful lot of incentive, I make myself, I make myself get up in the morning have a little bit of a routine, basically because of the dogs to be honest … so I have to get up and I get up at a certain time and do things but apart from that, apart from the fact I go out and do some shopping every day or make myself go out, that's really, that's it, I've got nothing. Nothing to do.

In whatever form, often participants described the necessity of having dependents that provided a reason to get up in the morning. Similarly, John talked about the need to 'come up with' some motivation or find a hobby:

> So, I've got to come up with some sort of, things to do in effect, some sort, put some sort of motivation into my life you know, whether it's doing some sort of charity work or whatever or actually coming up with some sort of hobby that I want to do.

Though he had never 'had much of a hobby,' finding some activity suddenly had taken on a crucial importance in John's life now that his wife was no longer with him. For both John and Paul, it was the physical act of doing some form of hobby or work that they felt they needed in order to face the 'nothingness' of grief. It appeared they were attempting to build their own structure by thinking up things to do or getting out the house every day. These acted as distractions for them both, which they described as 'beneficial' to get them away from thinking about themselves or their wives:

> … a diversion, away from being here, get yourself out, go and join a club, go and do this and go and do that, go and meet people. (Paul)

> Life's very hectic at times, to be honest with you. And I suppose in effect that's been beneficial for me because it's, there's always been something to

think of apart from me thinking of myself and my wife you know … and I think that's the main thing for me is if I can keep busy then I can take my mind off my problem. (John)

Keeping busy through socialising, as well as household activities and family responsibilities, was of key importance for John and Paul in that it 'diverted' them away from 'here and myself' (Paul). Paul described how being around people he became 'outward' again but as soon as he came back home, he returned to his 'grey dark feelings.' For John it seemed that managing thoughts and feelings was itself a form of labour. John described how he 'put off' thoughts and feelings and concentrated on other activities such as driving or being with his grandchildren. At other times he explained, 'It'll hit me, and I have to stop what I'm doing and think about it.'

However, within this activity, John told me he was doing little for himself that brought enjoyment. Planning work and things to do was out of the need to have 'something in the pipeline,' which enabled him to 'get by.' While John was also open to counselling interventions, Paul was clear that he needed to deal with grief in his own way. He felt counselling could not provide anything he did not already know: the answer for Paul was through finding 'diversions' from his grief.

Laura found that the activities she used to engage in such as reading she was no longer able to do, and like John and Paul, the loss of her husband meant she lost the source of motivation in her life. Laura described how she would start but not finish anything:

It's too much effort to finish it, I get bored, and I have no motivation to move forward. Because when I get bored with something my husband would go, "Oh we've paid so much money for that and you're just going to leave it there, are you really not going to finish it?". He'd guilt me and encourage me to move forward, but there's no reason to move forward. There's nothing, there's no reason to my life. I go to work, I come home, I eat, I do the things I'm supposed to do.

It seems, being busy was a strategy to fill the space left by the loss of their partners. John reflected on how spending more time with his grandchildren would probably 'take her place.' For him resolution was in activities, maybe taking up golf or getting interested in bowls, John remarked, 'I think probably that's how it'll be resolved.' In these examples, it was as if the experience of grief gave rise to a need to be 'doing' where distractions gave a temporary anchor in the liminal impasse of a new and meaningless present. As Lewis (1961) described in *A Grief Observed*, grief gives life a 'permanently provisional feeling.' I noted this provisional feeling in participants' accounts where grief produced a lack of meaning, incentive and motivation. In the grief over his wife Lewis wrote about how there seemed little point in starting anything: 'I yawn, I fidget, I smoke too much' (1961, 30). This was a situation of suspended agency, where the practices that the participants undertook were a means to counteract the sense that everything had become the same in its meaning and purpose.

Negotiating Space and Objects

In interviewees' accounts, spaces and objects played interesting roles in the management of grief and memories of the deceased person. For instance, participants described visiting cemeteries and gardens. The influence of the material environment on the participants' ongoing relationship with the deceased person was evident and impacted in varying degrees. These 'everyday' rituals as I describe them often focused on the home and the practical tasks of running a household that gained a renewed significance in bereavement. As Hockey et al. (2005) identified, the practical aspects of everyday living such as shopping, socialising and cooking were intimately bound up with the 'emotional transition of bereavement' (136). In many respects, the home acted like a shrine to the memory of their deceased partner where the objects served to keep and sustain memories. But the attachment to the home could be ambivalent—both a comforting and upsetting reminder. The scene of 'going home' was described in several of the accounts:

> Going home is the worst thing really. Because that's like you open the door and you, and no matter what happens you expect her to be there,

> and she's not. But I find that hard even if I'm going down the shops or whatever. It's very hard going home. (Paul)

After the sudden death of her husband Tania described the need to move to a new house:

> I moved house nine months after he died. Just because purely it was such a huge house to keep on and the fact that we'd found him there, every time I walked through the door it was a reminder.

The death of a cohabiting partner or family member either fostered a greater (and often ambivalent) attachment to the house and possessions or, in the case of Tania, a need to move out into a new and different environment. Alternatively, bereavement could lead, in extremis, to homelessness as was the case for two participants, Jamie and Saadhia, following the death of a mother. An increased ambivalent attachment to the home was especially pertinent in John and Paul's account who, after long-term marriages, found that without their wives they lacked the motivation to keep things tidy in the house, having to learn how to cook or being unable to rid themselves of objects in the house. Paul feared that he was becoming a hoarder as he had become 'very lazy' as his wife was not around to 'chase' him and 'harass' him about things that needed to be done around the house. He was also unable to clear his wife's possessions. He remarked that other people had suggested he get rid of his wife's objects but for Paul it would be an act of 'betrayal':

> And people say "oh why don't you get rid of them why don't you do this and why don't you do that," I can't … She's got loads of clothes, loads of things, but everything is, the way I look at it Caroline, it's like a betrayal. To me, you know.

I interviewed Paul in his home so I had the opportunity to see some of the objects he described. In the living room there were walls of shelves filled with books and DVDs and there were clear traces of his wife, a selection of walking sticks resting in the corner of the room and a selection of women's perfumes on one of the shelves. When Paul explained there was 'too much' and 'lots of things,' I could see clearly to what he was referring. He explained how his wife was 'possessive' over her things and 'she knew exactly where almost anything was':

> … even a tiny little ceramic thimble she would say it's on the third shelf, little cabinet down there behind the so and so, she knew, oh yeah, she knew.

Paul was adamant that he would never clear her things out of the house, but I did ask him what he thought might happen if he were to get rid of those objects. Paul paused before telling me he simply could not see himself ever doing it. The attachment was not to his own objects and possessions, only his wife's and those things they shared together. John, too, had a similar struggle finding he was still living in the house with things exactly where his wife had left them. John was aware that this was not necessarily what he 'should' be doing, detailing his experience in a bereavement support group where some of the group members spoke about how they got rid of the deceased person's belongings straight away. John acknowledged that, in keeping his wife's clothes and leaving the house unchanged, he was 'still hanging on to her':

> I'm just, I'm not, I don't want to lose her. And I know I have to … it's sort of like I don't want to lose her yet. And you think, at other times I think to myself, "Oh, that's being silly" but I just, well it doesn't hurt anybody just leave it as it is, it's only going to affect me so why worry about what other people are going to think.

The only motivator to clear the house of his wife's things was 'what other people think' and yet John contemplated that leaving things as they were was not really hurting anyone. In her exploration of how bereaved people used objects in their grieving and memorialising of the deceased person, Gibson (2004, 2008) utilised the psychoanalytic concept of 'cathexis' (Freud 1917) to portray how bereaved people held on to material objects, not only psychic objects, as a mode of transitioning through their grief. Gibson argued that the objects of the dead carry powerful symbols of their presence noting that the transition through grief often followed a move away from these objects, the objects acted as an intermediary enabling the transfer of the attachment from the deceased person to be integrated back into the ego. However, I argue that for some participants, there was a constant need to maintain their obvious presence in the everyday life of the bereaved person. Objects would 'animate' the presence of the deceased (Hockey et al. 2005) temporarily as part of the mourning process or, in the case with Rose, objects would become more permanently animated by her deceased husband, becoming what Gibson (2004) described as 'melancholy objects.' Rose told me:

> I've got this knitted old English sheepdog, massive thing, but if you put him upside down in the bed beside, it looks just like, it looks just like Simon laying there! And he came everywhere with me … So it was just like he was there.

Not only did the character of the deceased person animate objects but was also was relocated in space. So, while Rose's husband was now brought back to life through her sheepdog toy, her husband's ashes were also somewhere out in the river Thames:

> I just poured him out and … it goes straight down. No, you would not know he was there. And I was just literally pouring him around … It was amazing. And because I always say um, I always used to say if Simon was turning in his grave, I think he's out to the Thames by now, well out in the Thames by now.

I went to visit Rose in her home to conduct the interview. Rose had remained living in the house she shared with her husband, being alone for 26 years. Following the death of her husband, Rose began to hoard objects. She showed me around her home and her 'clutter' as she described it, which had filled some of the rooms of the house so that it was impossible to enter. As we spoke we sat in the living room surrounded on either side by boxes of Rose's belongings. Rose showed me her bedroom that had just enough space for her to climb into bed with a computer and a TV positioned for easy viewing. From how Rose portrayed it, she had an almost indifferent relation to the objects that congregated around her, as though the stuff had accumulated due to a lack of interest rather than out of a strong attachment. This lack of care was in stark contrast to how she described her husband's control over the home environment; not only in how the house appeared but, in the running, and organisation of their family, where he was very much head of the family.

Some of the participants acknowledged that being left with the sole responsibility of the household at times felt overwhelming, leading Paul to become lazy or for Anne to move to a smaller home. John told me he had 'a freezer full of food' he did not need. For John while some objects were retained and provided with meaning, other objects, such as too much food, became unwanted clutter. For the participants, holding on to objects was a way of holding on to the person who had died, yet conversely, the rejection of the home could be a rejection of the influence—positive or negative—the deceased person may have had over the home. This was captured in Rose's ambivalent connection to the objects she hoarded, where she told me that in the event of a fire there was nothing she would attempt to save. Yet her statement was belied by the quantity of belongings that surrounded her. Rose contended her hoard had formed out of indifference rather than attachment, and her indifference was a result of the dominant role her husband had played in their home. However, I argue Rose's accumulation of objects could be read as one of resistance to her husband and the way he controlled the home. In his absence, Rose in her hoarding was reclaiming the space as her own; crowding out her husband's influence, leaving only enough space for her husband that Rose could comfortably manage.

Grief Work in Practice

So far, I have presented the experiences of bereaved people navigating their way through a new and liminal landscape and the strategic and social activities that involved engaging in everyday rituals and practices and negotiating space and objects. I emphasised the important role of the ordinary and mundane activities that might alternatively be viewed as 'distractions' from grief work but were described by the bereaved person as crucial to their ability to get on with daily life. This is a trope common in the understanding of grief work, where it is understood that grief can be dealt with successfully via certain methods.

This belief in the work involved in overcoming grief stems from the early psychological studies interpreting Freud's (1917) 'detaching' of the ego from the lost object as formal work to be undertaken in the individual psyche. This was further emphasised by Worden's (1991) 'tasks' of grief, where the language used clearly denoted grief as an active rather than passive process that unfolded naturally. The active need to intervene in grief was based on the premise that left unattended, grief could transform into pathological forms, or 'unlimited' mourning as Gorer (1965) termed it, which had negative consequences for the individual and society. Efforts to ward off the possibility of being 'derailed' into 'complicated grief' (Shear 2012), led to the creation and need for bereavement counselling, and bereavement care professionals whose responsibility was to ensure grief remained on a 'normal' course.

As discussed in Chapter 2, whether formal 'grief work' is of benefit to the bereaved person remains debatable, with some studies finding bereavement counselling to be ineffective and potentially harmful (Schut 2010). However, this is outweighed by discourses that highlight the 'socio-economic costs' of bereavement, positioning bereavement as a public health concern (SECOB Project Research Group 2013; Stephen et al. 2014). Positioned as a 'risk,' the need for expert intervention and the management of grief is legitimated as an economic and social responsibility. Grief, much like birth and death, is no longer an ordinary life event but a risk, an extraordinary event to be governed and one that normalises the role of experts intervening into the ordinary.

As Hockey and Small (2001) have discussed, within bereavement counselling there appears a proliferation of specialisms but a marginalisation from the mainstream. This might be due to the nature of bereavement that does not favour brief time-limited therapies such as cognitive behavioural therapy more commonly used in mental health care services, to manage conditions such as depression. Bereavement counselling and its person-centred focus remains little changed and, in many respects, has not incorporated the research findings of the grief and bereavement literature into practice. This is, perhaps, a result of the emphasis on grief as 'normal' and 'natural' and a subsequent shying away from any forms of 'medicalising' grief. Yet it also indicative of the gap between bereavement care practice and the implementation of empirical evidence.

In what follows I draw on interviews with bereavement counsellors and support workers from four different organisations to discuss the various models they used and how they were transferred into practice. I also discuss my participation in a Grief Recovery UK workshop, designed for personal development as well as training to become a certified 'Grief Recovery Specialist.' I highlight some of the key components that were described as key to the bereavement counselling process[1] though what makes 'grief work' effective in practice was often described in more nuanced terms, where bereavement practitioners shied away from prescriptive statements. The reluctance to make prescriptive statements about grief work reflected how the term 'recovery' in grief and bereavement literature is contested and often controversial (Balk 2004, 2008). Contrary to the embrace of recovery in mental health care services, recovery from grief was not something that was always agreed as being possible, indeed, recovery could seem like a dirty word. The 'Grief Recovery Method' (James and Friedman 2009) provides a contrast to the ambiguities of the bereavement counselling endeavour, as an organisation that makes clear and strong 'truth claims' about the possibility of recovery from grief through the undertaking of a series of specific actions and exercises. I discuss these conflicts as well as agreements on what recovery from grief entailed and how it was achieved, or not, through the assistance of the expertise of bereavement professionals. As highlighted in Chapter 2, there lies a tension between the proclamation of grief as natural and normal and the justification of external intervention into individuals' grieving. I explore how this tension persists in the facilitation of the grief process, where the knowledge of grief lies not in individual experience but the expert's understanding of it.

The Type of Counselling Approach and Method

The counsellors and support workers deployed a number of models of grief in their practice as well utilising humanistic counselling approaches. The approach employed by the majority of counselling practitioners was a client/person-centred model derived from the work of Rogers (1951) and drawing on an eclectic approach. The person-centred model was central to volunteer training at Cruse Bereavement Care. Counsellors at London based bereavement service Caris (Christian Action and Response in Society) had completed or were undertaking counselling qualifications before working as bereavement counsellors. Consequently, Caris counsellors tended to have a broader range of influences in their approach. Some counsellors demonstrated an integrative approach that touched upon a number of different theories and techniques including Bowlby's attachment theory, Gestalt therapy (Wertheimer 1938), mindfulness (Kabat-Zinn 1994) and referred to psychodynamic approaches and utilised concepts such as transference and countertransference, the unconscious, with an emphasis on childhood experiences (derived from the work of Freud).

Rogers' (1951) person-centred approach emphasises the client as expert. It is a non-directive approach that holds that the client knows her or himself best. The role of the counsellor is to be skilled in empathetic understanding and non-judgemental listening in order to allow the client to express their feelings. Roger's theory is reliant upon the idea that humans have an inherent potential, and tendency to growth and to be whole. This positive view of the person is the 'organismic self,' which innately seeks self-actualisation. However, people also possess a 'self-concept' produced and affected by others around them that can conflict with the organismic self if one's self-concept becomes distorted which can happen when there is a lack of positive regard and approval from those around them. Thus, the role of the therapist is to enable the client to become fully functioning and bring congruence between the phenomenal field of experience and the conceptual structure of the self. If achieved, this would represent freedom from internal strain and anxiety, and the capacity to use talents and abilities, realise potential, move towards complete knowledge of self and maintain responsibility for determining one's actions.

The interviewees also drew on grief models with many making reference to the dual-process model (Stroebe and Schut 1999) (nine out of twelve participants), along with Worden's tasks (three participants made explicit reference), continuing bonds (mentioned by five participants) and the stages of grief (also mentioned by five participants). Also popular were the ideas of 'growing around grief' conceptualised by Tonkin (1996) and the 'grief wheel.' These models featured in the grief and bereavement specific training that the counsellors and volunteers received at Cruse and Caris and were used in an 'integrative' way. Here models were used in a pick and mix fashion depending on 'the individual and their pathway,' and 'making use of whatever is available.'

Representatives of the organisations to whom I spoke employed different systems for the number of sessions a client received. For example, Cruse and St Christopher's had a limit of twelve sessions, offering six sessions in the first instance. Caris was unusual in that it offered an open-ended service, where counsellors had an opportunity to build relationships over time with clients: a difference the counsellors believed affected how they worked. Often time limitations were due to organisational restraints that demanded proof of the success of the intervention.

By way of contrast, the Grief Recovery Method (GRM) clearly states it is not counselling or therapy. A senior member of Grief Recovery UK, Ellen, appeared quite dismissive of bereavement counselling and of the service provided by Cruse. Speaking of her experience: 'I've had counselling, I think what they call person-centred, whatever that means, and I really didn't like that.' Ellen was critical of the lack of choice in bereavement care and described it as a 'disservice to the bereaved.' For her the GRM presents something very different, and better. Ellen told me: 'It's my goal that by the time I retire people won't say Cruse automatically they'll say Grief Recovery. That is my mission to knock Cruse off that.'

The GRM is a series of steps, described in the Grief Recovery Handbook; first created by John W. James. The steps involve a number of activities that must be followed in the stated order. For example, the first is to write a 'loss history graph,' which details all the losses people have experienced in their life, loss being broader than death and encompassing 'the loss of hopes, dreams and expectations.' The second step is to write a 'relationship history graph' for the relationship with whom people wish to find 'completion.' This graph documents the key aspects of a relationship with the chosen person (deceased or alive) on a timeline. The third and final step is to write a 'completion letter' to the person, which again has a very strict format. The key to each activity is that the letter had to be read out to another person. Along the way there are a number of exercises and concepts to learn, from the 'six myths of grief' to 'short-term energy relieving behaviours' (STERBs). For Ellen the novelty of this approach could not be understated:

> Now I believe, that until John James put the words grief and recovery together nobody else had … and that's why we changed our name from grief recovery to the grief recovery method, so that we could trademark it.

When I asked Ellen whether the GRM utilised any of the other dominant grief theories, she replied: 'Nope. That's all head stuff.' The GRM is against 'intellectualising' grief declaring that grief is a matter for the heart. The dominant ideas around grief were thus ignored by the GRM, due to the fact they were seeking an 'intellectual solution to an emotional problem.' Ellen told me that the 'growing around grief' idea made her 'angry' because it's 'simply not true.' Rather, in the GRM grief is 'chucked out' and gotten 'rid of' through completion.

Below, I explain further the different perspectives among the participants concerning what recovery from grief involves. However, here I want to note the seeming ambiguity in the role of the bereavement helper who in different settings occupies the position of counsellor, support worker, volunteer or 'coach' who provides a 'toolkit.' In the rest of this chapter, I intend to separate where possible 'counsellor' and 'bereavement support worker' to acknowledge the difference in levels of training among the participants. Furthermore, in bereavement work and in contrast to work within mental health care, personal experience of bereavement is often a desirable feature of a potential candidate that can substitute for any lacking in formal counselling qualifications and training, as I describe next.

The Making of the Bereavement Expert

> A lot of us have got backgrounds with personal experiences, which has led us to do what we do now. So, you get a connection - it's not formal counselling, it's professional we are all properly trained and its professional - but at the same time there's lots of empathy and, can't say friendliness, but just connection and empathy. (Susan)

Like Susan quoted above, the majority of bereavement care practitioners I interviewed spoke in some capacity of their own experience of loss and how the knowledge of loss either provided them with the incentive to become a bereavement counsellor or how it enhanced their work. Susan described how at Cruse 'a lot of the counsellors and supervisors' were drawn to the work at Cruse because of their own experiences. Many of the participants told me of their own personal experience of loss in order to explain why they became engaged in bereavement work. Getting involved in bereavement counselling was a way to 'give something back' and do something 'positive' following their loss. They also told me that having such experience meant that they had something to offer as counsellors, even without formal counselling training. This, some of the participants claimed, was because the mutual experience of loss was considered to produce a 'connection' where the potential counsellor could 'understand how it feels.' A personal experience of grief was considered to complement the person-centred approach to practice that encouraged the counsellor to imagine and feel the world of the client, despite the Rogerian approach encouraging empathy rather than a sharing of the experience. In one case, it was not even the experience of bereavement by death that led her towards bereavement counselling. Caris counsellor Claire described how her experience of illness impacted on her:

> I felt, I know something about loss, and I know something about looking at it in the face in a way and finding meaning in it. And I think that was, I think that was what led me to think yeah bereavement counselling is what I will apply for. (Claire)

In all cases, being aware and reflective about one's own 'loss background' was included in the bereavement counselling training, albeit in different ways. For example, at Caris, counsellors would create their own 'grief map' of the losses they experienced. This was understood as part of the necessary personal development of the counsellors that would raise awareness of any 'unconscious' thoughts and feelings around grief and bereavement that might become problematic in the counselling encounter and prevent the counsellor from listening to the client. A background or experience of loss might be an incentive to getting involved in bereavement counselling, but in a person-centred approach while self-awareness was key to being able to focus fully on the client's needs the personal experiences of the counsellor should not enter into the counsellor–client encounter.

Grief Recovery UK explicitly embraced the practitioner's personal experience of loss in the training of their 'grief recovery specialists.' In fact, personal experience was considered key to being able to train others. At the Grief Recovery training workshop I attended, all trainees had to undertake the 'personal workshop' which had to be 'completed' in order to undertake the extra day of specialist specific training. Further, being able to speak about one's own experience is key to the method. As Ellen described:

> We don't use a professional mask in grief recovery we don't make our faces blank, we show our human emotions and we share our personal stuff which is a complete no-no [in other methods].

Ellen here was highlighting the difference between the GRM and counselling where personal disclosure is not standard practice; indeed, disclosure from the counsellor goes against the counsellor/client contract. In the GRM the idea is that the 'leader goes first.' As demonstrated at the workshop, Ellen showed us her own loss history and relationship graph, spoke openly and copiously about her deceased husband as well as her father and even her current relationship and wedding plans. She noted: 'Counsellors would never do that. No, no, no.' Within the GRM however, the emphasis is on 'telling the truth' and showing 'real stuff.' The claim to 'realness' is a repeated theme, displayed clearly in another publication *Moving Beyond Loss* (Friedman and James 2013) which is subtitled: 'real answers to real questions from real people.'

Speaking about one's loss history was thus used to reveal the 'authenticity' of the GRM in contrast to the 'masks' of counsellors. Yet arguably, the 'mask' of counsellors is a means to create important boundaries between counsellor and client. For Ellen, the principle of 'leader goes first' created 'safety' but it could also create confusion. At one point during the facilitation of the Grief Recovery workshop Ellen began to cry as she went through her 'relationship graph,' asking one of the group to give her a hug. Listening to other group members in training the following day questions were raised over her credibility, insofar as some being unconvinced she had gotten 'over' the death of her husband. Even Ellen was somewhat aware of the confusion:

> It's a really bizarre thing, I have to constantly tread this fine line between Ellen the widow and Ellen the Grief Recovery specialist. So, I wear the two hats.

This contrasted with how Caris counsellor Wendy spoke about the boundaries of the counselling setting. These boundaries existed not only in the counselling room itself but needed to be embodied by the counsellor. Wendy believed the lack of strength of these boundaries would then show themselves when the counsellor was taken outside of the familiar setting, to a client's home, for example, where the counsellor and client were away from the familiar props of the counselling encounter:

> My view on it is the boundaries only became confused if the counsellor is confused about what counselling is. And you can be in a consulting room because someone else set the room up, you can appear to be a counsellor much more, but actually fundamentally if the boundaries are confused in the home setting then that's because the counsellor is confused. So, it shows up weak counsellors more but if you're not a weak counsellor then it's a marvellous setting … so there has to be an ownership on the counsellor's side about what boundaries matter and what one's don't.

However, as the GRM does not claim to be counselling, the parameters were quite different. The role of the specialist is to 'teach the steps' of the handbook: 'We're not messing about with your head, we're not analysing anything,' declared Ellen. Subsequently, the potential specialists need not undertake formal training or an application process. Instead, they were required to attend the four-day workshop[2] and have 'an open mind and open heart.' Following the workshop, people were then 'licensed' as 'Grief Recovery Specialists' either to set up their own one-to-one or group sessions using the GRM, charged at a price of their choosing, or incorporate it into their existing work.

Counselling as Normalisation

> And it was almost when I gave her permission, to say look it's completely understandable and it's completely normal that you would be upset … It's completely normal to be feeling the way you're feeling … and so to be able to dispel that myth, to help to normalise feelings, because I think that's a big part of bereavement counselling: it's about normalisation. (Linda)

As Linda described, a big part of bereavement counselling is about 'normalisation' and 'normalising feelings.' However, there was some ambiguity around how 'normal' and 'abnormal' were defined. Grief was described as individual and unique but then also a 'process' that was 'natural' and 'normal.' Normal and natural were often used interchangeably and when I explored with interviewees what was meant by 'normal,' many of them had difficulty providing an easy answer. They emphasised that normal could be quite broad. Describing the activity of 'normalising' grief was intended to make people experiencing grief feel better, rather than to state there is a 'normal way' to grieve. As Charlotte put it: 'When I talk about normalising emotions it's more about being in a world where it's okay to feel like all you want to do is lie on the ground and stare at shoes.' But normal was also a measure in models of grief, or as Susan mentioned, 'photocopies of all the emotions' that she would use so that clients could 'see them all written down' and learn that what they were feeling was normal, 'it gives them something concrete.'

Normal emerged as something to be achieved, as something that has been lost in grief, yet at the same time the grief process itself was judged as either normal or not. The use of the term 'normal grief' implied some form of movement forward, in contrast to those who got 'stuck.' Cruse bereavement support worker Susan used the 'growing around grief' model to measure clients' return to 'normality.' Susan drew me a diagram to demonstrate, drawing 'the grief' as a circle in the centre and then circles that would expand around the grief, as she described:

> And so, you can, after the first few sessions you get a feel if they are totally immersed in all that or if they are not, you can start (draws circle) went back to work for two weeks you can put that outside there, meet up with friends now and again. So that's the grief but … a person's got a little bit, is in the normal world … so even though that's their grief, there's a bit of normality going on, restoration if you like round there.

Grief could be categorised into types, whether 'straightforward' and 'run of the mill' or 'complicated' and 'risky.' Cruse's Early Intervention Project, for example, aimed to identify 'complicated grief' even before it developed into 'prolonged grief disorder.' The project was designed to provide support to people within six months of being bereaved and who may show signs of developing prolonged grief disorder. Thus 'complicated' grievers were separated out from the 'run of the mill' grievers. Participants' inability to express clearly what was normal highlighted the conflict that, at times, appeared when emphasising both the individual and unique feelings of the grieving client and the belief in a 'natural process' of grief.

Furthermore, constructing grief into a process standardised the time limit on grieving, establishing a time limit on grief signalled when grief should end, and recovery should begin. Having a sense of the 'normal' course of grief gave those working within bereavement care an idea of when grief stopped being normal and started being 'prolonged.' However, 'normal' tended to be emphasised by the bereaved participants and the bereavement care practitioners not in order to imply one 'norm' but to embrace a diverse range of behaviours under the category of 'normal.' On the one hand, this meant 'normal grief' could encompass a wide range of feelings and behaviours. Especially for the bereaved participants, the meaning of grief was very personal and reflected the idiosyncrasies of their relationship with the deceased person. On the other hand, while it was agreed that grief was individually expressed, from the practitioner perspective, common traits could be identified. The role of 'normalising grief' was for bereavement counsellors and support workers a way of reaffirming grief as a 'natural' human emotion.

Emotion Work

> We are working with the emotions, grief is all about emotion. (Ellen)

As Ellen identified, grief was all about working with emotions, and my interviews highlighted how participants drew on a variety of, sometimes conflicting, metaphors and images to describe the work of grief. Grief was often described as a space to be worked through and moved out of: 'You can't go around it, you can't go under it, you can't go over it, you have to go through it' (Ellen). But grief was also described as something that was 'inside' the person that needed to be 'externalised.' For example, grief work was described as 'pulling,' 'hoiking,' and 'bringing up emotions.' Furthermore, emotions and grief were described as having a life of their own and could be resistant to being managed. Emotions were viewed as 'fluid' and unable to be contained and could inhabit different bodies and be 'transferred' on to different people. For example, Charlotte described how in transferring feelings of grief, people may not recognise their feelings until another bereavement or loss:

> Because they'll then transfer those feelings on to something else or someone else. Or say for example you had a mum and a dad, and the dad died, and the mum and the dad had divorced, and the kid was always, grew up with the mum and the mum would say oh that's a terrible person and then the dad dies. The kid's still not allowed to grieve for the dad because mum's still there and mum's still saying what a terrible person this was but

when mom dies you lose your mom and then you also go, 'shit I lost my dad as well!'

For this reason, as trauma counsellor Tony told me, emotions had to be 'worked through' and 'dealt with' otherwise they would 'catch up with you' and 'come back and bite you on the bum.' In these differing interpretations, grief was both something to be actively moved through but also something that moved the individual. Grief was something inside to get rid of, or outside the person and in the way. Similarly, the emotions that were provided by the person when they were alive, in particular if they were bad or abusive feelings and not only positive, could leave a space in the bereaved person's life where they looked for ways to inflict that feeling upon themselves. Charlotte described to me this transfer of emotions, which led to further discussion:

Charlotte: This person might go and then I won't have this shitiness so where am I going to get this shitiness from? I'll have to do the shitiness to myself.

Interviewer: I'm thinking about how people internalise an emotion. It's almost like that feeling is there but it can inhabit different bodies.

Charlotte: Yes, it's like a possession. It is like a possession, which I am only realising now as I am talking about it, which is making me very interested.

Interviewer: What is the task then when someone has taken on these feelings, is it to try and get rid of these feelings?

Charlotte: I guess it would be getting them to see that, to acknowledge it … how can you do that for yourself now that they've gone, now that role is no longer there's. Can you take on that role for yourself … I mean that's the whole thing: what's your shit, what's somebody else's shit.

The client was provided with different forms of agency in each interpretation, either as possessing the control to move out of grief or possessed by grief itself, unable to resist the emotional sway of grief. As Árnason (2007) and Anderson (2001) both identified in their studies of the imagery used by grief counsellors, in my findings, spatial metaphors were employed based on the assumption of an individual inner space, what Rose (1985) termed the 'psy' space installed in the 'modern' individual. This inner space conjured the 'murky' depths of the client from which emotions could be 'brought up' and 'worked through.' Emotions were not always visible to the person experiencing them, but they could be named and identified by the counsellor, in an activity Claire described as 'colouring in a picture together.' The counsellor 'gaze' (Foucault 1973; Rose 1989) was enabled by the capacity to name and identify emotions and thoughts, colouring in the unknown depths of the client. The counsellors repeatedly remarked that what presented initially in the counselling encounter was not what was important, suggesting that the 'true' emotions could only be brought to light through the counselling process. These methods also required particular displays of emotions, so that crying was described by interviewees as 'raw' and authentic and laughing as 'avoidance.' This emphasis on the 'truth' of tears was most evident in the GRM, where at the training workshop tears were anticipated: we were given tissue boxes on our arrival. When a small group of the workshop attendees laughed during an activity they were swiftly told to keep quiet by the group leader, laughing being an activity of avoiding truth, a 'short-term energy relieving behaviour.' The encouragement to show emotions thus appeared to be limited to particular types of emotions. The appropriate type of emotional display was important because in each case emotional expression had been endowed with the claim to truth. It seemed whether one laughed or cried was not just a transitory affect of the body but a reflection of the deep inner workings of the psyche.

Agents of Change: Negotiating Recovery

The counselling contract is arguably established in the belief that people can (and need to) change and transform. In the previous section, I highlighted some of the key components of 'grief work' that laid the foundations for the possibility of change and recovery. In this section, I discuss how counsellors and bereavement support workers aimed to facilitate change and recovery. Using Foucault's ideas around building an 'aesthetics of existence,' I explore how the facilitating of recovery and change presents an opportunity for the 'crafting' of the self, for creating oneself as a 'work of art' (McDonald and O'Callaghan 2008). Counselling is a form of work based on the psychodynamic tradition of 'picking apart your perception of yourself' in order to 'rebuild it stronger.' This notion lies at the heart of the therapeutic endeavour, as Charlotte described:

> [S]omeone described it as all of your clothing and all your skin and bone and everything just being taken off and you're just this quivering little thing. … Then it's about putting stuff back together again. But in the way that you want it to look like, not in the way that you've had to make it look like.

Charlotte here describes the crafting process, remaking oneself in the image one desired. Implied in this notion was the belief in a 'thing' underneath all the 'clothing,' 'skin,' and 'bone' that could be transformed and rebuilt. I then asked Charlotte what she thought that thing was, once everything has been stripped away, she replied:

> The essence of the person, their spirit, the soul. The potential. I think I like that word more. The potential of the person. That's what I think is there. Once everything else has been stripped.

The word potential fits well with the ambitions of counselling and the belief that everyone has the capacity to flourish, a potential that can be nurtured, or indeed hindered in different ways. As mentioned earlier, the contract between counsellor and client also assumes that both parties were ready and willing for a transformation to take place. For bereavement counsellors, the change is brought about by the method they use: talking therapies. Talking about one's feelings in such a manner was seen to initiate the change and enable 'movement' and a 'reconfiguration' inside the person. In the GRM following the steps in the required order was what brought about change. In each approach, a method needed to be adhered to by the client under the promise of change and transformation. The components above are cited as providing the right environment for change to occur, such as establishing safety in order for people to 'vocalise their pain' and to talk about their feelings. Yet though the components of grief work seem fairly clear, how change actually happens did not appear to have a set formula in bereavement counselling. This contrasts with the GRM that has a clear pathway to 'completion.'

One of the key questions in this book is to ask what constitutes recovery from grief. The literature I reviewed in Chapter 2 shows the answers to this question were far from conclusive. In Chapter 3, I further analysed how the concept of recovery has been taken up and embraced in mental health care yet, in the process of mainstreaming, the meaning of recovery arguably has become hollow, used only as rhetoric that seeks to reaffirm dominant political agendas. Recovery from grief is particularly contentious in grief and bereavement research and theory and, as I have documented so far, straddles an uneasy divide between the emphasis on grief as 'natural' and grief as having a 'normal,' staged process. As Paletti (2007) identified, there appears to be an epistemological divide between researchers and practitioners over the use of the concept of recovery, a divide I explore next.

In interviews with bereavement counsellors and support workers while the term recovery was embraced, more often they preferred terms such as 'integration' or ideas about 'movement' and the client 'inhabiting' new identities. Though counsellors and those who work with bereaved people have an investment in helping them to recover or find relief from their grief, they acknowledged that grief was less well suited to the discourse of recovery than, for example, mental disorders, as what has been lost cannot be recovered. In bereavement counselling there is no resolution of the initial problem, as Wendy explained:

> Well I do say to our counsellors that bereavement counselling is just about the only counselling where there is no resolution of the initial problem. If you come to a counsellor with a phobia you can just get over the phobia or come to the counsellor with some childhood issue and work through it, but actually you can never bring back the person who died and so actually what the counselling is about is coming to terms with the fact you can't mend it, there's no mending this issue.

It is around this final problem that bereavement counselling and care is positioned as providing different but never quite complete solutions to grief. Formal measures were used in practice that aimed to capture a client's recovery; these include the CORE assessment forms. Though not designed for grief, these are used to measure a client's general mental state before and after a series of bereavement counselling sessions. Linda, who managed the new client assessments at Caris, described how the CORE-10 and CORE-OM[3] forms helped show the 'effectiveness' of the service but also comparing the forms before and after the counselling intervention allowed the client to 'see their own progress almost in black and white.' Grief models were also used in counselling sessions to enable clients to see their progress. Susan drew out the 'dual process' and 'growing around grief' models with clients which she claimed helped them see how well they were coping and how they were integrating back into the 'normal world':

> So, it's your new life that has emerged and that's the nice balance, you've got a nice big new life with your interactions and new relationships, friendships, whatever. It's never the same again … when you restore back into recovery, whatever you like to call it. It's a new life; it's a different life, you don't go back to the same old life. But the lovely idea being that the grief where this person that you have lost is integrated within your new life.

Linda, who used the 'grief wheel' with her own clients, explained why recovery was depicted as the higher point to represent hope and what has been 'gained' from the loss. In the 'grief wheel' recovery was depicted as an upward movement that could be achieved as long as one avoided 'deterioration' and stayed on course. In the 'grief wheel,' recovery was defined as 'accepting the loss and having an increased interest in socialisation, new lifestyle and behaviour patterns and having a greater sense of meaning and purpose.'

The grief wheel, and its companion models and measures, sought to provide a road map for both client and counsellor as they navigated grief and negotiated recovery. Behind the tick boxes however, grief often did not follow a straightforward journey. The Cruse Early Intervention

Project also used the CORE-10 to measure progress in their clients. The results for 2013–2014 displayed a 38% improvement over the six-session treatment. The use of a further tool, the 'bereavement compass,' showed a 33% improvement with 90% of those who used the service reporting feeling 'better' or 'much better.' However, in speaking with one of the volunteers about the telephone counselling service she portrayed a more ambiguous story of success. The service provided a limit of six sessions of telephone counselling. I asked the volunteer, Jane, whether she thought six sessions was enough time to see any improvement. Jane hesitated before telling me that in some people she did see some changes, but with others there was no change at all. Jane further suggested it could make things worse. Six sessions were not enough time to 'bring up' all the emotions and then work through them effectively. Clients could be left with more 'unresolved problems' than they started off with.[4]

Accounts from bereavement counsellors and support workers did not provide a unified vision of what recovery looked like. Participants described the processing of finishing with a client as a 'long process' that involved 'constant reviewing.' Caris counsellor Claire described it as 'very sort of drip, drip, drip' and 'not anything like a clear road.' Many counsellors and support workers described a mutual intuitive sense of knowing when the 'work is done' and 'it's time to say goodbye' by a change in the 'feel' of the counsellor–client relationship.

There were, however, markers that practitioners observed and looked for to signal when the 'work was done.' These involved recognising that the client was taking an interest in their own life again and had started talking more about her or himself than the person they had lost. It could also be evidenced by practical things such as thinking about going back to work, taking up hobbies, doing new things and meeting people. These new activities were often described as ways of internalising the lost person into the client's new life, as Charlotte explained:

> So, people look for ways to keep the deceased in their life but in a way, which allows them to live. So, you might find some people take up hobbies which remind them of the lost person which then gets them into a place where they're meeting people and doing new things but they are

> also internalising the person that they've lost through this new activity, because maybe it's rock climbing or singing or salsa dancing and the person that they've lost was into that.

What was being described was thus a shift in the client's identity that allowed them to have or rediscover choices via a 'loosening' of the grip of grief. Counsellors and support workers observed how a client's identity could transform in the counselling encounter to inhabit a different sense of self. The participants often drew on particular cases to illustrate their ideas, avoiding generalisations where possible, and emphasising the individual context. Further, they appreciated that ways to recovery were individual and idiosyncratic and there was not a 'normal' way. In the person-centred approach the client was the only expert on what was appropriate grieving behaviour for them, as Wendy explained:

> If a client is going to the grave every day and happy to do that and finding it supportive and not intrusive, then good for you and who cares if you do that for the rest of your life if that's good for you. But you might get another client who feels that going every fortnight is too much and is getting in the way and they can't stop themselves and they feel like its unhelpful and so, who can decide what's normal and not normal, only the client can.

As argued above, the components of normalisation and safety were key in tailoring an individual specific recovery. At the same time, there was acknowledgement that societal norms had levels of restriction on expressions of grief and recovery and permitted certain behaviours over others. Recognising the normative requirements on emotional expression, Charlotte described the process of recovery as 'a really difficult dance to do' one which 'nobody knows what the steps are, nobody knows what the bloody music is.' For her, and the other counsellors, the counselling setting was an opportunity to experiment with revealing thoughts and feelings not permitted elsewhere.

There was some agreement among the bereavement practitioners that recovery was a sense of 'moving forward.' Movement and 'stuckness' were key metaphors used by all bereavement counsellors and support workers, implying the natural process of grief and the bereaved person's success or failure in making his or her way along this linear course. These descriptions of 'moving forward' and 'stuckness' mirrored the contrast between linearity and liminality. Recovery-orientated activities, such as letting go of the deceased person, were largely viewed as a conscious decision, a choice that was fostered by the building of 'ego strength' experienced through the counselling process. On occasion Freudian terms were employed to identify this movement as a 'reinvestment in energy' from mourning the person who had died back to the client's self (or ego), as Linda explained:

> ... what we're hoping at the end of counselling is they'll be more forward-thinking. Because the process of grief means when somebody works their way through it then they're able to reinvest all that energy that they spend in grieving and ... start to withdraw that energy from that grief and for the mourning of that person, and they start to reinvest that energy in themselves.

This enabled clients to become 'forward-thinking' and think about the future, moving away from the past and into something new. The future was depicted in contrast to the 'nothingness' of grief, but there was not always a clear vision of what lay beyond.

However, in the GRM that sets out a clear path to recovery through their method of 'completion' there is no scope for ambiguity. Completion is gained through the writing of a letter that has a very specific format, as presented below:

> Dear.... I have been reviewing our relationship and found some things that I want to say...
> I apologise for...
> I forgive you for...
> I want you to know (significant emotional statement)

The letter is designed to be written to the person with whom clients wanted to get 'complete,' to rid any 'unresolved communications' they might have. The letter had to be ended properly by writing 'goodbye' to complete the communication. Not saying goodbye risked leaving someone incomplete. The letter then had to be read in front of another person in order to become complete. At the workshop when some of the group members questioned why the completion letter had to be heard by another living person we were told: 'I don't know, it just works.' In our interview, Ellen further explained that they had found through testing that reading the letter to the air or a mirror or a grave did not produce the same effects. During my attendance at the workshop, I struggled to identify in the explanation of completion what precisely was special about the method. I wrote in my fieldwork diary how completion was positioned like a 'magic wand':

> Completion was described in such a way that it felt like a magic wand. And the method was so all encompassing – it heals every type of loss! It was as though it could do anything. It was the only answer. Ellen was evangelical about its virtues. (Fieldwork Diary, September 2014)

When I asked Ellen whether there might be other ways to get complete, she permitted that maybe there were, but then stated she might have thought the same before she knew what completion meant. In the GRM then, recovery can only be achieved through a specific activity without which people are incomplete. Yet even completion does not provide the permanent recovery it promises. Completion letters could be written a number of times to the same person. Ellen described how she needed to get complete again with her father, revealed when she started to cry at the workshop. 'There's some more stuff I've got to get complete with, that's why I started crying.' I asked Ellen in our second interview whether completion was then a temporary thing. 'Inevitably it almost is,' replied Ellen, 'But you can be as complete as possible.' The purpose of 'getting complete' was to communicate all the 'unsaid' things you needed to say. Yet even for Ellen, new thoughts and feelings emerged that needed communicating, and so completion became an ongoing process. The act of completion was emphasised as crucial, but it was a misleading term to describe a process that did not appear to have an end point.

Thus, recovery emerged through the frameworks, models, and methods as a contested site with boundaries never quite defined. Recovery becomes an ongoing project only glimpsed at for a period in the counselling encounter. The GRM's promise of completion is flawed as Ellen acknowledged that completion can only last temporarily. Recovery and completion are forms of work carried out in the promise of self-integration and eradication of 'incomplete communications.' However, it is possible to wonder, as I did at the end of the Grief Recovery workshop, what might be so wrong about being incomplete. Yet 'incompletion' is not a desirable option when at the heart of the theory of recovery, and in turn happiness, is the belief in an autonomous self-contained subject with conscious control over choices. Incompletion is a threat to the continuity of this sense of stable personhood and one that risks disintegration.

Failing to Perform Grief

Resistance in the counselling setting was depicted as an unwillingness to adhere to the method, as well as a failure to manage emotions appropriately, where emotions were either too excessive or lacking. This was demonstrated in the Grief Recovery UK workshop during a small group exercise when a few of the group members burst into laughter. The small group was quickly told by the workshop leader to quieten down. Over the weekend, as a group we had been encouraged to show our emotions whatever they might be. 'Let that be okay with you' was the repeated mantra referring to the coming to terms with the feelings of grief we experienced. However, in this incident it became apparent that what were deemed 'true' emotions were limited to sadness and tears, encouraged by the individual tissue boxes placed under each chair. Laughter was interpreted as an avoidance tactic and not a display of emotion. Laughter and other emotions were framed not as merely bodily responses but as a display of moral character. Therefore, laughing at the workshop was a moral failure, a sign of avoiding the work of recovery and of preventing 'completion.'

The moralistic nature of grieving is showcased in 'disenfranchised' forms of grief (Doka 1989). Disenfranchised grief refers to feelings of grief that are deemed socially inappropriate. Arguably in modern western societies a hierarchy of grief exists (Robson and Walter 2013), revealing a disjuncture between individual feelings and the social role one is expected to perform. Goffman (1959, 1963) in his concept of 'front' and 'back' stages described how people put on different performances in different contexts. The 'front stage' is where people perform the ideal or socially appropriate image of themselves. This role is shaped by the desired impression on the 'audience'—the significant others that surround them. Maintaining the performance is vital as a 'minor mishap' can lead to the image that is fostered being 'discredited.' Rose explained how, at the funeral for her husband, she was 'laughing and joking' rather than crying, where the vicar thought her sister-in-law was the one widowed who, unlike Rose, was dressed in 'the full regalia' and wailing. After the service a family member came up to Rose to exclaim, 'But you could have least have cried!'. Rose had failed to play the widow, a failure that was highlighted in the rest of her narrative where she described a handful of incidents where she had cried over her husband's death. The implication was that the emotion of grief must be in proportion to the weight of the role one occupied. It seemed that Rose's lack of grief was disproportionate to her role as widow. Yet her grief was defined only by the display of particular emotions. Rose's failed performance on the 'front stage' highlights the discrepancy between the front and back regions in a person's life. The fear of being discredited—of a 'spoiled identity'—reveals the precariousness of positioning identity in the social arena (Goffman 1963).

However, as different approaches to grief might show, what can constitute a failed performance is context dependent and thus varies considerably. This counters the idea that grief is 'natural' and only shows itself in particular forms, such as tears and not laughter. Two literary figures showcased in twentieth-century classical works of fiction illustrate well the disjuncture in role and displays of grief. Meursault, Camus' narrator of *The Stranger* (Camus 1942) and John, in Huxley's *Brave New World* (Huxley 1946) in different ways both display inappropriate performances of grief following the death of their mother. Camus' *The Stranger* begins with the death of Meursault's mother. His emotional state following his mother's death later further incriminates him after he murders a man. As Meursault faces trial the prosecution described that he'd 'shown no emotion' on the day of his mother's funeral. His 'calm' appearance and apparent lack of remorse implicated his guilt further. Commenting on the character Meursault, Camus (1982) described him as someone 'condemned because he does not play the game.' Rather than merely a social failure or outcast as Meursault is treated in the novel, Camus described him as someone unable to lie, who remained steadfastly to his truth and his true feelings even if they were socially provocative, and ultimately not only discredit him but condemn him to death. In a similar way, John is the outsider in Huxley's *Brave New World* embodying the old 'savage' ways of the past. John, at the event of his mother's death openly showed signs of distress, and caused a scene:

> The Savage stood for a moment in frozen silence, then fell on his knees beside the bed and, covering his face with his hands, sobbed uncontrollably. The nurse stood irresolute, looking now at the kneeling figure by the bed (the scandalous exhibition!). (Huxley 1946, 228)

Both John and Meursault refused to play the game but remained 'true' to their feelings, a truth contrary to the society in which they inhabited. John found himself in a society where ageing and death did not exist. People did not grow up in families and have a 'mother,' and human relationships were pragmatic with the 'individual' of little significance. In the two stories, emotions—in their revelation, or failure to be revealed—showed one's true human character, suggesting how closely connected emotional display and human nature are considered. In each case the showing and not showing of emotions made them both appear less than human to others around them. The need to manage grief is revealed in these points of failure that caused disorder in social norms. Both characters became a site of disgust in their social faux pas.

Disgust also carries symbolic meaning as argued by Douglas (1966) who described how 'dirt' is constructed as a by-product of systematic ordering and classification. Dirt offends order and must be managed: 'uncleanness or dirt is that which must not be included if a pattern is to be maintained' (41). Drawing from the ideas of Douglas, dead bodies provoke disgust by their association with 'dirt' and fears of contamination. For instance, stories of bereaved people who keep the bodies of a deceased person at home feature in the media shrouded in a sense of disgust and repulsion (Collins 2012; Porter 2014; *The Local* 2014). However, in some non-western cultures keeping the dead body of a family member in the home for several months or more is a traditional custom, such as the Torajans in Indonesia who also periodically bring out deceased people from their graves to give them new clothes and gifts (Bennett 2016; Sieber 2017). Bereaved people, I suggest, have the potential to provoke similar feelings of disgust and fear depending on their proximity to the deceased person. Staying too attached, but also not attached enough, can produce negative judgements. Meursault and John's actions caused disorder that needed to be excluded by their removal from society in order to maintain the pattern. Yet disorder also provides the material for the pattern by reinforcing social norms.

The person who fails to perform on the 'front stage' is discredited causing feelings of shame and embarrassment (Goffman 1963). Douglas described how cultures have provisions for dealing with ambiguity and anomalies. Some of the practices I have detailed here, such as the obligation to carry out 'grief work' and the public performance of socially appropriate emotions are arguably practices that seek to control and manage grief in different ways. At the Grief Recovery workshop the small group had to stop laughing and 'play the game.' Those who refuse to play the game have a high price to pay taking Meursault and John's fate as symbolic examples.

Resisting recovery and failing to recover, is framed not only as a failure of moral will but also a resistance of one's true potential. And yet the promise of recovery as revealed in the GRM's notion of completion is inevitably a temporary one that requires continual work to maintain. Recovery is thus the constant horizon of potential, both motivator and cruel promise, but never quite reached. In this way, the methods and models developed to guarantee recovery are always in demand when the journey to recovery rarely meets its summit and work of the griever seldom ceases.

The Work of Recovery

What is clear so far is that from the perspective of the bereavement practitioner it is unanimously agreed that grief requires work and is helped by expert intervention: an unsurprising view for those that are invested in the field of bereavement support. Indeed, it could be argued that becoming a counsellor is also part of the recovery of the counsellor as many of bereavement counsellors and support workers explained the motivation for becoming a counsellor was influenced by their own loss experience. In their view, the value of counselling work and talking through emotions or following the steps in the Grief Recovery Handbook are without question the most effective means to relieving the pain and suffering of grief. In this framing recovery and non-recovery emerge as an unwillingness or inability to do the work and of the approaches I considered, the GRM presented the most extreme example where the method was the only true means to recovery.

Describing grief as 'work' is an appropriate metaphor when personal life is increasingly framed by productivity rather than leisure time. Marx (1976), in his description of 'The Working Day,' argued how in a system of capitalism the day is ordered so that the body remains consistently productive. A neoliberal capitalist system of politics and economics that exists in the UK relies upon 'techniques of temporalisation' (Binkley 2009) to enable high levels of productivity that also impinge on how leisure time is experienced. Accordingly, grief work is a technology of the self that is gladly undertaken by the client, for the intervention has been rationalised in terms of individual freedom and happiness. In Chapter 3, I discussed the ways in which contemporary government had become invested in individual happiness and well-being, where recovery from unhappiness had political and economic benefits. Bereavement care too is increasingly framed as reducing the 'burden' of bereavement and preventing the 'risks' of complicated grieving. However, in the counselling setting, the move towards recovery becomes more of an ethical rather than a political goal phrased in notions of potential and the freeing and fulfilment of the self through making the right choices. In this way, as Rose (1998) argued, psychological expertise becomes a 'relay' between government and individual private lives, where public values are bound to private authorities.

Here I argue that counselling becomes an arena for the crafting of the self with the intention to bring one's identity more in line with one's true nature. Evolving into one's true nature, clearly had its limits and what constituted self-fulfilment and the 'good life' were demarcated by the behaviours and activities that were read as problematic and getting stuck. What constituted recovery was not always made clear and some practitioners insisted that they did not have an agenda or goal in mind when dealing with a client. However, the investment in the notions of individual choice, autonomy, self-awareness, and forming a coherent identity are clearly tied to the achievement of recovery or integration. These features were considered an unquestionable good. Governing individuals in terms of their freedom, however, presents an ethical obligation to the client, which makes the stakes of refusal all the greater. Refusing to recover in such a way may condemn someone to never recovering or to a performance of recovery that sooner or later will falter. It also ignores the way in which counselling is implicated in the construction of the social realities to which it seeks to adjust its clients (Árnason 2007).

I suggest that the dominance of the notion of 'grief work' frames the everyday activities described by the bereaved participants at the start of this chapter. Distractions and 'energy relieving behaviours' were viewed as only a way to help keep grief at bay for a little longer, a wave that would, according to dominant discourses of grief, overwhelm you at some point. However, these behaviours and distractions, and not just formal forms of grief work, were used by bereaved people as forms of identity preservation and repair. In the accounts of the bereaved participants, negotiating the ongoing presence of the deceased person could be ambivalent, and the home space and objects often became the stage upon which the desire to both 'hold on' and 'let go' was played out.

Acknowledging the ambivalent nature of relationships with others dead or alive is I argue a better lens through which to view the experiences of the bereaved person than describing such a state as 'stuckness.' Using such a term as being 'stuck' fails to recognise that there is a great deal of movement and negotiation happening.

Yet the stuckness of wanting to hold on and let go is also a double-bind, where the desire for an ever out-of-grasp past resists the construction of a new identity and future. For bereavement practitioners, being able to construct a new future was an important part of recovery. Though the transition from an assumed future with another person to having to make plans on one's own met with mixed success across the participants' accounts. For example, bereaved participant John, in his wife's absence, had no desires or wishes for the future:

> [M]y future basically was, was with my wife. That's the only thing I'd ever thought about really that we'd be living together until old age and sitting in front of a fire all that sort of thing, reading the paper or something that things would, that that would be my future. And that's probably part and parcel of the trouble I've got, trying to come to some sort of resolution as to what my future is now, in that I always saw my future as being with her.

In the absence of a future all that remained was a persistence to keep going through the use of different forms of grief work, distractions, and material objects and spaces. I noted how recovery was not necessarily something with which participants identified: the vision they articulated was more one of 'muddling through' (Anne), or a 'road that's not ever gonna run out' (Paul). Similar sentiments appeared across participants' accounts, detailing a tiring process of picking oneself up and 'plodding.' These stories could be viewed as the unglamorous face of recovery, stories of plodding and exhaustion and getting on with it. 'Getting on with it' might seem a limited goal in the face of the transformative power of recovery, or it is possible that stuckness was the search for bigger and better fantasies than the normative vision of recovery, where the future was still under revision and identity remained in flux.

Notes

1. A detailed discussion of these components can be found in: Pearce, Caroline. 2018. 'Negotiating Recovery in Bereavement Care Practice in England: A Qualitative Study.' *Bereavement Care* 37 (1): 6–16.
2. Further details of the workshop available at: https://www.griefrecovery-method.co.uk/train/.
3. The CORE-OM is a 34-item generic measure of psychological distress. The CORE-10 is a shorter version which includes ten items. More details available at: http://www.coreims.co.uk/About_Measurement_CORE_Tools.html.
4. The Early Intervention Project was a pilot project funded by the Department of Health and is no longer running.

References

Anderson, Michael. 2001. "'You Have to Get Inside the Person' or Making Grief Private: Image and Metaphor in the Therapeutic Reconstruction of Bereavement." In *Grief, Mourning and Death Ritual*, edited by Jenny Hockey, Jeanne Katz, and Neil Small, 135–143. Buckingham: Open University Press.

Árnason, Arnar. 1998. "'Feel the Pain': Death, Grief and Bereavement Counselling in the North East of England." Durham University, Unpublished Doctoral thesis.

———. 2001. "Experts of the Ordinary: Bereavement Counselling in Britain." *Journal of the Royal Anthropological Institute* 7 (2): 299–313.

———. 2007. "'Fall Apart and Put Yourself Together Again': The Anthropology of Death and Bereavement Counselling in Britain." *Mortality* 12 (1): 48–65.

Balk, David E. 2004. "Recovery Following Bereavement: An Examination of the Concept." *Death Studies* 28 (4): 361–374.

———. 2008. "A Modest Proposal About Bereavement and Recovery." *Death Studies* 32 (1): 84–93.

Bennett, Amanda. 2016. "Where Death Doesn't Mean Goodbye." *National Geographic*, April, 53–67.

Binkley, Sam. 2009. "Governmentality, Temporality and Practice: From the Individualization of Risk to the 'Contradictory Movements of the Soul.'" *Time & Society* 18 (1): 86–105.

Camus, Albert. 1942. *The Outsider*. London: Penguin.

———. 1982. "Afterword." In *The Outsider*. 2nd ed. London: Penguin.

Collins, Nick. 2012. "Hans Rausing Hid Wife's Body as He Could Not Cope with Her Dying." *The Telegraph*, December 14.

Doka, Ken J., ed. 1989. *Disenfranchised Grief: Recognising Hidden Sorrow*. Lexington, MA: Lexington Books.

Douglas, Mary. 1966. *Purity and Danger: An Analysis of Concepts of Pollution and Taboo*. London: Penguin.

Foucault, Michel. 1973. *The Birth of the Clinic: An Archaeology of Medical Perception*. London: Routledge.

———. 1988. "Technologies of the Self." In *Technologies of the Self*, edited by Luther H. Martin, H. Gutman, and Patrick H. Hutton, 16–49. Amherst: University of Massachussets Press.

Freud, Sigmund. 1917. "Mourning and Melancholia." In *The Penguin Freud Reader*, edited by Adam Philips, 310–326. London: Penguin.

Friedman, Russell, and John W. James. 2013. *Moving Beyond Loss: Real Answers to Real Questions from Real People*. Lanham, MD: Taylor Trade.

Gibson, Margaret. 2004. "Melancholy Objects." *Mortality* 9 (4): 285–299.

———. 2008. *Objects of the Dead: Mourning and Memory in Everyday Life*. Carlton, VIC: Melbourne University Press.

Goffman, Erving. 1959. *The Presentation of Self in Everyday Life*. London: Penguin.

———. 1963. *Stigma*. London: Penguin.

Gorer, Geoffrey. 1965. *Death, Grief and Mourning in Contemporary Britain*. London: Cresset Press.

Hockey, Jenny, Bridget Penhale, and David Sibley. 2005. "Environments of Memory: Home Space, Later Life and Grief." In *Emotional Geographies*, edited by Joyce Davidson, Liz Bondi, and Mick Smith, 135–146. Aldershot: Ashgate.

Huxley, Aldous. 1946. *Brave New World*. London: Harper & Bros.

James, John W., and Russell Friedman. 2009. *The Grief Recovery Handbook: The Action Program for Moving Beyond Death, Divorce, and Other Losses Including Health, Career and Faith*. New York: William Morrow.

Kabat-Zinn, John. 1994. *Wherever You Go, There You Are: Mindfulness Meditation for Everyday Life*. New York: Hyperion.

Lewis, C. S. 1961. *A Grief Observed*. London: Faber and Faber.

Marx, Karl. 1976. *Capital Volume One: A Critique of Political Economy*. 1867. London: Penguin.

McDonald, Matthew, and Jean O'Callaghan. 2008. "Positive Psychology: A Foucauldian Critique." *The Humanistic Psychologist* 36 (2): 127–142.

Paletti, Robin. 2007. "Recovery in Context: Bereavement, Culture, and the Transformation of the Therapeutic Self." *Death Studies* 32 (1): 17–26.

Porter, Steven. 2014. "'Wife Carried on as Man Lay Dead in Home." *USA Today*, June 4. http://www.usatoday.com/story/news/nation/2014/06/04/wife-lived-with-man-dead-in-home-nine-months/9947321/.

Robson, Patricia, and Tony Walter. 2013. "Hierarchies of Loss: A Critique of Disenfranchised Grief." *Omega* 66 (2): 97–119.

Rogers, Carl. 1951. *Client-Centred Therapy: Its Current Practice, Implications and Theory*. London: Constable and Company.

Rose, Nikolas. 1985. *The Psychological Complex: Psychology, Politics and Society in England, 1869–1939*. London: Routledge & Kegan Paul.

———. 1989. *Governing the Soul: The Shaping of the Private Self*. London: Free Association Press.

———. 1998. *Inventing Our Selves: Psychology, Power and Personhood*. Cambridge: Cambridge University Press.

Schut, Henk. 2010. "Grief Counselling Efficacy: Have We Learned Enough?" *Bereavement Care* 29 (1): 8–9.

SECOB Project Research Group. 2013. *Socio-Economic Costs of Bereavement in Scotland: Main Study Report*. Aberdeen: SECOB.

Shear, Katherine. 2012. "Grief and Mourning Gone Awry: Pathway and Course of Complicated Grief." *Dialogues in Clinical Neuroscience* 14 (2): 119–128.

Sieber, Claudio. 2017. "Cleaning the Dead: The Afterlife Rituals of the Torajan People." *The Guardian*, October 12. http://www.theguardian.com/world/gallery/2017/oct/13/cleaning-the-dead-the-afterlife-rituals-of-the-torajan-people.

Small, Neil, and Jenny Hockey. 2001. "Discourse into Practice: The Production of Bereavement Care." In *Grief, Mourning and Death Ritual*, edited by Jenny Hockey, Jeanne Katz, and Neil Small, 97–124. Buckingham: Open University Press.

Stephen, Audrey I., Colin Macduff, Dennis J. Petrie, Fu-Min Tseng, Henk Schut, Silje Skår, Anne Corden, John Birrell, Shaolin Wang, Cate Newsom, and Stewart Wilson. 2014. "The Economic Cost of Bereavement in Scotland." *Death Studies* 39 (1–5): 151–157.

Stroebe, Margaret, and Henk Schut. 1999. "The Dual Process Model of Coping with Bereavement: Rationale and Description." *Death Studies* 23 (3): 197–224.

The Local. 2014. "Woman Slept Next to Mother's Body for 5 Years." November 18. http://www.thelocal.de/20141118/woman-slept-next-to-mothers-body-for-5-years.

Tonkin, Lois. 1996. "Growing Around Grief—Another Way of Looking at Grief and Recovery." *Bereavement Care* 15 (1): 10.

Wertheimer, Max. 1938. "Gestalt Theory." In *A Source Book of Gestalt Psychology*, edited by Willis D. Ellis, 1–11. London: Routledge & Kegan Paul.

Wetherell, Margaret. 2012. *Affect and Emotions: A New Social Science Understanding*. London: Sage.

Worden, J. William. 1991. *Grief Counselling and Grief Therapy: A Handbook for the Mental Health Practitioner*. 2nd ed. London: Routledge.

5

Emotions, Bodies, Practices

One undisputed claim made by all participants, whether counsellor or client, was that grief was a natural and normal emotion. This was stated as a self-evident premise, yet on closer inspection this is a multi-layered statement. Describing grief as 'natural' acknowledged the understanding that grief was a universal human emotion; the 'cost' of the human inclination to make attachments. In Chapter 2 I reviewed the theories of grief that have dominated the field of grief and bereavement research over the last century, since Freud first proposed his theory of mourning and melancholia. In reviewing how grief has been conceptualised I highlighted some key assumptions in the literature, concerning the universality of grief. Studies of grief that drew on the work on Bowlby, who in turn drew on Darwin's understanding of the emotions, promoted the view of grief as an intrinsic biological reaction to loss (Parkes 1972). This affirmed grief as an essentially human emotion, with other researchers attributing facial expressions and psychological symptoms to accompany this human response.

In the previous two chapters I have explored how people make sense of and manage grief, often reaffirming the notion that grief is both normal and natural. In this chapter I challenge these assumptions by

C. Pearce, *The Public and Private Management of Grief*,
https://doi.org/10.1007/978-3-030-17662-4_5

highlighting the role of emotions, bodies, and practices, commonly overlooked in a predominantly psychological and psychodynamic view of grief. I draw on theories from the sociology of emotions, affect theory and cultural theory to explore how emotions, bodies, and practices are enacted in theories of grief, and crucially how to account for the subjectivity of the bereaved person, situating the theme of the penultimate chapter on how identities come to be inhabited and resisted. By drawing on this alternative literature I seek to challenge the disembodied view of the bereaved person that appears in dominant grief theories and bring into the view the embodied, relational, and liminal aspects of grief. In this respect I also challenge the Cartesian (Descartes 1649) divide between the understanding of mind and body that persists in theories of grief and the study of emotions more broadly.

I begin this chapter by explaining the concept of liminality and describe how I have used this concept as a basis on which to problematise the boundaries around emotions, bodies, and practices. Drawing on the work of van Gennep (1960) and Turner (1969, 1974, 1982), I argue that following bereavement people may find themselves in a space of liminality where their sense of identity is destabilised, and the usual order of everyday life has been suspended. I suggest that bereaved people are liminal bodies, 'matter out of place,' due to the threat they pose to the dominant understandings of the emotions and the body.

Then I focus on emotions, bodies, and practices in turn to explore further how an emphasis on liminality can provide an alternative perspective to conceptualising grief. First, I refer to the large field of research into understanding and categorising emotions. Rather than emotions being discrete and easily measurable, I argue that the interdisciplinary study of the emotions has yet to find a conclusive answer to the question: 'What is an emotion?' Further, I describe the recent 'affective turn' where emotions are being rethought as non-conscious bodily processes, as a way to reconsider grief as an embodied and relational experience. Secondly, this leads me to a focus on the 'lost' body (Tanner 2006) in grief theories, and I highlight literature that has emphasised the embodied experience of grief. Within this I return to Freud's theory of mourning and melancholia through the work of Butler (2003, 2004, 2010) to explore grief as an instance that reveals a radically relational model of self, foregrounding vulnerability and precarity as fundamental to the human condition. In emphasising the relational aspect of bodies, I argue that in a society that privileges individual autonomy and recovery, bereaved people become problematic bodies to be managed.

To bring together the discussions on the body and emotions, I borrow Wetherell's (2012) concept of 'affective practices.' I suggest that an analysis of practice can allow for an account of grief that views it as both a bodily felt, affective experience and also something that is managed and maintained through social practices. Emphasising the role of practices and social activity, I seek to build an alternative way of theorising grief where grief is not something that exists purely in the psyche but is a socially constructed object, framed and produced by various discourses, including the theories put forward by the bereavement counsellors in the previous chapter and the psychiatrists and psychologists outlined in Chapter 2. In the final section I piece together the vision of the person that is implied in the claim that grief is both an embodied, felt experience that reveals the fundamentally relational nature of human beings, and yet also a socially constructed category that refers to a range of emotional behaviours, none of which I argue can be defined conclusively as 'natural.'

Grief and Liminality

In his anthropological studies van Gennep (1960) defined liminality as the middle phase of a 'rite of passage' undergone by members of tribal societies, which comprised of: the initial stage of separation from one's group or society, the middle stage of liminality, and the final stage of reintegration. Turner (1969) described those in a liminal stage as 'threshold people' who elude the classifications that normally locate people in space. In this liminal period the characteristics of the subject become ambiguous. As Turner states: 'Liminal entities are neither here nor there; they are betwixt and between the positions assigned and arrayed by law, custom, convention, and ceremonial' (95). In a state of liminality, people exist outside not only their own social position, but all social positions. Being 'betwixt and between' causes one to literally and figuratively lose one's sense of being in the world.

Recognising grief as an experience that destabilises familiar boundaries around identity, social norms and behaviour it follows that a state of liminality can provide opportunity for creativity and subversive acts due to the eradication of the normal structures that tend to inhibit or obstruct behaviour (Turner 1974). Turner (1982, 47) describes how: 'Liminality is both more creative and more destructive than the structural norm.' However, in such a state people might be prone to suggestibility, social influence, imitation, and contagion, for under liminal conditions there is no structure against which to measure objectively. Stenner and Moreno (2013) suggest that when the taken-for-granted is swept away, people can easily lose 'grasp of external reality' and their 'sense of inner self-coherence.' This means that the ambiguity of liminality from which stems its potential may also be the scene of disease, despair, death, or suicide: of a breakdown without replacement of well-defined social ties and bonds (Turner 1982).

Rituals such as funeral rites and traditional burial customs have historically been considered as aids to move people through the mourning process. Van Gennep (1960, 147) described mourning as a transitional period that was entered through 'rites of separation' and emerged from by 'rites of reintegration' into society. He highlighted the fact that often the duration of the mourning period would correspond exactly with societal ideas about the amount of time it might take for the deceased to become incorporated into the world of the dead. Before this reincorporation, both mourners and the deceased are suspended in a space between the world of the living and the world of the dead. In contemporary western societies, interventions such as bereavement counselling, or popular self-help books that proscribe steps through the process, similarly act as guides through the liminality of grief to what is considered to be an agreed 'good' resolution. Conceptualising grief as an experience of liminality problematises the idea of a linear process of grief often promoted in grief theories. Rather than a phase in a staged process, I propose an understanding of grief as something from which people do not always recover, where the liminal phase can become the new permanent reality for bereaved people. Describing grief as a liminal space then, I am not suggesting grief follows the logic or structure of ritual, but on the contrary, is an experience where familiar structures have been destabilised.

Rosaldo (1993) critiqued the way the anthropology of death and mourning had focused on ritual at the expense of the study of the emotional experience of grief, highlighting the problem of studying grief through the logic and order of mourning rituals. Rosaldo argued that the overemphasis on ritual meant that the ritual process had been conflated with the process of mourning; rituals were viewed as 'containing' emotions and conveying social and cultural attitudes towards death. Rosaldo drew on his study of the Ilongot tribe in the Philippines, whose members felt impelled to hunt and chop off the head of a person following bereavement. The 'rage' expressed by the Ilongot's, Rosaldo argued was an example of the way the study of mourning rituals had failed to convey the emotions of grief.

However, Rosaldo's critique of the anthropological study of grief still relied upon an understanding of grief as a universal emotional experience that is, for instance, overwhelming and powerful, which as Árnason pointed out (1998) is a particularly western notion. This is highlighted in the way Rosaldo described how sharing the common experience of bereavement enabled him to understand those of a different social and cultural background. In what follows I address the common assumption that emotions are universal, biological phenomenon and suggest instead that overwhelming emotions such as the rage discussed by Rosaldo are also shaped and constructed by the social context.

In the western philosophical tradition there is a division between essence (nature) and existence. Traditional thought considers essence as more fundamental than existence. Existentialists, notably the work of Sartre, sought to argue that existence precedes essence emphasising how actions constitute a person's identity and value, in the belief that people create their own value and meaning rather than it being predetermined. This view links to broad debates on the meaning of existence as well as predetermined essence but also suggests the productive aspect of actions and rituals and how they serve to create meaning and identity. For Bloch and Parry (1982), mortuary practices served to reassert social order at death. They further describe how social order is itself a product of rituals: social order does not exist prior to ritual. Ritual thus has a productive role in the liminal space of grief in reasserting current norms of grief and recovery but also the potential to create new ideas about grief. In exploring ritual, Durkheim (1915) saw emotions as being central to ritual action. For him, rituals reinforced social values, fostered identity and built solidarity aided by emotional responses. In the Durkheimian view, ritual practices and emotions are thus intertwined and may play an important role in producing social stability, particularly at moments when people are undergoing periods of liminality. Davies (2011) also emphasised the role of the body in such ritual action in his term 'moral-somatic' processes, which referred to how people respond to social values through embodied action.

According to Turner (1969) becoming reincorporated into structure, as in the final stage of a rite of passage, is a way to control the danger the liminal person poses to the smooth running of society. For example, the time restraints placed on grieving, as demonstrated in the diagnosis of 'prolonged grief disorder' where the display of grieving symptoms at six months following bereavement might signal the need for clinical intervention, could be seen as a way to reintegrate people who have been cast into liminality back into a linear ordered sense of time. These rituals and customs serve to provide staging to the process, not in order to close down options but to facilitate a productive 'becoming' (Turner 1969). In using the concept of liminality to describe the experience of grief, I argue that the final stage of reintegration, or 'recovery,' is socially and culturally constructed. What constitutes recovery or reintegration, while achieved or resisted with varying degrees of success, is something that must be continually negotiated and maintained, and this negotiation takes place within the shifting boundaries of the liminal space of grief.

Next, I highlight the intertwined nature of emotions, bodies and practices that play an important role in enabling people to find meaning and construct identities in the liminal space of grief. Furthermore, ritual practices, whether a funeral or a bereavement counselling session, seek to manage people across the transitional space of grief, maintaining the boundaries and 'margins' of what is taken to be reality in society. As Douglas (1966, 122) has argued, pulling margins 'this way or that' is a dangerous act that can alter 'the shape of fundamental experience.'

By drawing upon liminality, I am attempting to illustrate the 'vulnerability' (Douglas 1966) of taken-for-granted assumptions about grief that persist in modern western societies. Bereaved people have the potential to resist and challenge these boundaries by existing between the divided worlds of the living and the dead and inhabiting this margin, or space of liminality.

Theorising Emotions

So far in this book I have argued that even among studies that analysed the socially constructed nature of grieving behaviours, grief was still assumed to be an entity located somewhere in internally felt emotions that could be differently shaped and expressed. In a similar way, the study of the emotions has historically rested on the Cartesian divide between body and mind, and emotion and reason, where the biological and the social constructionist understanding of emotions have been unhelpfully positioned as separate phenomena that can only be studied in isolation. However, as I discuss here, the study of the emotions has long been a focus of numerous disciplines from the biological and psychological, to the philosophical, sociological, and anthropological and more recently as a focus of neuroscientific research.

Nevertheless, defining emotions has remained a contentious topic across the disciplines. As Dixon (2012) has shown, a glance at the history of the term 'emotion' reveals that what actually constitutes an emotion is not as fixed as it has been purported to be by researchers of the emotions. Dixon detailed how 'emotion' did not become a word to describe mental states until the mid-nineteenth century, prior to which the terms 'passions' and 'affections' were more commonplace. The term emotion gained favour along with the rise of psychology as a discipline that sought to move away from both the religious connotations of 'passions' and the medical usage of 'affections.' The term emotion, Dixon describes, originally denoted a physical agitation or disturbance in people and animals alike and later came to be accompanied by mental feelings. Thomas Brown, who first established the term 'emotions' within psychology in 1820, admitted that emotions cannot be defined

(Dixon 2012), and later James' essay published in 1884 entitled 'What is an emotion?' (1884) captured the sentiment yet concluded without an answer. It is not surprising that something that could not be defined from the outset continues to resist easy classification. Yet the meaning of terms generally considered to designate emotions—such as anger, fear, sadness, happiness, disgust or surprise—appear obvious not only to researchers who have produced vast fields of studies under such categories but also in everyday discourse where the terms seemingly possess a universal understanding.

The belief in a set of basic emotions, commonly including the ones listed above, was arguably a development beginning with Darwin's (1872) theory of the emotions as primitive, innate and involuntary instincts. Darwin's description of grief, for example, described the expression of grief in terms of a contraction of the 'grief muscles' that produced a particular facial expression. In Darwin's understanding there was no acknowledgement of the cause of, or the context of, emotions but rather they were something that passed through the body over which the person has no control. The evolutionary view of emotions then, was that these were common to all humans and non-human animals.

The belief in a universal set of emotions was extended in the work of Ekman (1992, 1993) who carried out studies in which people from a range of cultural backgrounds were asked to identify different emotions from facial expressions; from this research Ekman concluded there was a set number of 'basic emotions' common to all humans. Ekman's work was and remains highly influential while the ambiguous origins of the term emotions have been somewhat lost. Instead, emotions have been classified further into varying numbers of primary and secondary ones. Kemper (1987) outlined four primary emotions—happiness, fear, anger and sadness—that qualify as such due to having five features, which are:

1. Evolutionary survival value
2. Appear in earliest stages of human development
3. Universally recognised in the face
4. Have unique autonomic responses
5. Emerge in all social relations

Secondary emotions were formed from a combination of primary emotions, for example anger and sadness constitute the secondary emotion of grief. For while it is believed that primary emotions are 'hard-wired,' it is unclear whether secondary emotions are innate or culturally defined. Primary and secondary emotions are also described as 'lower' or 'higher' emotions where, as Descartes (1649) noted, the higher emotions emerged from initial 'lower' emotions. Lower emotions were thus considered as body automatic responses to external stimuli, whereas higher emotions demanded the intellect and involved cognition.

However, many have found fault in Ekman's extensive studies (Barrett 2006; Mead 1975), not least with his interpretation of the research findings. Ekman's results showed that how people identified emotions from facial expressions varied considerably; presumably if emotions were universal, they would be similarly identified across all participants. Ekman's model also relied on facial expressions as being the defining feature of emotions, as though emotions are purely bodily responses rather than viewing facial expressions as communicative and intentional.

In the 1970s, sociologists began to address the neglect of emotions in the discipline, highlighting the culturally diverse appearance of emotions as well as exploring how emotions are socially constructed (Dixon 2012; Harré and Parrott 1996). According to Turner and Stets (2005), biology had become the 'black box' sociologists refused to enter. The dualism of emotion and reason in the foundational, and overly masculine, works of sociology by Durkheim, Marx and Weber, as Williams (2001) identified, served to perpetuate the understanding of emotions in sociology as irrational and separate from the rational mind. A challenge to this thinking emerged in different forms: feminist critiques of the rational body, a growth in interest in the role of the body in social theory, and research into consumer culture and emotional labour (Hochschild 1983; Lupton 1997; Shilling 1993; Turner 1984). The sociology of emotions sought to bring together the social, cultural, and biological to rethink emotions as not only a bodily agitation, but as intentional and involving a moral order (Harré and Parrott 1996).

One sociologist, Harré (1986), critiqued the psychological study of emotions and what he saw as the psychologist's belief in an abstract 'it' that assumed the existence of emotions as discrete entities and studied them as such. Rather, for Harré, emotions could not be studied without close attention to the local language and 'moral order' in order to understand the differences in the meanings and uses of emotions. Harré proposed a need to explore emotion 'vocabularies' that would focus analysis on the strategic use of emotion. He also noted the need to acknowledge the social function of emotional displays and the system of rules that maintained and taught emotional expression. However, it is only after focusing on language, discourse, and social rules, Harré claimed, that the physiological details of the various bodily 'perturbations' that accompany the activities can be engaged with and tracked, as the extent to which the perturbations are important and how they are managed will vary according to local culture.

Harré's argument, by separating the analysis of language and the body presents an example of how the Cartesian divide between mind and body is often repeated in the study of emotions. Ahmed (2004) described this thinking as either an 'outside-in' or 'inside-out' perspective. An outside-in perspective would consider emotions as properties of social and cultural practices that 'get inside' the individual whereas an inside-out perspective would see emotions as something innate to the individual that emanate from within out onto the world. For example, Harré above was arguing for an outside-in study of the emotions, where the discourse of an emotion produces bodily perturbations; whereas psychological theory tends to interpret emotions are something 'inside' that comes 'out.' One example of this view can be found in a book by Hatfield et al. (1994) on 'emotional contagion' that argued emotions can leak out of one individual and can be 'caught' and 'infect' others. Their argument highlights well the problems with thinking about emotions as something that can come from outside and 'infect,' or 'leak' out from inside. In each case emotions are viewed as things that people have or gain, or that they catch and have little control over.

As detailed in Chapter 4, the bereavement practitioners presented grief as something indeterminate that could move location, defined according to both the 'outside-in' and 'inside-out' theory of emotions. Grief was alternately described as a possession (something internal) or something one could be possessed by (external to the person).

Both groups of participants—practitioners and laypeople—described how grief could be triggered or appear without warning, and that grief was capable of being able to 'hit you' unexpectedly. Grief was either inside a person and needed to be externalised as presented in the Grief Recovery Method, or something that became incorporated as a permanent part of the body, as reflected in the 'growing around' theory of grief.

Following Ahmed (2004), I contend that rather than stating people come to be infected by or leak out emotions, emotional expression can blur the boundaries between bodies. This way of thinking about emotions therefore maintains neither an 'outside-in' nor an 'inside-out' perspective. The recent interest in the study of 'affect' provides a way of theorising emotions that attempts to overcome this divide between emotions and bodies. The trend towards studies of affect regards emotions as both biological and social phenomenon, capable of inhabiting and moving between bodies. The use of the term affect refers to the human bodily capacity to affect and be affected. From this, two different meanings have emerged in social and cultural analysis: one is to develop the notion of embodiment to appreciate the non-verbal, non-conscious aspects of human bodies. This also includes thinking about emotions as less structured and less socio-linguistically fixed (Ngai 2005). Second, the affective turn has heralded an ontology that thinks beyond or 'post' human. The capacity to be affected by other bodies but also non-human objects and the environment at large is seen to provide a way of overcoming divides between not only mind and body, but nature and culture; self and other. In this way affect theory owes much to feminist work on the body (Haraway 1991) but is greatly inspired by Deleuze and Guatarri (1984, 1988) and a select group of neuroscientists (Damasio 1994; Massumi 2002).

Biology is reconfigured in affect theory so that biological explanations for social behaviour are no longer considered essentialist and reductionist but as a creative space that injects potentiality in understandings of the human body. This is curious considering that the term 'affect' has quite a different legacy in psychology where affect is often used interchangeably to refer to emotions that are innate, largely physiological responses that can be categorised and measured. By contrast, the embrace of biology by certain cultural theorists writing on affect, depict a dynamic, mutable material body that defies all boundaries. Affect theory is positioned as a response to 'old' structuralist or constructionist social and cultural theory that distanced itself from biology as well as a theorising of the body and emotions that over-valued rationality and reason producing tidy disembodied accounts. The body in affect theory rather is not fixed but fluid, composed of 'lines of flight' (Deleuze and Guattari 1984) or intensities rather than Freudian drives.

Affects are characterised by their movement and how they are 'transmitted' between bodies. For Brennan (2004), the transmission of affect counteracts western notions of the 'affectively contained' individual by showing how the social and psychological produce physical, bodily changes. Affect seeks to capture the 'puzzle' of suggestibility that therapists and analysts described as the concept 'transference' (Blackman 2013). As Blackman details, this notion of suggestibility captured in psychoanalytic understandings of the unconscious or psychic realm lost favour but has now returned in a scientific and biologically informed manner. Psychoanalytic understandings of grief in Freud (1917) and Klein (1940) relied upon a belief in the way in which people incorporated others within themselves, described as object-relations or attachment, where the ambivalence experienced at the actual or imagined loss of the object risked destabilising the ego or self. However, affect theory that depends on neuroscientific findings tends to dismiss psychoanalysis as part of the theoretical framework that promoted the bounded and separate human being. Yet arguably the melancholic presents the perfect affective subject, for the melancholic has no conscious knowledge of what has been lost in her or himself; the boundaries between the deceased and the living, self and other, are blurred and fluid.

Many scholars privilege the use of affect over emotions. Fox (2013, 2015), for example, claims that affect can go beyond what he considers the limitations of the sociology of emotions. Emotions are only a sub-component of a broader 'affective interactivity' between bodies and non-human entities. Viewing emotions in this way overcomes the distinctions between structure and agency, nature and culture to which Fox claims sociology falls prey. Thus, Fox borrows from Ahmed (2004) to suggest a mode of studying emotions that looks at not what emotions are but what they do. This shifts attention away from the individual to address 'emergence' rather than 'substance.' Tracking the impersonal flows of affect is Fox's attempt to decentre the human, individual, rational actor as the starting point of enquiry to explore how the individual is but one element in the circulation of affects.

However, a key problem in Fox's argument, which is often repeated in other writings on affect, is that the flow or intensity of affect is given undifferentiated power. So, while I agree that an acknowledgement of the ways in which people are relationally constituted is beneficial for destabilising the notion of the autonomous individual, attention needs to be given to precisely the different ways in which people are affected, as well as how people might not be similarly affected by the same 'flow' of affect (Anderson 2009). The emphasis is overwhelmingly on how affect flows but not how affect gets stuck, on how some bodies become stuck rather than move in a continual flow (Ahmed 2004, 2010). Thinking about how some bodies get stuck might allow researchers to consider what makes it possible for a body to become affected and what makes a body resistant. The overemphasis on the 'free' and 'flowing' nature of affect and emotions negates the role of bodies and structure (Stenner and Moreno 2013).

The affective turn is an interesting move in the study of emotions that has shed some light on the importance of thinking about the affective capacities of bodies. However, the multi-disciplinary study of the emotions remains conflicted over the question of what emotions actually are. Situating the study of grief within this broader multi-disciplinary field is important in order to challenge the idea that grief is a 'natural' and stable category of the emotions. From this starting point the study of grief takes quite a different perspective.

Theorising Bodies

While suggestions of the biological underpinnings of grief reactions are present in psychological theories of grief, the body remains markedly absent. Grief is understood as an emotional response that occurs in the individual psyche. Tanner (2006) has argued that within theories of grief the body becomes 'lost' where mourning is described in symbolic, disembodied terms. For Tanner, grief is unavoidably an embodied experience and definitions of mourning that disavow the embodied dynamics of grief reflect a cultural discomfort with the 'rupture of autonomy' manifest in both the fact of embodiment and recognition of intercorporeality (Csordas 1990, 2008).

The discomfort with intercorporeality in western theories of the body is all the more present when dealing with dead and dying bodies. The body in death is a reminder that human beings are in constant flux and subject to change. As Hallam et al. (1999) have noted, there has been a under theorising of the body in death studies. Where embodiment has appeared, it has tended to imply bounded, alive bodies. They argue that embodiment needs to expand its focus to 'vampires': the 'disembodied dead,' to selves not bounded by the body; and to 'vegetables,' mortal, permeable and not autonomous bodies. Switching focus to the socially dead/biologically alive and the socially alive/biologically dead, circumvents the Cartesian dualism between body and mind to a human embodiment which situates itself at and beyond the boundaries of the body.

It would seem that some bodies are allowed to be present and others are encouraged to be absent. Bennett and Bennett (2000) found in their study of bereaved people who had experienced the presence of the dead that their participants would move between a materialist domain of thought and a supernaturalist domain to make sense of their experiences. The study revealed how participants in the narration of their experience drew on the sorts of modern rational discourse that classified dead bodies as separate from living ones, as well as the participants' own fears of being considered delusional at seeing and feeling the dead. Within a rationalist logic, experiencing the presence of the dead would be considered illusionary and dismissed. The authors argued the need to embrace alternative ways of thinking that would allow for such experiences of the presence of the dead to be considered as equally rational and real.

The ways in which certain bodies are made absent also reveals the boundaries placed on bodies to perform and appear in socially normative ways. Howarth (2000) argued that a scientific approach to mortality is the product of modernity that relies on the assumption that life and death are clearly separate. Bereaved people appear to embody this divide, posing a problem in a society orientated around life and troubled by death. The division between life and death, claimed Howarth, is not a fact but rather a false boundary borne out by a modern need to segregate and classify. What is needed is not to find yet another model of grief, but to work to blur the boundaries between life and death.

Hockey et al. (2010) drew on Douglas's (1966) notion of 'matter out of place' to describe how certain bodies, in particular dying and dead bodies, become matter to be managed. This 'polluting' of boundaries is managed through ritual, which Douglas (1966, 97) described as separating the person from their old status and segregating them 'for a time' before publicly declaring their entry into a new status. The 'danger' lies in this act of being in transition: of being neither one state nor another. The person who is in transition and indefinable is himself or herself in danger and emanates danger to others. 'Complicated grievers' for example may be considered polluted and in need of classification due to what is considered their proximity to the deceased person. The bereaved person is thus 'betwixt and between' the margins of life and death: they are not wholly living, as their bereavement means they are emotionally distanced from the world as they cling to the memory of the dead, but nor are they wholly dead, for of course they are in fact literally alive.

'Out of place' bodies also gain a level of power due to being on the wrong, or neither, side of the boundary. As Foucault's work (1973, 1976) has demonstrated, non-normative bodies require forms of discipline that act upon the body through 'bodily regimes.' Power over bodies, or 'biopower,' is not total and fixed but mobile and ever changing just like human biology. Where power is present so also is resistance, or at least the possibility of resistance. Foucault alluded to bodily agency in his concept of 'biopower' where he described 'life' as a force that resists and escapes power and can never be quite fully controlled (Foucault 2003). Foucault argued it was the materiality of the body, prone to errors and dysfunction, which necessitated the need for power in the first place. Yet what are considered as 'errors' or abnormal are precisely dependent on the historical context.

Foucault received criticism for his failure to explain resistance (McNay 2009), but I interpret Foucault's description of biopower as one where resistance is not necessarily conscious or intentional but a description of how 'unruly' bodies can challenge boundaries. Resistance is the failure to embody the 'figure of man' I referred to in the introductory chapter that underpinned Foucault's work and which he sought to challenge. People and actions then get read as resistant when they do not fit into the discursive 'régimes of truth'; when for instance they blur the boundaries between mind and body. Resistance to power therefore finds its possibility in that 'life' which escapes power, in the materiality of the human body that cannot be quite grasped by power and discourse.

Next, I consider how practices, both rational and symbolic, can act to 'control' this 'danger' posed by the liminality of grief. But first I want to consider how people might continue an embodied connection to a person after they die, as it is 'holding on' to the deceased that bereavement researchers have identified as the problem in need of professional intervention and management among bereaved people.

The continuing bonds theory, discussed in Chapter 2, was first proposed as an antidote to theories that emphasised detachment from the deceased as the way to resolution or recovery. However, I argue the continuing bonds theory tends to rely upon the individualised and largely disembodied subject it attempted to critique. Ribbens McCarthy and Prokhovnik (2013) similarly have critiqued the notion of 'internalising' the dead person that the continuing bonds theory describes, contending that it remains predicated on the mind/body split by psychologising and locating the deceased other within the individual's psyche. Instead Ribbens McCarthy and Prokhovnik recommend the need to move beyond the binary thinking that is implied in models such as the continuing bonds theory to think about how people maintain a material and embodied relationality after death.

Ribbens McCarthy and Prokhovnik highlight how within a western secular framework that assumes the mind/body and life/death divide, it is unclear what happens to personhood following the death of the body. However, for Ribbens McCarthy and Prokhovnik while the biological body dies, the embodied relationship does not. The material presence of the dead person remains as well as the 'us' formed in the relationship between the two bodies. This 'us' remains written in the body of the living person as an ongoing embodied presence. In contrast to the disembodied continuing bonds theory, Leichtentritt et al. (2016) in their qualitative study found that bereaved people made attempts to blur the boundary between living and dead bodies, 'by focusing on physical aspects of the post-death relationship using their own body as well as that of the deceased' (5). The exploration of the ways in which the bereaved person experiences the presence of the deceased in their absence has led a number of authors to consider the notion of 'absence-presence,' positioning the grieving person at the boundaries between the living and the dead and blurring the edges of the bounded subject (Frers 2013; Meier et al. 2013; Maddrell 2013).

An embodied approach focuses on how absence becomes not only something to be dealt with through individual psychic work but shifts bodily orientation in space. As Krasner (2004) argues, grief is a 'series of slight physical adjustments based on the fact that a body that was always here, in a certain relation to our own, is now gone' (219). Grief is the experience of the absence of a body by which one was once orientated and constituted. For Krasner, grief has a disabling or crippling effect as the particular physical relation in space has been disrupted. He illustrates this through reference to literature and descriptions of people stumbling, reaching out and falling in the face of grief. Bodies become compromised in grief and have to renegotiate themselves in space.

Krasner describes how grieving can be considered a bodily disposition because bodies are already in relation to each other in varying degrees of intimacy. The experience of absence is rooted in the corporeal 'embeddedness' of people. Absence emerges because bodies are already in a state of 'being-in-the-world' with others, whether human or non-human (Frers 2013). Frers further explains that, to experience absence, the object must have already been part of the person's 'habitus.' Here, Frers draws upon a concept popularised by Bourdieu (1990). Habitus is a generative form of identity where the social is internalised into the body consciously and unconsciously, creating a set of ever-evolving bodily dispositions, practices, habits and tastes. As Krasner illustrates, this habitus is disorientated in the event of loss. The presence of absence is the disruption of expectations, a disruption that is experienced bodily and in space. This idea was also captured in

Parkes' concept of the 'assumptive world' that describes how what is lost following bereavement is not only a person but the sense of reality from which the bereaved person made assumptions about world they inhabited.

Arguments that emphasise the embodied nature of grief often do so in opposition to Freud and what is considered to be his disembodied theory of grief. However, I return to Freud to demonstrate how psychoanalytic theories of loss and attachment support a relational embodied concept of the self. As described in Chapter 2, for Freud relationships were fraught with ambivalence due to the way in which people identified with others, where the continuation of one's understanding of oneself was in part or wholly reliant upon the endurance of another object outside of oneself. The loss of the loved object thus brings that ambivalence to the fore. From Freud and Klein's understanding of internal objects and how they come to be internalised, the work of grief is not about 'taking in' what is 'outside' but an acknowledgment that for the object to be lost 'it must have already existed within the subject' (Ahmed 2004, 160).

Butler (2003, 2004, 2010) draws upon Freud's theory of mourning, to describe how grief reveals a fundamental human dependency on others. Loss and vulnerability follow from being socially constituted bodies. Yet what grief displays, writes Butler, is that people are in relation to others in ways of which they are unaware, challenging the notion of an autonomous subject who is in control. The work of mourning in Freud came to be interpreted as a discrete process with stages and tasks, yet Butler notes that Freud kept changing his mind on when mourning is successful. For Butler, Freud's theory instead suggests the ways in which people are liable to 'coming undone' by others. Butler directly attacks the notion of grief theories by arguing that grief is not something that can be 'worked through' but rather something larger than one's plan or choices:

> I do not think for instance one can invoke the Protestant ethic when it comes to loss. One cannot say, "Oh I'll go through loss this way, and that will be the result, and I'll apply myself to the task, and I'll endeavour to achieve the resolution of grief that is before me". I think one is hit by

waves, and that one starts out the day with an aim, a project, a plan, and finds oneself foiled. (Butler 2004, 21)

Butler positions the relational subject as the given form of the subject, and in doing so she builds on Freud to explain that dependency rather than autonomy is the fundamental state of human beings, elucidated by the experience and expression of grief. The autonomous individual for Butler, rather than being a reality, is 'an accomplishment, not a presupposition, and certainly no guarantee' (2004, 27). Butler highlights that people are not only constituted by their relations with others but dispossessed by them. In this framework 'severing ties' is impossible because the 'I' cannot be thought without 'you.' However, ambivalence arises in the struggle between the desire to grasp control and maintain autonomy and the reliance upon the other needed to exist.

This ambivalence is evidence of the way in which objects become incorporated into the self, but further how people do not precisely know the ways in which they are attached to the objects in which they invest. Ahmed (2010) describes the melancholic figure as one who does not know what has been lost. Melancholia is not an inability to let go but an inability to perceive what needs letting go of. As in Klein's theory, melancholia arises because the person does not know how to lose (Kristeva 1989). The presence of ambivalence also reveals a different view of agency where the attachment that sustains life at the same time destroys autonomy. Berlant (Berlant and Edelman 2014) employs the term 'non-sovereignty' to describe this, invoking the psychoanalytic notion of the subject's constitutive division that keeps subjects from fully knowing or being in control of themselves. Borrowing from Berlant, melancholia and the refusal to recover or let go of attachments to the dead can be read not only as a sign of pathology but understood as an active choice to not be sovereign. This is explained further in Berlant's (2011) concept of 'cruel optimism,' which describes how a relation of desire to an object can become cruel by becoming an obstacle to flourishing. Berlant's concept is instructive for grieving for while recovery is constructed on the understanding that detaching from the lost object leads to successful mourning, yet it is the object, as Berlant describes, that is the anchor that sustains hope. So while an attachment to the deceased person might act to impede the ability to 'move on,' that same attachment provides a sense of self, and belonging in the world. This is the cruel nature of the optimism for the lost object where the bereaved person is then suspended in the space of liminality, for to let go and leave the object of desire is to leave the anchor for optimism, and yet staying with this fantasy produces unhappiness.

I have discussed literature that has emphasised the body and embodiment in the experience of grief. I have also discussed literature that has enabled me to view the relational and affective aspects of bodies, and the importance of this relational nature for understanding the experience of grief. However, these bodies are also potentially problematic in a culture that favours autonomous individuals where the boundaries between mind, bodies and emotions are clearly demarcated. From the literature I have just discussed, I argue this is a proposition that is unsustainable and which has led to the shortcomings of the dominant grief theories. In the next section I focus on practices as a way to bridge together the two discussions on emotions and bodies, and to centre in on how people are managed, and manage themselves, in the liminal space of grief.

Managing Emotions and Bodies

Here I argue that a focus on practice can help to resolve some of the shortcomings of the perspectives on affect, as well bring together ideas on how emotions are embodied in practice. I draw on an argument first proposed by Wetherell (2012) in her discussion of affect theory and emotion and her concept of 'affective practices.' Wetherell argues that the generic category of autonomous affect is unhelpful and that instead affect needs to be situated and studied as part of an embodied process of meaning-making. Wetherell also argues for the need not to abandon discourse, as many affect theorists have done, but to explore through an analysis of practice how affect interacts with and informs discursive meaning-making. An analysis of 'affective practices' is thus not one necessarily concerned with following 'flows,' but human behaviours that seek to preserve, construct and negotiate identities and meaning.

According to Scheer (2012), a focus on practice in the study of emotions can help to bridge dichotomies between structure and agency. Practices not only generate emotions but emotions themselves can be viewed as a practical engagement with the world. Practices can be considered as 'vehicles' for emotions or emotions can be considered practices in themselves. In doing so, both Wetherell and Scheer use a Bourdieusian understanding of practice. In Bourdieu's (1990) understanding, subjects are not prior to practices but products of them. Bourdieu explained this through his concept of 'habitus.' As discussed earlier, for Bourdieu the individual internalises the varying conditions of objective social structures and norms producing particular bodily dispositions. These learned behaviours become unconscious and habitual. Practices are then guided by a 'practical sense,' which is informed and shaped by the norms and the society in which one lives. Bourdieu's concept provides an embodied understanding of practice as well as an understanding of what might predispose a person to express emotion in a particular way. From his model of practice Bourdieu's also argues that certain emotional practices, including facial expressions, are learnt or inherited from the society in which one lives, and are not necessarily 'natural' displays of emotion.

Thinking about emotions as practices also repositions emotion as no longer opposed to rationality but as potentially central to rational action (Barbalet 2001; Turner and Stets 2005). Barbalet (2001) argued emotions should be understood as essential to social structure and processes, as well as the routine operations of social interactions, where emotions provide direction and give purpose to action. Viewed from this perspective, emotions do not derail rational behaviour but give it meaning. If emotions distract persons from their purposes, then, at the same time, emotions establish those purposes afresh. Barbalet further described how emotions such as confidence and shame serve to produce and maintain social structures, highlighting how emotions can produce change but also conformity and sameness.

Ngai's (2005) description of 'ugly feelings' provides a way of thinking about emotions that are not necessarily transformative or disruptive. Ugly feelings are 'minor' feelings like anxiety or irritation that do not bring about a release or catharsis but rather serve to perpetuate the situation that caused them originally. Thinking about affects that suspend agency is an interesting counter to the authors who write about the transformative potential of affect. I argue it is a useful way to think about the place of the affective in the everyday and how the practices people carry out in the act of 'reproducing life' (Berlant 2011) are imbued with the affective. For example, the organisation of the working day has a particularly important role in modern western societies that are governed within a neo-liberal capitalist system. Binkley (2009), drawing on Foucault's concept of 'technologies of temporalisation' discussed how the organisation of time is central to producing 'docile' and obedient bodies. As I described in Chapters 3 and 4, time has an increasingly significant role in how grief is both defined and treated, with designated time periods marking the line between normal and complicated grieving. If grief is an emotion that suspends agency, reintegration and recovery become reliant on time-limited interventions that reorient the bereaved person into a linear sense of time.

The ways in which affective practices are carried out in the ordinary working day is further captured in Hochschild's (1983) understanding of 'emotional labour.' Based on Marx's theory of labour (1976), Hochschild described how waged labour was not only physical but required emotional work. In her study of air flight assistants, she explored how the employees traded on smiles and were trained and encouraged to express positive emotions as an unpaid part of their job. For Hochschild these 'feeling rules' that existed in the workplace were part of a broader emotional management that governed people's interactions in their day-to-day lives, and a form of exploitation. However, when emotional management becomes institutionalised as part of company policy, Hochschild argued this led to a commodification of emotions since what is being sold as part of the service is a display of appropriate emotion. At its simplest, part of the emotional labour was to smile at customers and at its most taxing not to show negative emotions to difficult or abusive customers. Staff thus became alienated from their 'authentic' feelings through the required performance of emotions. These performances were either 'surface acting,' where the person pretended to feel an emotion but did not deceive themselves as to their 'true' feelings; or 'deep acting' where the pretence became indistinguishable from the 'true' feelings, causing a transformation in how the individual felt and related to their emotions.

While Hochschild's belief in natural 'authentic' feelings is problematic, her analysis of how emotions are utilised in work practices illustrates how everyday practices become a way of managing the emotions. It also demonstrates the performative nature of emotions. In Hochschild's understanding of 'deep' and 'surface' acting, the performance of emotions can never be understood to be 'real,' rather that the real, the unmanaged and spontaneous emotion had to be rescued from the processes of emotional management. Yet I would argue that performance is central to affective practices, and that the performance itself might be considered the 'real' emotion. Goffman (1959) claimed that even the most 'authentic' appearing performances are managed. For Goffman, emotions were just another 'move' in the 'game' of controlling and managing the impression one gives to others. Emotional expression was not about relaying the true character of a person but a response to the requirements of the social encounter. Authenticity was something that was achieved by the persuasiveness of the performance that required adhering to the 'feeling rules.' Further, for Goffman even those emotions performed in private, in the absence of an audience, were socially performed.

Affective practices can also be studied as a way of understanding how people construct and maintain identity and not only how they might hide or perform it. Valentine (2013) used the concept of 'affective practices' to explore responses to death and bereavement through her analysis of people's narratives about their continuing relationships with the deceased person. Valentine drew on the work on affect to illuminate the role of the body and emotions in managing identities of bereaved and deceased people. For Valentine, affective practices referred to the 'behaviour designed to preserve relationships, identities and continuity of being' (2013, 385). Grief provided the epistemological site for exploring how individuals made sense of the mix of ordinary and extraordinary in the experience of bereavement. Valentine described how people managed post-mortem relationships through situated affective practices, such as memorialising the dead through formal and informal rituals. These affective practices were a means to repair identities shattered by the event of loss. The practices of meaning-making and continuing attachments to the deceased were not something that simply happened as a result of a psychological state, but arose out of strategic social action (Unruh 1983, 349).

In terms of identity repair following bereavement, there has been a considerable amount of research on how bereaved people use material spaces as a way to actively manage the liminality of grief (see, e.g. Hockey et al. 2001; Horsley 2008; Maddrell 2013). These studies have shown the meaning of spaces has a role to play in how death and grief are experienced, not only in the spaces of the cemetery or the funeral home (Horsley 2008) where death is expected to be, but also as a site of creativity and agency where the landscape is adapted to accommodate formal and informal grieving rituals, such as roadside memorials. Maddrell (2013) has described in her work on informal public memorials how absence becomes a dynamic 'absence-presence' located in material spaces, not just in the psyche. This forms what she calls a 'third emotional space' where informal memorials serve to mediate between private and public, and between the living and the dead. What these studies have demonstrated is how people come to inhabit spaces such as the cemetery to manage the liminal experience of grief, and further that these spaces too are liminal in that they forge a unique space between the living and dead. However, these spaces also become identifiable places in which to locate the deceased person, and in effect bring some order to what might be felt as the disorientating experience of grief. Here, the dead are not only divided from the living, but they are in effect 'stored' so that the living may here interact with the dead, before returning to their lives away from this socially designated space of bereavement and death.

Affective practices can be seen as everyday performances and behaviours that emerge in response to social encounters or events, performances that might be differently interpreted as conforming to or resisting the dominant 'feeling rules.' Affective practices are also important modes of preserving and maintaining identity, where identity is something constructed through everyday actions not something occurring inside the individual psyche. Describing emotions as practices, I argue, is a way to overcome the problems of viewing emotions as uncontrollable intensities that come from 'outside-in' and equally the difficulties in arguing for a set of basic emotions that emerge from 'inside-out' of the body. It also allows space to reconsider the important role of discourse in constructing ideas and norms around appropriate emotional behaviours. Following Bourdieu's notion of practice, emotional expression is understood as a learned and habitual bodily practice and not something that is merely repressed or induced by feeling rules, as in Hochschild's argument. The management of emotions can be thus understood as more akin to Foucault's (1988) 'technologies of the self' where individuals act to govern their own behaviour for different ends through various practices. In Chapter 4, I focused on different types of practices that seek to manage grief, often in order to achieve the end goal or recovery, but I also highlighted practices, such as interacting with spaces and objects, that act to preserve and construct identities both of the bereaved person and the person who had died.

So far in this chapter I have drawn on literature that has differently emphasised the intertwined nature of emotions, bodies and practices or rituals that combine together to produce different experiences of grief. In closing, I now turn to consider what type of body or subject emerges from this way of conceptualising grief, as opposed to the autonomous resilient individual that recurs in the overly psychological view of grief.

Theorising 'The Blob'

In speaking of affective practices, it might feel as though a conscious, rational actor has replaced the ambivalent melancholic figure discussed earlier in this chapter. Yet to emphasise the analysis of affective practices is to move away from categories that govern and constrain behaviour to thinking about how the category of an emotion does not determine the actions and feelings felt in its wake. I argue a focus on practice can allow for the study of grief that acknowledges that people might come to inhabit the structure of grief differently, conforming to or resisting feeling rules.

In this attempt a quite different, yet unclear, vision of the bereaved person and grief emerges. The body is both material and beyond materiality, coherent and emotional, possessing the capacity to be affected by others and also to remain resistant to them. This understanding of the body as always in flux is made possible through a relational ontology of the body. This resonates with Deleuze and Guattari's (1984, 1988) 'nomadic' form of subjectivity where the body is viewed as a constant process of becoming. The nomadic subject has 'no terminus from which you set out, none which you ought to arrive at' (Deleuze and Parnet 1977, 2). The aim of the nomadic subject is not integration but rather disintegration, captured in Deleuze and Guattari's concept of the 'body-without-organs' that poses a radical counter to the question of 'being this or that sort of human' (Deleuze 1990). The 'body-without-organs' describes a subject not constrained by binaries, whether the divide between the living and dead, or the mind and body.

While Deleuze and Guattari seek to affirm the potential of the human body and liberate it from what they see as unnecessary boundaries, as the name suggests, the 'body-without-organs' views the material matter of the body itself as something from which to be freed. This is often where the disembodied accounts of affect heavily influenced by Deleuze and Guattari derive. However, is there really nothing to be said for the human body? This is the question Bloch (2011a) posed as he attempted to account for how people can be both in process and relational beings and yet also have some type of biological consistency that makes people identifiably human. Bloch begins his essay by describing the 'universalist vs culturalist' debate that has plagued the history of the social sciences in the attempt to define 'human nature.' Critiquing the social construction of the culturalists, Bloch argued that in the attempts by the social sciences to capture the 'individual' and 'self' there has been a failure to consider people as natural organisms. Bloch then proceeded to propose a model of the human which, to avoid the ontological underpinnings of categories such as 'self,' he called 'the blob.' The 'blob' is created simultaneously by biology, psychology, history and culture. Bloch's model of the blob is an attempt to reconcile the ideas of the social sciences, namely anthropology, and those found in the life sciences and to explain the multiple and incomplete visions of the human that are produced when in 'the never-never land of culture without minds and bodies' or in 'the never-never land of minds and bodies without culture and history' (Bloch 2011b).

Bloch distinguished three different levels that compose the blob. The three levels exist on a continuum, where neither element can be separated from the other.

- The 'core self': This involves a sense of ownership and location of one's body and a sense that one is the author of one's own actions. This is a type of selfhood which Bloch suggests is shared by all animate creatures, but implies no reflexive awareness whatsoever.
- The 'minimal self': This concerns a sense of continuity in time. This level involves the short-term memory required to organise episodes and the ability to use information from the past to inform behaviour in the present and the future.
- The 'narrative self': It is the narrative aspect of the blob that allows memories to be formed into an autobiography. However, having an autobiography is distinguished from being conscious of and using language to speak about one's autobiography. Bloch here makes a distinction between two rhetorical styles: those that tell stories about themselves and those that do not.

Bloch makes this point concerning the 'narrative self' to emphasise that this does not imply a difference in the nature of the blob but rather a difference in style and means of expression. It is here that culture has a clear role to play in shaping the type of stories people might tell about themselves. Yet as Bloch points out, it is not possible to say how much influence culture has until the epistemological status of the thing claimed has been clarified.

Bloch's analysis provides a conceptualisation of the self that avoids having to fall on one side of the 'universalist vs culturalist' debate. Here, mind and bodies are on a continuum, and emotional expression is both bodily and socially informed: there is no way to distinguish them from one another. Biology and the environment in which one is situated (including other people, language, social norms and social structures) are always engaged in a process of negotiation. This shape and form does not exist prior to this negotiation, at least only in the form of the blob that allows such negotiation with the environment to be possible in the first place. Drawing on a Foucauldian ontology that suspends judgment on the 'nature' or essence of the human body, this can enable the exploration of questions of how people account for themselves rather than asking what people are.

In this chapter I have tackled two areas of concern that I argue have been largely overlooked in past and recent grief and bereavement research. As discussed so far, much grief research is based on an assumption of an autonomous individual subject with grief as a natural emotion. Through this a paradoxical grieving figure emerges who is at once a rational and resilient actor and yet liable to 'come undone' by the loss of another. I argue that the study of grief has been short-sighted in its understanding of emotions and bodies, and I have turned to literature from the social and cultural sciences to bring new insight to theorising grief. In this attempt I have highlighted the 'unbounded,' relational and unconscious aspects of the body as well as exploring how emotions might not be understood as things one innately has or 'catches' from elsewhere but something one does through practices, whether extraordinary or mundane, which give form both to the affect and to the body itself. By centring the discussion on the concept of liminality my aim has been to suggest that theorising grief is best begun with no 'a priori' assumptions of what constitutes grief and the person who experiences it. I have also addressed, as Hockey et al. (2010) have done previously, the impasse between social constructionist arguments that claim human beings see and experience their environment in culturally specific ways and the everyday experiences of the immediacy of bodily emotional and sensory responses to that world. I argue that biology and the social environment are in a constant process of interaction, out of which the shape of the person and their grief emerges.

Focusing on the relational nature of grief, what has emerged is an embodied subject whose boundaries are fluid and porous and formed in relation to others, whether those others are alive or dead; problematising the notion of the autonomous, bounded body. The bereaved person is shaped and undone by relations with other bodies and spaces: intimate, political and social. This body becomes open to intervention when it falls on the wrong side of the boundary and becomes a negotiated and contested site, ever vulnerable and precarious to the power of others. This shapeless evolving 'blob,' making its way through the liminal space of grief, comes into view as a category or kind, an entity with form, on the boundaries and intersections of the lines of power, discourse and truth that lay claim to the body, mind or brain of the bereaved person. Echoing Foucault's notion, subjects are produced on the 'axes' of the regimes of truth. In these intersections a constant negotiation is occurring; how well a person might endure in these categories depends on a capacity for performance, how well they can play the game, what space there is for resistance, and what opportunities the shifting composition of lines (institutions, individuals, groups, discourse) allows.

References

Ahmed, Sara. 2004. *The Cultural Politics of Emotion*. Edinburgh: Edinburgh University Press.

———. 2010. *The Promise of Happiness*. Durham and London: Duke University Press.

Anderson, Ben. 2009. "Affective Atmospheres." *Emotion, Space and Society* 2: 77–81.

Árnason, Arnar. 1998. "'Feel the Pain': Death, Grief and Bereavement Counselling in the North East of England." Unpublished Doctoral thesis, Durham University.

Barbalet, J. M. 2001. *Emotion, Social Theory, and Social Structure: A Macrosociological Approach*. Cambridge: Cambridge University Press.

Barrett, Lisa Feldman. 2006. "Are Emotions Natural Kinds?" *Perspectives on Psychological Science* 1 (1): 28–58.

Bennett, Gillian, and Kate Mary Bennett. 2000. "The Presence of the Dead: An Empirical Study." *Mortality* 5 (2): 139–157.

Berlant, Lauren. 2011. *Cruel Optimism*. London and Durham: Duke University Press.

Berlant, Lauren, and Lee Edelman. 2014. *Sex, or the Unbearable*. London and Durham: Duke University Press.

Binkley, Sam. 2009. "Governmentality, Temporality and Practice: From the Individualization of Risk to the 'Contradictory Movements of the Soul.'" *Time & Society* 18 (1): 86–105.
Blackman, Lisa. 2013. "Habit and Affect: Revitalizing a Forgotten History." *Body & Society* 19 (2–3): 186–216.
Bloch, Maurice. 2011a. "The Blob." *Anthropology of This Century*, May 1.
———. 2011b. "The Blob." *Anthropology of This Century*, October 1.
Bloch, Maurice, and Jonathan Parry. 1982. "Introduction: Death and the Regeneration of Life." In *Death and the Regeneration of Life*, edited by Maurice Bloch and Jonathan Parry, 1–44. Cambridge: Cambridge University Press.
Bourdieu, Pierre. 1990. *The Logic of Practice*. Stanford, CA: Stanford University Press.
Brennan, Teresa. 2004. *The Transmission of Affect*. New York: Cornell University Press.
Butler, Judith. 2003. "Afterword: After Loss, What Then?" In *Loss: The Politics of Mourning*, edited by David Eng and David Kazanjian, 467–474. Berkeley and Los Angeles: University of California Press.
———. 2004. *Precarious Life: The Powers of Mourning and Violence*. London: Verso.
———. 2010. *Frames of War: When Is Life Grievable*? London: Verso.
Csordas, Thomas J. 1990. "Embodiment as a Paradigm for Anthropology." *Ethos* 18 (1): 5–47.
———. 2008. "Intersubjectivity and Intercorporeality." *Subjectivity* 22 (1): 110–121.
Damasio, António R. 1994. *Descartes' Error: Emotion, Reason, and the Human Brain*. New York: Putnam.
Darwin, Charles. 1872. *The Expression of the Emotions in Man and Animals*. London: John Murray.
Davies, Douglas J. 2011. *Emotion, Identity, and Religion: Hope, Reciprocity, and Otherness*. Oxford: Oxford University Press.
Deleuze, Gilles. 1990. *Negotiations 1972–1990*. New York: Columbia University Press.
Deleuze, Gilles, and Claire Parnet. 1977. *Dialogues*. New York: Columbia University Press.
Deleuze, Gilles, and Felix Guattari. 1984. *Anti-Oedipus: Capitalism and Schizophrenia*. London: Athlone Press.
———. 1988. *A Thousand Plateaus: Capitalism and Schizophrenia*. London: Continuum.

Descartes, Rene. 1649. *The Passions of the Soul.* Translated by S. H. Voss. Indianapolis: Hackett Publishing.
Dixon, Thomas. 2012. "'Emotion': The History of a Keyword in Crisis." *Emotion Review: Journal of the International Society for Research on Emotion* 4 (4): 338–344.
Douglas, Mary. 1966. *Purity and Danger: An Analysis of Concepts of Pollution and Taboo.* London: Penguin.
Durkheim, Emile. 1915. *The Elementary Forms of the Religious Life.* London: George Allen & Unwin.
Ekman, Paul. 1992. "An Argument for Basic Emotions." *Cognition and Emotion* 6 (3/4): 169–200.
———. 1993. "Facial Expression and Emotion." *American Psychologist* 48 (4): 384–392.
Foucault, Michel. 1973. *The Birth of the Clinic: An Archaeology of Medical Perception.* London: Routledge.
———. 1976. *The History of Sexuality, Volume 1: The Will to Knowledge.* New York: Vintage.
———. 1988. "Technologies of the Self." In *Technologies of the Self,* edited by Luther H. Martin, H. Gutman, and Patrick H. Hutton, 16–49. Amherst: University of Massachussets Press.
———. 2003. "1976." In *Society Must Be Defended: Lectures at the College de France 1975–1976,* 239–264. London: Allen Lane.
Fox, Nick J. 2013. "Flows of Affect in the Olympic Stadium." *Sociological Research Online* 18 (2): 2.
———. 2015. "Emotions, Affects and the Production of Social Life." *The British Journal of Sociology* 66 (2): 301–318.
Frers, Lars. 2013. "The Matter of Absence." *Cultural Geographies* 20 (4): 431–445.
Freud, Sigmund. 1917. "Mourning and Melancholia." In *The Penguin Freud Reader,* edited by Adam Philips, 310–326. London: Penguin.
Goffman, Erving. 1959. *The Presentation of Self in Everyday Life.* London: Penguin.
Hallam, Elizabeth, Jenny Hockey, and Glennys Howarth. 1999. *Beyond the Body: Death and Social Identity.* London: Routledge.
Haraway, Donna. 1991. *Simians, Cyborgs, and Women: The Reinvention of Nature.* New York: Routledge.
Harré, Rom. 1986. *The Social Construction of Emotions.* Oxford: Blackwell.

Harré, Rom, and W. Gerrod Parrott, eds. 1996. *The Emotions: Social, Cultural and Biological Dimensions*. London: Sage.
Hatfield, Eliane, John T. Cacioppo, and Richard L. Rapson. 1994. *Emotional Contagion*. Cambridge: Cambridge University Press.
Hochschild, Arlie Russell. 1983. *The Managed Heart: Commercialization of Human Feeling*. Berkeley: University of California Press.
Hockey, Jenny, Bridget Penhale, and David Sibley. 2001. "Landscapes of Loss: Spaces of Memory, Times of Bereavement." *Ageing and Society* 21 (6): 739–757.
Hockey, Jenny, Carol Komaromy, and Kate Woodthorpe, eds. 2010. *The Matter of Death: Space, Place and Materiality*. Basingstoke, Hampshire: Palgrave Macmillan.
Horsley, Philomena A. 2008. "Death Dwells in Spaces: Bodies in the Hospital Mortuary." *Anthropology & Medicine* 15 (2): 133–146.
Howarth, Glennys. 2000. "Dismantling the Boundaries Between Life and Death." *Mortality* 5 (2): 127–138.
James, William. 1884. "What Is an Emotion?" *Mind* 9 (34): 188–205.
Kemper, Theodore D. 1987. "How Many Emotions Are There? Wedding the Social and Autonomic Components." *American Journal of Sociology* 93: 263–289.
Klein, Melanie. 1940. "Mourning and Its Relation to Manic-Depressive States." In *Love, Guilt and Reparation and Other Works 1921–1945: The Writings of Melanie Klein, Volume I*, 344–369. London: Hogarth Press.
Krasner, James. 2004. "Doubtful Arms and Phantom Limbs: Literary Portrayals of Embodied Grief." *Publications of the Modern Language Association of America* 119 (2): 218–232.
Kristeva, Julia. 1989. *Black Sun: Depression and Melancholia*. New York: Columbia University Press.
Leichtentritt, Ronit D., Michael Mahat Shamir, Adi Barak, and Ayelet Yerushalmi. 2016. "Bodies as Means for Continuing Post-death Relationships." *Journal of Health Psychology* 21 (5): 738–749.
Lupton, Deborah. 1997. "Consumerism, Reflexivity and the Medical Encounter." *Social Science & Medicine* 45 (3): 373–381.
Maddrell, Avril. 2013. "Living with the Deceased: Absence, Presence and Absence-Presence." *Cultural Geographies* 20 (4): 501–522.
Marx, Karl. 1976. *Capital, Volume One: A Critique of Political Economy*. London: Penguin.
Massumi, Brian. 2002. *Parables for the Virtual: Movement, Affect, Sensation*. Durham, NC: Duke University Press.

McNay, Lois. 2009. "Self as Enterprise: Dilemmas of Control and Resistance in Foucault's the Birth of Biopolitics." *Theory, Culture & Society* 26 (6): 55–77.

Mead, Margaret. 1975. "Review of Darwin and Facial Expression." *Journal of Communication* 25: 209–213.

Meier, Lars, Lars Frers, and Erika Sigvardsdotter. 2013. "The Importance of Absence in the Present: Practices of Remembrance and the Contestation of Absences." *Cultural Geographies* 20 (4): 423–430.

Ngai, Sianne. 2005. *Ugly Feelings*. Cambridge, MA: Havard University Press.

Parkes, Colin Murray. 1972. *Bereavement: Studies of Grief in Adult Life*. Harmondsworth: Penguin.

Ribbens McCarthy, Jane, and Raia Prokhovnik. 2013. "Embodied Relationality and Caring After Death." *Body & Society* 20 (2): 18–43.

Rosaldo, Renato. 1993. "Introduction: Grief and a Headhunter's Rage." In *Culture and Truth: The Remaking of Social Analysis*, 1–21. Boston: Beacon Press.

Scheer, Monique. 2012. "Are Emotions a Kind of Practice (And Is That What Makes Them Have a History)? A Bourdieuian Approach to Understanding Emotion." *History and Theory*, 51 (2): 193–220.

Shilling, Chris. 1993. *The Body and Social Theory*. London: Sage.

Stenner, Paul, and Eduardo Moreno. 2013. "Liminality and Affectivity: The Case of Deceased Organ Donation." *Subjectivity* 6 (3): 229–253.

Tanner, Laura. 2006. *Lost Bodies: Inhabiting the Borders of Life and Death*. Ithaca and London: Cornell University Press.

Turner, Bryan S. 1984. *The Body and Society: Explorations in Social Theory*. London: Sage.

Turner, Jonathan H., and Jan E. Stets. 2005. *The Sociology of Emotions*. New York: Cambridge University Press.

Turner, Victor. 1969. *The Ritual Process: Structure and Anti-Structure*. Chicago: Aldine.

———. 1974. *Dramas, Fields, Metaphors: Symbolic Action in Human Society*. Ithaca and London: Cornell University Press.

———. 1982. *From Ritual to Theatre: The Human Seriousness of Play*. New York: Performing Arts Journal Publications.

Unruh, David R. 1983. "Death and Personal History: Strategies of Identity Preservation." *Social Problems* 30 (3): 340–351.

Valentine, Christine. 2013. "Identity and Post-mortem Relationships in the Narratives of British and Japanese Mourners." *Sociological Review* 61 (2): 383–401.

Van Gennep, Arthur. 1960. *The Rites of Passage*. London: Routledge & Kegan Paul.

Wetherell, Margaret. 2012. *Affect and Emotions: A New Social Science Understanding*. London: Sage.

Williams, Simon. 2001. *Emotion and Social Theory: Corporeal Reflections on the (Ir)rational*. London: Sage.

6

Inhabiting and Resisting Identities

Laura: You know when you read the novels, the old novels where there's a widow in there and she's on the side-lines of everything's that's going on, she's no longer in that part of the family. Because I was always a bit the matriarch in the family, bossy boots, and that role's gone for me now … my role has definitely changed within the family, being a widow.

Interviewer: Your external identity has changed to other people.

Laura: Yes, yeah. And that's bizarre for me because, as you see, I still wear my wedding ring. Three years on and I will wear it until I die. Because I don't see myself as a widow, I still see myself as his wife.

In this chapter I focus on identity following bereavement to consider how new identities are formed, or old identities are sustained, as bereaved people come to move across the liminal space of grief. The bereaved people I interviewed described how, after bereavement, they felt like a completely different person as well as being treated differently by others. Initially, it was a realisation that one's external identity had changed despite feeling like the same person. As demonstrated in the excerpt above, for Laura there was a disjuncture between how others saw her and how she viewed herself: "as his wife." The disjuncture

C. Pearce, *The Public and Private Management of Grief*,
https://doi.org/10.1007/978-3-030-17662-4_6

felt by Laura revealed how her identity was in transition, 'betwixt and between' (van Gennep 1960) social positions. To those around her, Laura had lost her previous identity and status, yet Laura was not willing to accept the new status of widow.

This liminal identity could be unsettling to others, as the bereaved person comes to embody the divide between living and dead people, polluting the clear boundaries between life and death. For example, Paul remarked how as a sociable extroverted person he was treated as a "pariah" where people would avoid contacting and visiting him. The way in which people avoided her after her husband's death made Anne feel as though "[bereavement] might be a contagious disease." Equally, being placed within this new undesirable category was a motivator for Tania, who acknowledged the gulf between the identity she had come to inhabit and who she wanted to be, she described: "I just wanted to be Tania again rather than the woman whose lost her husband." I describe three key identities that emerged, identities that provided different trajectories through the liminal space of grief. These three trajectories I outline—'recovered,' 'relational' and 'resistant'—are identities that might only be temporarily inhabited, rather than an end point in the journey.

I suggest that the ways in which people make sense of and perform grief informs the types of identities they come to inhabit. In Chapter 4, I presented how grief is something that is performed through formal and informal practices. As Valentine (2013) has suggested, these 'affective practices' enable the repairing of the identities of the bereaved person as well as the preserving of the identities of that of the deceased. Different individuals and groups through a variety of practices constructed the three trajectories detailed here such as: psychiatric diagnostic categories, psychological research, counselling practice and individual narration. In each case the identity of recovered or unrecovered is negotiated and contested by the different parties. As people move in and out of these identities, what comes to be considered 'resistant' or 'unrecovered' is in constant shift.

In closing the chapter I discuss the temporary nature of grieving identities and my search for the person experiencing 'complicated grief.' Complicated grief or resistant identities could be identified through acts of performing grief too well or not enough, and they could also be what a person comes to inhabit when they fail to narrate the 'right' story. But these identities are produced, inhabited and resisted in different ways.

Constructing Identities

So far, I have been tracking the grieving subject and the different forms grief takes whether 'complicated' or 'recovered.' This subject, I contend, in line with Foucault's work on subjectivities, does not exist as a material reality apart from how it is constructed by discourses and practices on grief and recovery. In the same way that a genealogical approach seeks to problematise ideas, Foucault rejected the idea of starting out with a theory of the subject (Foucault 1984, 290), a view that informs the notion of identity I describe here. For Foucault there is no true ethical human subject: the subject is created and is contingent on the historical context. The idea of what a subject is depends on the prevailing discourse and explanations provided by the relevant authority at a given time. Foucault's study of human subjectivity encompassed the ontological (the nature of human beings); the epistemological (how the subject is known); ethical (the type of selves people should seek to be), and technical (the forms of conduct and practices people undertake in order to achieve desirable traits). In terms of the ontology of the subject, Foucault's work focused on effacing the particular image of 'man' that had dominated western history, rather than assuming a materiality behind it. For Foucault the subject was not a 'substance' but a 'form' where the body was to be understood not as a brute fact of nature but as a historical entity. A genealogy of subjectification takes a particular understanding of the human as the site of a historical problem rather than as the basis of a historical narrative. What aims to be revealed is not a universal nature of the subject, but rather the multiple forms of knowledge that are constructed around the subject. These different forms of knowledge 'arm' the subject with a truth that does not reside within (Foucault 1984).

Rather than composing a history of the person, the aim is to construct a genealogy of the relations to the self. This is achieved by focusing not on revealing the 'truth' of the subject but highlighting the ways in which 'one plays' at constituting oneself in different situations and contexts. In the course of detailing how different bodies are produced and managed, the body emerges as a contested site, not a constant but shaped and manipulated by different contexts. Subjects are constituted into various forms through an ethical relation to the norms and games of truth that govern a particular historical context. This production of identities Foucault described as the process of subjectification. Deleuze (1990) described the process of subjectification as the relationship to force or power that, depending on where the line is folded, establishes different ways of existing. It is within these 'folds,' as Deleuze puts it, that the 'self' emerges.

Subjects are not, however, merely formed by forces of power but develop as 'ethical' subjects through the ways in which people come to relate to themselves. Foucault (1988) described how people turn to work on themselves through practices he called 'technologies of the self.' 'Technologies of the self' refers to the ways in which individuals experience, understand, judge, and conduct themselves. Foucault explained that 'technologies of the self':

> … permit individuals to effect by their own means or with the help of others a certain number of operations on their own bodies and souls, thought, conduct, ways of being, so as to transform themselves in order to attain a certain state of happiness, purity, wisdom, perfection, immortality. (1988, 18)

Foucault's explanation of power allows for the understanding of how people govern themselves in the promise of transformation into a happier, purer and wiser self. Power, in Foucault's terms, is thus productive rather than merely repressive; the presence of power produces identities as opposed to repressing them. Furthermore, the 'governing of the self' changes how people relate to themselves. People work on themselves through different 'bodily régimes,' for example, carrying out 'grief work.' The management of abnormality, which is the focus of these technologies, is carried out not only by authorities but also by the individuals themselves, as they are encouraged, in Foucault's view, to become 'happier' or 'recovered' in the name of becoming ethical subjects.

Taking Foucault's approach in the analysis of data, I suspended belief in an essential human subject, which enabled me to identify a number of different 'subjects' that appeared in the research findings. In this book I have described 'figures' of grief, where I refer to representations of types of grief. These representations are public, cultural figures, promoted by media, literature or political discourse, and that come to impinge on the type of person the bereaved person might judge him or herself to be. In my analysis of 'bereaved people,' bereaved people are 'clients' and 'service users' but also 'experts.' Bereaved people are 'citizens' of a nation obligated to work and be happy and also act as 'individuals' or as a 'community.' The bereaved person is also represented by cultural 'figures' such as 'widows' that proscribe behaviours and characteristics. Bereaved people can be diagnosed as 'complicated,' or considered 'normal.' Further, bereaved people are often characterised by their continued relationships with deceased people, suggesting a relational and distributed sense of personhood.

In Chapter 5, I introduced Bloch's (2011) description of 'the blob' to explain how the categories of 'subject,' 'individual,' and 'citizen' are social constructions that provide different forms to the 'blob.' In accordance with this conceptualisation, I view individual identity as a construction that people come to inhabit. Identity is a collaborative construction in that it is not formed purely through individual choice, which would presume an autonomous self-determining subject (Giddens 1991), but identity is formed by interaction with other people and social structures. In this view I am applying Foucault's conception of subjectivity as something that emerges through negotiation with authorities and discourse, and by engaging with relational models of the self, leaving space to consider how people come to make choices about their identity, and the extent to which those choices can be seen to be 'conscious' or 'unconscious' ones.

Recovered Identities

Recovered identities can be identified and claimed in different ways. On the one hand, recovery is an objective measure in mental health care. Service users are actively claiming, and being encouraged to claim, an identity that is 'recovered.' In this setting, recovery has become conflated with assumed notions of what it means to be a functional citizen yet the criteria of what is deemed to bring quality of life are rarely questioned. *A Journey to Recovery* (Department of Health 2001) described the importance of recovery to the rights of a citizen, where those rights included: having an acceptable place to live, a meaningful occupation, access to further education and training, access to information on entitlements and benefits, and engaging in 'ordinary social activities.' For instance, recovery colleges deliver courses on how to stop smoking, how to eat better, and how to get a job. In these models of recovery there is an implicit judgement of how one should successfully live out their personal lives. As observed by social scientist Diana Rose, 'For all that [recovery] goals are meant to be "personal", certain goals are not permitted. You cannot decide to go to bed for a month' (Rose 2014, 217). In speaking of the recovery model, one of the study participants and mental health service user Donna described that adhering to the model was as though "you need to recover from being yourself."

On the other hand, subjective definitions of recovery offer myriad ways of living recovery, which embrace the non-normative ways people might live. Throughout the findings discussed in this book there was a conflict between these two types of recovery, often defined as 'clinical' and 'personal' recovery, which was not easily reconciled. This was demonstrated in the recovery model itself that, in transforming a subjective feeling into an objective measure, had faced considerable criticism. The debate over the uses of the term recovery in grief and bereavement also brings these issues to the fore, where recovery appears in different guises such as 'integration' and 'adaptation.' As described in Chapter 4, bereavement practitioners showed caution over using the term 'recovery,' concerned about the medical connotations of 'recovery,' and instead spoke of "change", "movement" and "newness."

Being recovered also described internal shifts in the psyche: a withdrawal of energy from the deceased person or an integration of the loss into the bereaved person (Freud 1917).

However, there is a sense of recovery implicit in these descriptions in that bereaved people are understood to be coming back to 'normal life.' If considered in terms of a 'rite of passage' (van Gennep 1960) recovery signals the return from liminality: changed, but stronger and more efficient. Grief casts people out into liminal space erasing past identities but providing various props to navigate one's way back. Recovery is a transformation for the better but it is also a transformation back into normal life. For example, one of the bereaved participants, Tania, described how following her husband's death she just wanted to get "fixed", expressing an urgent need to be "me" again. A number of the bereaved participants described a moment of recognition that their identity had changed, and the struggle to return to their previous self or come to terms with a new identity. For example, I asked Tania whether there were moments in her grieving where she felt like she was no longer herself, to which she replied:

> Yeah and it annoyed me because I remember thinking I am not this weeping wailing depressed woman, I'm not a depressed person by nature. I've always, always been quite optimistic and it used, it just really upset me, sitting on my own at night thinking this is not me, this is just not me.

Tania acknowledged that she was "quite dependent" on her husband and narrated a sense of disbelief and surprise at the person she had now become. Anne too, had married her partner in her early twenties and finding herself alone was a new experience in her adult life. This was coupled with being forced to take sole responsibility for their family and children. As other people acknowledged her change in identity, Anne recognised for herself that her identity had changed:

> I'm a different me. I can't be that person, because that person is reliant on having another half. And I have to be a different me, I have different priorities, I have different ways of looking at things, and I'm harder. It's just, you can't see life the same way anymore.

This recognition could then lead to making changes or taking specific actions. For Tania and Anne this change in identity provided the impetus to transform their lives in what they felt were positive ways. Changed circumstances provided Anne and Tania with new confidence and both told me that they were a "better person" now. But this was, as Anne described, an "interesting conundrum", for while Anne liked the fact she was "stronger" she described how she would rather be "back there", when her husband was alive.

Tania's changed identity was a process of striving to be "me again"; for Anne it was a process of learning to be a new person without her husband. She explained a scene from one of the *Harry Potter* films, to describe the feeling, where Harry Potter's godfather died and fell through a curtain, but it was a one-way door and Harry could not go through. For Anne this was illustrative of how her husband had gone in one direction and Anne had gone in another, which had sent her on a new journey. She described this movement into a new life as jumping from one set of train tracks to another:

> I think of train tracks where his track went that way, my track went that way. I fought so hard physically to bring time back and to follow that track … and it just diverges and diverges … So, it's just a different journey in my view … And I felt almost like I was the one who died because I have started a new life. It's like being jumped off one set of train tracks and on to another set of train tracks that are heading off in a different direction.

Despite her efforts to follow her husband's train journey they were headed on two different journeys for better or worse. Anne had entered a new "blitzed landscape" that was a far distance from the "simple person" and "normal" life she used to share with her husband. Anne found she no longer recognised herself or the world in which she had arrived. In this way, the journey Anne described captured a 'rite of passage,' where Anne moved through liminality to a new identity.

As these accounts demonstrate, becoming 'recovered' required considerable internal psychic work as well as practical forms of work discussed in Chapter 4. Being recovered also required continual maintenance work on the behalf of the bereaved. The Grief Recovery Method's (GRM) notion of 'completion' promised recovery yet it became evident that completion was only a temporary measure. Completion did not signal an end, rather it was a fantasy that forced all those who desired it to constantly carry out the task of 'getting complete' by writing completion letters. If completion was invariably temporary, it was difficult to see the difference between completion and being incomplete. Senior member of Grief Recovery UK, Ellen, told me that "you can be as complete as possible." Yet the concept appeared self-defeating in that it demonstrated how people themselves appeared to be unable to remain as whole, integrated beings, but rather tended to experience losses, and formed relationships that meant disregarding 'completeness.' The promise of recovery is a powerful one as it implies that no matter what might threaten the stability of the self, one can prevail. The interest in resilience promotes a similar narrative of hope, that people can 'bounce back' from adversity, and furthermore that resilience is a natural human capacity. A recovered identity was a concrete reality witnessed in the performance of being a good citizen or by a CORE-10 form ticked off in a counselling room that demonstrated progress. However, being recovered also remained a fantasy fostered by a 'cruel optimism' (Berlant 2011) that a resolution could be attained, forcing people into a continual search for completion.

Relational Identities

> Somebody's going to suffer grief in a relationship at the end of the day because you're not going to go together. And when that happens it's the most, well ooh can't describe it. I can't describe it; it just tears you apart inside. (Paul)

For the bereavement counsellors, bereaved people were given an identity as normal or abnormal, recovered or unrecovered. By contrast, the interviews with bereaved people highlighted the presence of the dead person and how identity was structured relationally. In the bereaved participants' narration of grief, it was apparent how much of their sense of self was, and continued to be, structured by the presence and absence of the now deceased person. In Butler's (2004) interpretation of Freud's theory of mourning, grief is an experience that reveals the fundamentally relational nature of humans. The ways in which people 'come undone' by loss exposes the means by which a person's sense of identity is dependent on others. This precarious nature of the self proposes an explanation of subjectivity that is not an autonomous bounded subject but formed in relation with others, and subsequently faces the threat of destruction in the loss of those others.

Thus, the narration of identity was not solely an individual activity but involved the 'impressions' (Ahmed 2004) of the person who had died. For all participants their relationship with the deceased person was both close and long-term. Following bereavement, participants narrated the difficulty in facing up to the realities of entering relationality and the risks involved in the possibility of losing the other. It was a risk that, as Paul acknowledged above, while known, was one which people were unable to face up to until it actually happened. For Derrida (2001), all relationships bring with them a sense of mourning in that the formation of a bond rests upon the inevitability of separation. The precarity of ties can feel ameliorated by the consistent presence of the other person but in bereavement, the loneliness, loss and ambivalence come to the fore. The feeling of loneliness was particularly marked for John and Paul who had spent the majority of their adult lives married and living with one partner and now found themselves alone. As Paul described:

> The only way I can describe it is literally part, half of my life has disappeared. The light has gone out of my life and it's a sod to deal with it.

Paul narrated at length the life he had with his wife emphasising how close they were, never spending a night apart for forty years. For Laura, being in a couple had provided the confidence to be herself, a self-confidence which had been lost along with her husband. She found she was reluctant to attend social activities without her husband who was six feet tall and "built like the side of a barn." The description of his physical presence illustrates how her husband provided "grounding" for Laura:

> It makes it quite hard to be social, which has got worse since my husband died, much, much worse. Because I have no grounding. He grounded me and would say "Oh don't be silly" and there's no-one to do that now … So I think becoming a widow highlights your inadequacies … You're not quite so sure of yourself as you are when you're in a couple.

Being in a couple provided a protective cushion almost from the outside world to which Laura felt exposed without her husband. After the death of her mother, Saadhia described how the sense of safety and "belonging" had gone, narrating a story of an intimate relationship with her mother. Saadhia struggled after her mother's death, finding herself unable to maintain a job. When she was evicted from her flat she described feeling that "there was no-one holding my hand." After finding herself homeless and seeking help from a local shelter, Saadhia looked to her mother for inspiration to enable her to remain "strong":

> Mum, she's still there, but she would want me to sort things out and get on with it rather than sit in a corner crying for her.

The presence of her mother persisted in the new life Saadhia was forming, which involved finding a place to live and attending counselling sessions. However, the consequences of no longer being a 'unit' were not necessarily easily resolved. For instance, Saadhia and Paul described how they would still hear the voice of their deceased mother and partner. Paul illustrated this to me by mimicking his wife's voice and the distinctive way she said his name. For Rose, her husband's presence featured in her life in a more encompassing way. Rose regularly spoke with her husband and felt his presence at certain times and places:

> As I say, I'm not really psychic but sometimes Simon really feels as if he is here, certainly driving he takes over. If I'm driving through (place name anonymised) or somewhere in that area that I don't know, I go oh Simon

> where am I and I'll just go purely on to autopilot and I'll start driving around and I'll find I'm at the main road, and I'll go thank you Simon! Love you! Bless you! I've told him I love him and bless him much more than, I don't think ever told him when he was alive. Yet we've more conversations, we've better conversations now he's gone than when he was here! (laughs) … I just talk to him as if he was here. You lose things, he's amazing. Brilliant at finding things. You lose a CD or a memory stick and you're looking everywhere for it and you can't find it and you go Simon please help us.

It seems, the virtual presence of Rose's husband was useful, preventing her from getting lost and helping to find lost objects. Because of this presence Rose explained that she hadn't really grieved. When I asked Rose why she thought she had not grieved she replied: "It's because he's with me." Recalling two incidents where she felt she had grieved over her husband's death, Rose described that she shortly received a sense of reassurance from her husband:

> I got this this, not exactly a hug, but a feeling of it's alright thank you very much, we've got work to do. So, I wiped my eyes and got on.

The partnership Rose had with her husband had continued 26 years after his death, and I asked Rose whether she had a desire for another partner, she responded:

> No! No as I say, he's company enough quite honestly if I want to talk to anyone I can sit there and I know his reactions to conversations so much so I know exactly how he would answer things. So sometimes I would come home upset and I would go Simon what do I do now and I feel him just say right okay, we'd sit down let's go through what is the problem and I would hear his thoughts.

Rose remarked that she felt a closer bond with her husband now in his death than when he was alive. She narrated the story of how they met and how they "were always destined to be together" and "absolutely in sync all along." Rose described also how she had begun to take on the characteristics of her husband and how other people had commented she sounded, "just like what Simon would have said." The continuing intercorporeality of Rose's relationship with her husband illustrates Ribbens McCarthy and Prokhovnik's (2013) argument that the personhood of the deceased person continues to exist through the body of the remaining partner.

However, the way Rose narrated her relationship was full of complexities. So, while she said it felt as if "we're still together" she also described the peace she had not being with anyone and being her "own person." Her husband and the conversations they had certainly seemed to bring her comfort and reassurance and meant she appeared to have not experienced some of the pain of grief expressed by other participants. Her seemingly "melancholic" attachment to her husband was counteracted by how she acknowledged her role had changed since her husband's death. In the absence of her husband she was no longer "just the washer up-er," but the head of the family. She described the funeral as her first social activity without her husband, wearing red clothes and "larking about with his mates from work." Rose's grief was cushioned by the on-going presence of her husband and yet her life was also one in which she experienced more freedom in his absence.

The ongoing presence, or the ongoing 'absent-presence' (Maddrell 2013) of the deceased person, could prove overwhelming, as it was for Saadhia before she began to incorporate her mother's memory to build a new life. For Rose however the presence of her husband was a helpful companion. Yet this post-death identity of her husband appeared in contrast to how Rose had described her relationship with her husband when he was alive. Therefore, it was not only Rose's identity that had changed but also her husband's. For all the participants, as they narrated their experiences to me they would speak at length of the character of their partner or family member, constructing and re-constructing their identity. This was most marked in Rose's account where, after death, she was provided the opportunity to develop the relationship with her husband to what suited her; changing his identity so that she was no longer the "follower on." In this way there was no ambivalence about her relationship with her husband that made his continuing presence comfortable to live with.

After death, the relational identity one inhabited in a partnership might continue, but that partnership also continued to change and develop. I suggest, the way in which the relationship developed was due to the level of control the participants' felt they had over the deceased person's presence. Maintaining control meant the presence of the deceased person could be incorporated into the self rather than becoming overwhelmed by memories or hearing voices. Finding this sense of control meant that the relationship could be shaped to one's choosing. In other words, it was a way of overcoming the ambivalence that existed in the relationship when the other person was alive.

While attachments can be viewed as adaptive from an evolutionary perspective, grief is the 'maladaptive' response to separation of those attachments (Archer 1999; Bowlby 1980; Parkes 1972). Parkes (2006) described bereavement as the 'price of love' that 'starts a search that is doomed to fail.' This contradiction of human relations is often bypassed in models of grief that encourage detachment from the deceased person, an idea attributed to Freud, even if Freud himself seemed uncertain of its validity. The struggle to understand why people make attachments only to mourn them lay at the heart of Freud's theory of mourning and melancholia. Successors of Freud offered psychodynamic explanations of the choices and investment that people make in significant others, but it appeared that this complexity of human relations was also absent in theories that promote 'continuing bonds.' Rather than overcoming the self/other divide, the continuing bonds theory relies on it, where continuing bonds involves an individual making choices about how they want to incorporate the dead person into their life. Similarly, within Ribbens McCarthy and Prokhovnik's (2013) argument for an embodied view of continued bonds, an 'enfleshed' or separate presence of the dead is largely unproblematic, yet the presence of what is bodily absent can often be contentious. This material presence persists as 'us' but also may persist with the deceased as a separate other with intentional agency. The continuing bond is one-sided, making it not the continuation of a relationship but the formation of a new attachment to an idealised version of the deceased person. For Rose, who continued the relationship with her husband by regularly speaking to him, the relationship was much improved by his death. Her husband's new post-death identity produced a more suitable and compliant partner. The fact that Rose had some control over her life allowed for an equality in their relationship that was absent when he was alive.

The ambivalence that emerges in grief, I argue, also reveals how people are in relation with others in ways that they cannot always control. For Freud all relationships, as Carel (2007) points out, are fraught with ambivalence. Identifying with another always places the self at risk of losing control. Ambivalence imbued the continued relationships, as participants wrestled with gains in the midst of a great loss. In Chapter 4, I described how the bereaved participants interacted with their home space and objects that became the stage upon which the desire to both 'hold on' and 'let go' was played out. Acknowledging the ambivalent nature of relationships revealed more than describing such behaviour as 'stuckness,' which glosses over the movement and negotiation involved in managing such ambivalence. However, I also argue that ambivalent feelings of wanting to hold onto and let go of objects or a person also presented a double-bind for the bereaved participants as what they desired was also the obstacle to a new identity.

Carel (2007) argues that the melancholic views the true reality of the process of attachment, comprehending the devastation of not only the person but their sense of self invested in the lost object. The melancholic is thus not delusional but sees the true extent of what has been lost, while the successful mourner carries out the work only to repeat the same process again, risking once more loss and devastation. Klein's (1940) theory proposed an alternative by showing how by restoring one's lost 'good objects' one can resolve ambivalence by incorporating the positive and reducing bad feelings.

The presence of ambivalence revealed the key issues of power and control in bereaved participants' ongoing relationships with the deceased. Foucault (1984) defined power as being formed relationally, even romantic relationships, he claimed, were not free of a need to enact power over each other. In other words, people are always non-sovereign in relation to one another, non-sovereignty describing a condition of never being fully in control of oneself or of others (Berlant and Edelman 2014). Identities formed in relation are always reliant on the other, the construction of identity dependent on how one is addressed and how one inhabits and responds to that address (Butler 1997). Grief and the experience of loss, perhaps like few other experiences, reveals the hold people have over each other. When viewed from a relational perspective, grief is, as Berlant (2008) has described, an experience of 'irreducible boundedness': a sharp separation from the other whom one had imagined to be a part of one's self. This gap between self and other can be experienced as loneliness, as it commonly was among the participants. Thus, the act of attaching to a new person must always remain optimistic to overcome the inevitable risk of loss that is posed when entering into relationality. However, the optimism required for the construction of this relational identity could also become 'cruel' (Berlant 2011) and an act of resistance, as I describe next.

Resistant Identities

Here I reflect on what I describe as 'resistant' forms of identity. I use resistance to refer to those forms of identity that are framed as examples of people failing to recover. For the bereaved participants the resistant identity emerged as an image of something to keep away from. As Tania describes, it was witnessing "career widows" that gave her the incentive to get "fixed" by seeing the life and identity she wanted to avoid:

> I do remember going to the WAY (Widowed and Young) Foundation, they had a coffee morning … and there were women - I can't, I don't know, they were just not like me. I just remember walking in going I wouldn't be friends with any of you in real life at all. I remember sitting down, they were all chit chattering away, I just sat there and burst into tears, this older lady came along and she said: "I'm ten years down the line and it does get better" and I remember looking at her thinking, "Oh my god." And I made my excuses and left and thought I don't want to be like this, I don't want to be sat around in widow's groups like this ten years down the line… I wouldn't go back there, I've never been anywhere else to do with WAY. But I remember that terrified me I just drove home in floods of tears going, "Oh my god this is it, I do not want to be like this woman ten years down the line."

It seems, rather than fostering a sense of membership, attending the WAY support group produced a strong sense of not belonging, allowing Tania to demarcate herself from the other women as being "not like me." Tania explained how she and her friends could "spot" the career widows as those women who seemed "quite stuck" and not wanting to "move on," using similar terms—'stuck' and 'move on'—as bereavement counsellors. For Tania too, recovery or its failure was an individual choice. The choice of words for describing this set of people—*career* widows—suggests the work that is also involved in remaining "stuck." Life's work becomes about widowhood, which for Tania was something to prevent.

The career widow was a negative identity in the double sense in that the career widow was formed by the inability to move on and perform grief successfully. Resistant identities, then, were those that performed grief almost too well, but it also included those who failed to perform grief at all. Rose described to me her husband's funeral where she said she was "larking about" with her husband's friends, only to be told by a member of the family "you could have at least cried!". Rose's 'failure' to perform the appropriate identity of the widow at the funeral permeated the rest of her narrative. In her one encounter with a counsellor Rose explained that the counsellor had tried to figure out why she "hadn't grieved." Rose's inappropriate display of emotion was construed as a failure to grieve and yet as detailed in the previous section, for Rose grieving was unnecessary for her husband was not lost but still with her. Reading resistance in the participants' accounts thus produced a more ambiguous picture of how resistance to grieving might be interpreted. Using the varying frameworks of recovery maintained by the bereavement counsellors, for example, meant the participants' accounts came into view as recovered and non-recovered depending on which framework was adhered to.

Largely, the bereavement counsellors and support workers interpreted failing to recover as a form of resistance to accepting the reality of the bereavement, or as a resistance to the method. Resistance could be identified by practitioners in a number of external displays of client behaviour but also through the avoidance of, or incorrectly performed, internal emotion work. Resisting recovery was explained more commonly through reference to "stuckness" or "getting stuck." Stuckness was easier to identify when framed by the assumption of time-limited grieving and the expectations that accompany the 'normal process' of grief. As bereavement counsellor Charlotte explained in response to my question: how do you know when someone is stuck?

> When its two and a half years later and they still cry at the mention of someone's, the person's name. When it's a year and a half later and they still have got all their clothes, when they can't say that the person is dead, when they still talk as if the person is alive.

Stuckness was signalled by a lack of movement or even a movement backwards. Stuckness was becoming "fixated," "immersed," and "overwhelmed" by negative and unhelpful thoughts. Stuckness showed itself in a variety of different behaviours, some of which as Cruse support worker Susan described were "easy to judge." These could include deterioration in general appearance and hygiene, disrupted eating and sleeping patterns, and substance abuse. Susan also used worksheets to help her identify when clients were not functioning at a reasonable level: deviant behaviours were marked by a shift from green to amber to "red alert." Other interpretations were less clear-cut but still common themes emerged in the practitioners' understanding of stuckness. For Susan some types of bereavement could "predispose" people to having complications in their grieving:

> There's certain types of death that pretty much, they predispose someone to the likelihood of it's not going to be easy. If it's a murder or an accident, road traffic accident something sudden, something traumatic.

Cruse's Early Intervention Project also highlighted pointers that could put people at risk of developing complicated grief, including being bereaved by a sudden death. Regardless of the type of bereavement, the interviews with bereavement counsellors, suggested that in general, unwillingness was the popular explanation of why people got stuck and failed to progress in their grief. In this unwillingness people actively "bury feelings" and fail to "open up." There is an inability to accept the death and they "don't seem to be willing" to go back to work or return to the "normal world" outside the "grief bubble." This 'hermit group of mourners' (Jordan and Neimeyer 2003) also remains resistant to the counselling method, a resistance that counsellors and support workers interpreted from the cancelling of or turning up late to sessions, or in how clients might save talking about "real" feelings to the end of a session. Some participants would speak of the unconscious nature of this resistance that drives particular behaviours such as forgetting to turn up for a session. According to bereavement counsellor Wendy, the client was unconsciously finding ways to keep away from the painful reality of loss. Wendy described how behaviours could be read to understand the unconscious:

> People who turn up for their appointments an hour early, even though they've been coming for a year at 11 they turn up at 10. Why do they do that? Because their unconscious was saying I really need to get there. Or people who forget their appointment even though they've been coming for a year at the same time, because their unconscious is saying we're not doing that this week. Quite often you have to look at behaviour and that gives some idea of what's going on unconsciously.

In other interpretations stuckness and resistance were simply being "unprepared to change." In the GRM this was due to a rigid belief system and old ideas that encouraged people to "push down" their grief. For Ellen stuckness could only be understood as the inability to "carry out the steps" for, as she declared, the GRM "can help almost anybody." In this thinking, the failure to recover will always be due to a lack of adherence to the method, and thus a failure of individual choice, as stated clearly by GRM Senior Member Ellen:

> Because I haven't seen the method fail. I have seen people fail the method.

While it was not so black and white for the other participants the reality of people getting stuck in grief was certainly acknowledged. This was partly attributed by some of the practitioners to the fact that a certain level of stuckness was what made a client eligible for counselling initially. For the most part stuckness was something that could be moved out of provided the client made the right choice and showed willingness for the method. However, there were admissions that some people could only be "taken so far" or, as mentioned above, some people were considered "predisposed" to complications. According to Ellen, people could be separated into three categories of response:

> Some people will never recover. Some people will bury it deep and act recovered. And it only needs the next knock and it can smash it all to pieces. And some people fully recover, and I would say I'm about as recovered as it's possible to get.

Arguably in the GRM everyone was stuck if they hadn't encountered or succeeded with the method. This point of view is a several-layered judgment that crucially presumes recovery, and its failure, are assessable by the monitoring of behaviours. For recovery can also be an 'act' or 'performance' put on when grieving feelings had not been adequately worked through. Resistance to the method and resistance to personal change, read from the point of view of the expert becomes the same thing when the method proposed is considered as the only reasonable means to gaining self-fulfilment. Resistance then is not only a disagreement with counselling or the Grief Recovery Handbook, but a resistance to all the things that recovery, completion, and integration encompass. Failing to recover in these terms is thus a rejection of flourishing, choice, and congruence in self-concept, and of hope, the future and its potential.

The government policy *No Health Without Mental Health* clearly stated that recovery was possible for the 'vast majority' of people. This view of recovery is evident in materials on mental health recovery, for example from the South London and Maudsley's (SLAM) Recovery college prospectus:

> Treatment and support from mental health professionals can be helpful but every person with mental health problems can become an expert in their own self-management. Whatever challenges you face, recovery

> involves finding the personal resourcefulness and resilience to take back control over your life and what happens to you. (South London and Maudsley NHS Foundation Trust 2015, 19)

In this understanding, recovery is possible, no matter how serious the person's difficulties; service users just need to find their personal "resourcefulness and resilience." Yet when recovery is always possible, and resilience is a natural trait that all possess if only enhanced, failing to recover becomes the (moral) fault of the individual. It is for this reason among others that the recovery model has received criticism from service users and others working within mental health care. Recovery is seen as a way of abdicating responsibility for mental distress elsewhere; that is to the person experiencing the distress themselves. For an increasing number of people, including the service users I interviewed, recovery is a shiny gloss on an unchanged and still coercive system, enabling cut backs on services, and eradicating long-term care through referring people to recovery colleges as a way to discharge them sooner (Braslow 2013; Harper and Speed 2012; Rose 2014).

The mental health recovery model has been critiqued further for relying on the standard 'deficit model' of illness it was originally designed to oppose (Harper and Speed 2012). As one of the interview participants Eva described, recovery had become a "stick" used to measure metal health service users against. Eva described a culture within one of the recovery colleges where recovery was something one had to achieve and then maintain. By establishing markers of recovery such as the 'recovery star,' it became possible for the relevant medical authority to make a judgement on whether or not someone was recovered. People then become responsible for adhering to prescribed ways of governing their lives, but the medical authority still remains intact—as psychiatrists become recovery experts and mental health care becomes 'recovery-orientated' and 'recovery-focused.' A contradiction then arises as recovery is described as a unique individual journey to self-control and autonomy over one's life, yet it is taught and learnt via a set of experts and in adherence to a set of predefined criteria. As the SLAM recovery college prospectus further demonstrates:

> The workshops and courses we run aim to provide the tools (…) to help you become an expert in your own recovery. (South London and Maudsley NHS Foundation Trust 2015, 6)

The outcomes of the recovery model have been criticised also for promoting normative values. Travis (2009), in her account of the rise of the recovery movement in the US, described the goal of recovery politics as inherently 'square.' But recovery politics is not only 'square' it has come to coincide with and reaffirm a neoliberal government agenda of autonomy and individual responsibility that has its interests in retaining the status quo (Braslow 2013). Indeed, a group called 'Recovery in the Bin,' set up initially as a Facebook group to express their disapproval at the 'neoliberal intrusion' on the word recovery, has now developed into a politically active and engaged community. The members of this group contend that 'recovery' has been colonised and used to discipline and control people with mental distress and they argue for a 'Social Model of Madness,' placing mental health within the context of the wider class struggle. Some members have claimed the title of 'UnRecovered' to replace 'Recovered,' as a valid alternative and in rejection of the neoliberal and market values now infused in the notion of recovery. This refusal of recovery is also a refusal to 'tell our stories.' Once the central act of liberation from oppression, telling one's recovery story is now viewed as an obligatory gesture to justify and validate one's experience; a form of 'disempowerment, under the guise of empowerment.' This shift from 'Survivors Speak Out' to 'patient porn' (Costa et al. 2012) acknowledges the performative promise of recovery, where service users feel the ideology of recovery is merely 'lip service.'

To recover from mental illness, to adhere to the model of recovery, involves a considerable amount of work on behalf of the service user. Recovery involves a range of activities such as attending recovery colleges, completing recovery plans, taking medication, getting a job, sustaining good relationships with others, eating well, not smoking, creating a new identity, being mindful and taking walks in nature. People using mental health services are increasingly finding themselves obligated to undertake this sort of 'recovery-work' in the promise of becoming well. A report entitled *Making Recovery a Reality* published in 2008 by the Sainsbury Centre for Mental Health describes how recovery can only be resolved if the person can gain hope. 'Without hope,' the report declared, 'they cannot begin to build their lives' (Shepard et al. 2008). Recovery, like happiness, appears as a 'mirage,' leading towards something that is not really there (Whitwell 1999). The promise of recovery possesses a cruel contradiction in that the highly prized ability to become autonomous and have self-control to manage one's life is only possible through submitting to experts who help people navigate their way through to recovery. The service user is taught how and what to desire, all in the name of self-fulfillment and individual freedom. And because recovery is always possible it can only be the individual's failure of will or resilience if they are seen to relapse or fail to recover in the terms that have been proposed.

Recovering the Identity of the Complicated Griever

In the course of conducting the research, meeting and speaking with different people and analysing a range of documents, I gathered insight into the identity of the complicated, 'unrecovered' person. Across the accounts of bereavement counsellors and support workers, differences emerged in how they identified the complicated griever. The responses comprised a number of identities: the one who failed to perform grief appropriately, the 'career widow' who became consumed with grief, and the person resistant to counselling methods who found themselves 'stuck' in grief. Overall, however, practitioners agreed that clients had to be willing and able to 'do the work.' The failure to do that work was what would contribute to a failure to recover. In this way, recovery and non-recovery were in the individual's hands, yet counsellors had the capacity to see resistance in their clients, a resistance that would be belied by how the clients might present themselves. For Freud (1914), the role of the 'physician' was not merely to reveal the 'patient's' resistance to them, as if the patient's suffering results from a kind of 'ignorance':

> … and that if only this ignorance could be overcome by effective communication … a recovery must follow … But the illness is not located in this ignorance itself, but in the foundation of ignorance, the inner resistances that are the cause of ignorance and continue to sustain it. (Freud 1914, 7)

Revelation will not resolve resistance for one may not know what made one ignorant in the first place, hence why it is sustained. Freud argued recovery was attained only through the patient's own discovery; the physician cannot just 'show' resistance to patient, which may only intensify the resistance. This was reflected in my findings where counsellors and support workers would opine that what the client first presented was often not the 'real' issue. Some counsellors spoke further of how clients remained unconscious of what was keeping them stuck, where the counselling setting was an opportunity to bring those unconscious feelings to light.

The role of the analyst for Freud was to judge what had been 'negated' and 'repressed' which he considered the thing that was producing resistance. The aim of the analyst is to acknowledge this resistance and encourage confession and awareness. However, Freud was clear that accepting the solution of the analyst had to be carried out on the patient's own terms. Furthermore, resolving the 'inner resistances' was not a straightforward activity. What was producing a client's resistance may not be a singular thing; this foundation of ignorance may be fostered by multiple factors. By contrast, in the GRM, resistance was understood only as resistance to the method. As I have argued, it follows that when a method is seen as being impossible to fail, only people can fail the method. Resistance in the GRM was identified in those who analysed too much and were unable to move from the head to the heart, or anyone who queried the method. At the workshop, some group members questioned the relevance of certain activities, but we were encouraged to "stop analysing" and to do the activities unquestioningly, and as such were provided with little evidence of their purpose.

Resistance was not then necessarily active, more a by-product of a discourse that left little room for critique. Incorporating Foucault's ideas on resistance, resistance was the corresponding discourse to power. People get read as resistant when they fail to be managed, when they fail to embody the subject that lies at the heart of the dominant theory, for example being 'self-integrated' or 'complete.' Resisting the method meant resisting completion, recovery and inner happiness. The shadow of 'non-recovery' at times perpetuated the search for recovery, as presented by the "career widow" who spurred Tania on to "not be like that." The unrecovered identity was a negative identity made apparent only by distinguishing behaviours by their distance from the norm.

Thus, the only way to read resistance was to explore what participants did not say and also acknowledge the limits of my listening. In this process I discovered that though I had set out to uncover the experiences of non-recovery, it was not an experience that could be discoverable via talk and the interview setting. For example, Saadhia narrated her experiences following the death of her mother in which she appeared to enter a downward spiral:

> My moods were going down and I was either eating so much to comfort myself or I was just like, "No I'm not doing it." I stopped, I stopped listening to music, the things I enjoyed I stopped doing all those … Emotionally inside I wasn't feeling good and I was feeling that I was going to go down and down … and I keep hearing my Mum calling me and I think it's real, when I wake up from this sort of sleep I'm like, "Oh my god" and she's not there and I can't look at her picture, I just can't do it. Because I'm just, then I'm just drowning in tears all the time … I got to a stage where I was drinking, I was smoking, and I just wanted to die basically.

Saadhia's was a story of self-destruction but it was also a story that ended in recovery. At the interview she told me that now she could speak about her mother at length whereas before she would be unable to speak without bursting into tears. I realised that the ability to narrate suffering was a privileged one in that being able to speak to me and respond to questions was only possible from a place of relative recovery.

Looking for people who failed to recover was a key aim of this research, but it became a paradoxical task. During the field work, the subject of 'complicated grief' and the people who might inhabit such a category felt like chasing 'moving targets' (Hacking 2006). When I attended the Cruse Early Intervention Project, which was designed to target those at risk of developing 'prolonged grief disorder,' I was told that 'everyone' in bereavement care knew that complicated grief existed and that only now was it receiving the recognition it deserved. However, I found that this embrace of the diagnosis was not reflected by the personal experience of complicated grief. The need to identify complicated grief was not it seemed a grassroots movement for recognition, indeed whoever was being diagnosed with complicated grief or prolonged grief disorder seemed particularly hard to find. In my interviews with practitioners I asked how someone with complicated grief might be identified. In the responses I received it was hard to pin down any specific characteristics, or the characteristics were too wide-ranging: from poor personal hygiene to unresolved childhood attachment issues. The complicated griever could be just about anyone it seemed.

This problem was illustrated when I met Jamie. I got into contact with Jamie through the cold weather shelter at the bereavement counselling service Caris which had carried out their own research into the links between bereavement and homelessness and were keen for me to engage with the area. Jamie had cancelled scheduled meetings on more than one occasion and it seemed the interview might not take place. He appeared to be a hard person to pin down with a hectic and disorganised life. In our interview he did not wish to be recorded. The notes I made following the interview were scattered and that is how I recall the interview. Jamie was unsure what to say, he told me he'd never spoken to anyone before about his experiences. He described incidents where he felt dismissed by other people and so decided not to speak to people about his feelings of grief. He told me about how his sister died suddenly when he was 16 and then years later his mother died of cancer. He told me how he had periods of depression, alcohol addiction, being made redundant and homeless. It was a story with little resolution where he had lost the two people he loved the most and now experienced a "missing link" in his life.

I found that listening to a story without resolution was difficult and uncomfortable to bear. On reflection, I felt a sense of responsibility to resolve his story and considering the mobile text messages I received from Jamie following the interview it appeared he was looking to me too to help resolve his story. Yet the resistance to recovery is as much a construction as the notion of recovery itself. I recognised I was reading Jamie's story as a resistance and a failure to recover because I was working within a particular construction of recovery. I soon realised that I was searching for a subject that did not exist, and that in my searching I too was becoming complicit with the construction of 'complicated grief.' I could only find the complicated grieving participant if I described them as such rather than the person identifying with the description. In other words, I was 'making up' (Hacking 1986) the complicated griever. I was using the classification to find the person who inhabited the classification but could not find the person who fitted within it.

Complicated grief, like other forms and varieties of grief—anticipatory grief, disenfranchised grief, protracted grief—is a category that relies upon a notion of 'normal' grief. Yet when that normal is destabilised and revealed to be non-existent, to declare that complicated grief exists becomes untenable. In the same way I have argued 'normal grief' is a construction of bereavement research and practice, so too 'complicated grief' is a social construction, one historically specific to contemporary society. If the categories of complicated grief and prolonged grief disorder are not serving a population in need, their purpose is to medicalise some forms of grief while normalising others. The act of diagnosing complicated grief serves to distinguish between two sets of symptoms, ones that are 'complicated' and ones that are 'normal.'

Furthermore, the category of complicated grief and the choice to diagnose it relies on a belief that people who are stuck will remain stuck, at least without external intervention. The choice of term—'stuck'—was particularly telling when considered within the linear process of grief. Getting stuck was getting in the way, taking too long and preventing the normal course. Yet, diagnosing people with complicated grief, in effect labelling people as stuck, was a means to lift people out of stuckness, something it was assumed bereaved people could not do for themselves. The diagnosis of complicated grief delineated a clear problem to be solved, which conceivably, allowed grief to become manageable in the psychotherapeutic setting. After all, as acknowledged by the bereavement practitioners, bereavement when compared with mental illness has no resolution, for the deceased person cannot be returned and the bereaved person also does not return to the life and self they knew before. The purpose of the diagnosis of complicated grief was thus twofold: to reiterate grief as a normal emotion (with a linear course), and to diagnose, in order to treat those that were stuck back to normal in line with the process practitioners described as 'normalisation.'

As the bereavement practitioners explained, 'normalising' grief was the key purpose of the counselling process. Making grief normal produced safety and provided the client the coherence to articulate feelings. Bereavement may cause one to confront one's own ambivalence and incoherence, producing the 'discrepancy' (Goffman 1963) in performance. Bereaved people may fail to recover by external estimations, but they may also fail in their own ethical standing, causing them to act in 'bad faith' (Sartre 1958). Performing grief according to the dominant discourses can thus provide comfort or at least the ability to remain out of view of the authorities that seek to manage 'abnormal' grief. The failed performances of grief described in this book then are less reflective of inner characteristics of the individual psyche but rather a product of the bounded categories that demarcate behaviours in normal or pathological forms. Depending on one's perspective, bereaved people became normal or abnormal as they move and negotiate the lines of power and discourse across the liminal space of grief. Complicated grief was not a thing to be found nor, as practitioners and researchers have claimed, a pathology that has always existed waiting to be defined. Rather the boundary between normality and abnormality—or recovery and non-recovery—was porous and thin. Normality, it emerged, is a performance that is always 'incomplete.'

References

Ahmed, Sara. 2004. *The Cultural Politics of Emotion*. Edinburgh: Edinburgh University Press.

Archer, John. 1999. *The Nature of Grief: The Evolution and Psychology of Reactions to Loss*. New York: Routledge.

Berlant, Lauren. 2008. "Thinking About Feeling Historical." *Emotion, Space and Society* 1 (1): 4–9.
———. 2011. *Cruel Optimism*. London: Durham and Duke University Press.
Berlant, Lauren, and Lee Edelman. 2014. *Sex, or the Unbearable*. London: Durham and Duke University Press.
Bloch, Maurice. 2011. "The Blob." *Anthropology of This Century*, May 1.
Bowlby, John. 1980. *Attachment and Loss Volume III: Loss, Sadness and Depression*. London: Hogarth Press.
Braslow, Joel Tupper. 2013. "The Manufacture of Recovery." *Annual Review of Clinical Psychology* 9: 781–809.
Butler, Judith. 1997. *Excitable Speech: A Politics of the Performative*. New York: Routledge.
———. 2004. *Precarious Life: The Powers of Mourning and Violence*. London: Verso.
Carel, Havi. 2007. "Death and the Other: The Ambivalence of Mourning." In *Dying and Death: Inter-Disciplinary Perspectives*, edited by A. Kasher, 81–90. Amsterdam: Rodopi.
Costa, Lucy, Jijian Voronka, Danielle Landry, Jenna Reid, Becky Mcfarlane, David Reville, and Kathryn Church. 2012. "Recovering Our Stories: A Small Act of Resistance." *Studies in Social Justice* 6 (1): 85–101.
Deleuze, Gilles. 1990. *Negotiations 1972–1990*. New York: Columbia University Press.
Department of Health. 2001. "The Journey to Recovery—The Government's Vision for Mental Health Care." London: Department of Health.
Derrida, Jacques. 2001. *The Work of Mourning*. Translated by Pascale-Anne Brault and Michael Naas. London: University of Chicago Press.
Foucault, Michel. 1984. "The Ethics of the Concern for Self as a Practice of Freedom." In *Ethics: Subjectivity and Truth*, edited by Paul Rabinow, 281–302. London: Penguin.
———. 1988. "Technologies of the Self." In *Technologies of the Self*, edited by Luther H. Martin, H. Gutman, and Patrick H. Hutton, 16–49. Amherst: University of Massachussets Press.
Freud, Sigmund. 1914. "Remembering, Repeating and Working Through." In *The Penguin Freud Reader*, edited by Adam Philips, 391–401. London: Penguin.
———. 1917. "Mourning and Melancholia." In *The Penguin Freud Reader*, edited by Adam Philips, 310–326. London: Penguin.
Giddens, Anthony. 1991. *Modernity and Self-Identity: Self and Society in the Late Modern Age*. Cambridge: Polity Press.

Goffman, Erving. 1963. *Stigma*. London: Penguin.
Hacking, Ian. 1986. "Making Up People." In *The Science Studies Reader*, edited by Mario Bagioli, 161–171. London: Routledge.
———. 2006. "Kinds of People: Moving Targets." In *Proceedings of the British Academy, Volume 151*, edited by P. J. Marshall.
Harper, David, and Ewen Speed. 2012. "Uncovering Recovery: The Resistible Rise of Recovery and Resilience." *Studies in Social Justice* 6 (1): 9–25.
Jordan, John R., and Robert A. Neimeyer. 2003. "Does Grief Counseling Work?" *Death Studies* 27 (9): 765–786.
Klein, Melanie. 1940. "Mourning and Its Relation to Manic-Depressive States." In *Love, Guilt and Reparation and Other Works 1921–1945: The Writings of Melanie Klein Volume I*, 344–369. London: Hogarth Press.
Maddrell, Avril. 2013. "Living with the Deceased: Absence, Presence and Absence–Presence." *Cultural Geographies* 20 (4): 501–522.
Parkes, Colin Murray. 1972. *Bereavement: Studies of Grief in Adult Life*. Harmondsworth: Penguin.
———. 2006. *Love and Loss: The Roots of Grief and Its Complications*. Hove: East.
Ribbens McCarthy, Jane, and Raia Prokhovnik. 2013. "Embodied Relationality and Caring After Death." *Body & Society* 20 (2): 18–43.
Rose, Diana. 2014. "The Mainstreaming of Recovery." *Journal of Mental Health* 23 (5): 217–218.
Sartre, Jean-Paul. 1958. *Being and Nothingness: An Essay on Phenomenlogical Ontology*. London: Methuen.
Shepard, Geoff, Jed Boardman, and Mike Slade. 2008. *Making Recovery a Reality*. London: Salisbury Centre for Mental Health.
South London and Maudsley NHS Foundation Trust. 2015. *SLaM Recovery College 2015/2016 Courses, SLaM Recovery College Prospectus*. South London and Maudsley NHS Foundation Trust.
Travis, Trysh. 2009. *Language of the Heart: A Cultural History of the Recovery Movement from Alcoholics Anonymous to Oprah Winfrey*. Chapel Hill, NC: The University of North Carolina Press.
Valentine, Christine. 2013. "Identity and Post-mortem Relationships in the Narratives of British and Japanese Mourners." *Sociological Review* 61 (2): 383–401.
Van Gennep, Arthur. 1960. *The Rites of Passage*. London: Routledge & Kegan Paul.
Whitwell, David. 1999. "The Myth of Recovery from Mental Illness." *Psychiatric Bulletin* 23: 621–622.

7
The Other Side of Recovery

In this book I have explored how recovery from grief is defined in theory, policy and practice. I have also discussed how those who experience bereavement negotiate the process of recovery. I used the concept of spatial liminality to explore the experience of grief: tracking bereaved people as they navigated their way through this virtual space. Within the liminal space of grief, I have focused on the boundaries between recovery and non-recovery and how different individuals, organisations and institutions established, maintained and negotiated these boundaries. To build my argument I drew on literature from multiple disciplines, namely: sociology, anthropology, cultural theory and philosophy. I argued for the benefits of interdisciplinary engagements in the study of grief, in particular the insights from the established field of the study of the emotions. However, my methodological approach has remained rooted in a sociological perspective, indebted to the work of Foucault, as I sought to 'problematise' and question taken-for-granted assumptions about grief. Ultimately my aim has been to explore the possibility of 'non-recovery' and what happens when people fail to recover (accordingly this chapter is entitled the 'other side of recovery'). From this enquiry emerged three themes: meaning—how people, whether expert

C. Pearce, *The Public and Private Management of Grief*,
https://doi.org/10.1007/978-3-030-17662-4_7

or lay, make sense of grief; practices—how grief and recovery are managed and performed; and identity—what type of identities people come to inhabit such as 'recovered' or 'complicated griever.'

Here I draw together the key conclusions. First, I summarise my argument for an alternative way of theorising grief; second, I attend to the concept of 'non-recovery' and explain why the failure to recover matters, and third I conclude my search for the 'complicated griever' by questioning the reality in this construction. In the closing sections I describe the theoretical and practical implications of this book and consider possibilities for further study.

Theorising Grief: An Alternative View

Problematising Grief as a Psychological Object of Study

Throughout this book I have highlighted the shortcomings in how grief is currently theorised by critiquing the overly psychologised view of grief and I have proposed an alternative way of theorising grief. I emphasised the need to look beyond the individual psyche to how grief is experienced, expressed and lived out in everyday life, acknowledging how grief is framed and influenced by political and economic concerns. As discussed in Chapter 2, the 'scientific' study of grief is a relatively modern development, and over the course of the twentieth century grief steadily became an object of psychological study. This shift is clearly demonstrated in the history of Cruse and presented in the work of Árnason (1998), where the support offered by Cruse, once dedicated to supporting widows with diverse matters such as pensions, financial budgeting and finding employment, is now almost solely concerned with the facilitation of bereavement counselling for adults and children. The rise of research into grief, institutions and organisations such as Cruse, along with academic journals and bereavement counsellor training, were formed that disseminated and implemented the findings of this research into practice.

In effect what was being created was a new discipline and profession, shaping bereavement care into what exists today. As part of this shift, grief became something that could be identified in people and measured, with its course defined as 'normal' or 'abnormal.' In other words, grief became something that could be known, upon which the growing field of professionals could make claims to the truth of grief. I have argued otherwise that the 'natural course' of grief is a socially constructed notion, which is revealed in the discrepancy between changing social norms around grieving behaviours and how people perform their grief. Later, a new wave of bereavement research critiqued the staged course of grief by taking into account the social and cultural elements of the experience of grief. However, these theories—such as 'continuing bonds'—retained the understanding of grief as a universal phenomenon. Despite the changes in how grief has been explained over time, sustaining a universal definition of grief assumes to know how all people feel. I have argued that the divide between 'natural' and 'social' aspects of grief is an impossible one. This is made apparent once grief is situated within the broader interdisciplinary study of the emotions, where the extent to which the emotions are shaped by biology or socially formed remains elusive.

I have demonstrated how the public space of grief continues to be redefined by the interests and policies of different groups, whether from psychiatry, the government or indeed the bereaved person his or herself. Over the course of the century it was not only grief that was subject to 'professionalisation' and in Chapter 3 I described the historical developments that shifted perceptions of mental distress and emotions, for instance the prevalence of shell shock in the First World War and the culture of trauma and recovery that followed. Within these shifts, the population's emotions and mental state came to be understood as something only experts could interpret and manage. Moreover, the rise of psychological self-help and counselling coincided with a professionalisation of the management of death and disposal of the dead body. Arguably, the change of responsibility in the management of death and dying resulted in people becoming deskilled in the management of their own grief. Yet at the same time, somewhat contradictory to this shift, the management of grief was increasingly framed as an individual responsibility. Rather than viewed as a consequence of this structural shift in the management of death and emotions from layperson to expert, struggling to make sense of grief was viewed as a failure, or resistance, on behalf of the individual who was 'unwilling' to make the right 'choice' to recover.

This structural shift thus became diagnosed in terms of individual will, where the individual became the cause of his or her problem. As such, victims who resisted recovery were blamed for their failure to do so. People entered into a new relationship with their emotions and accepted the role of the expert to guide and resolve their inner turmoil, and so the 'need' for bereavement counselling became self-fulfilling. Furthermore, within a political and social climate that emphasised happy emotions, with mental health defined as a 'burden,' the mental distress produced by grief became a problem from which people were *compelled* to recover. Recovery became an economic, political and social issue, and the rationale for expert intervention into the prevention and resolution of individual failures was validated.

Highlighting Relationality and Ambivalence

While the psychological perspective may certainly offer valid insight into the individual experience of grief, the dominance of the psychological perspective, I have sought to demonstrate, has transformed grief into a diagnosable entity, made measurable and classifiable by psychological tools and tests. As a result, knowledge about grief that lies outside the remit of psychological testing has remained out of view and invisible. One of the key elements of grief omitted in the psychological approach is the ability to capture the ambivalence of grief. Specifically, ambivalence creates a situation of suspended agency, which is why the concept of liminality captures well the ambiguous sense of self the participants described to me. Contrary to professional discourses, incorporating ambivalence can assist in overcoming the paradox within grief theories that promote a linear process to recovery. But more than this, the experience of grief as one of suspended agency destabilises the vision of the neo-liberal subject: the autonomous individual with the capacity to make rational choices. Therefore, I have argued that the emphasis on a linear course of grief, affirms the notion of personhood at the heart of models of recovery, such as those popularised within mental health care services.

Instead I have attempted to revive the Freudian claims that underpin much of the research that has promoted recovery from grief as a process of detachment from the deceased person. Rather I suggest that Freud's description of mourning and melancholia displays how grief reveals the relational nature of the self. Indeed, grief poses a paradox to the psychological understanding of grief as a process because the concept of personhood that underpins psychological study fails to allow for a subject who can remain attached to persons after their death. Relying on an autonomous, resilient subject has meant the grieving subject is an uneasy fit for psychological models of personhood, by presenting a subject that both requires attachment to others in order to flourish but is also devastated by their loss. This is, I suggest, an elaboration of the ways in which people attach to one another in living relationships. Drawing from psychoanalytic theory, the desire for another person is the desire for the idea or object that they present. After bereavement, the remaining person remains attached to the same idea or object. The ambivalence that can be felt in grief is a sign of the desire for the lost object. The continued bond is thus evidence of how the bereaved person learned to re-accommodate this lost object as an 'absent presence.' Freud's argument for detaching from the lost object was then, in a sense, the only way to truly recover oneself, if recovery means a return of the self before the attachment. However, this emphasis on detachment overlooks the ways in which people are reconfigured by their attachments and their relationships with others. It might be said then that there is no overcoming the ambivalence of grief, as there is no undoing the ways in which one has been reshaped by the person now absent.

My aim has been to make central the ambivalent relational subject, at times incoherent in his or her attachment to others. The presence of ambivalence marks this struggle of not knowing how to let go of the deceased person—or of holding on in the wrong way—a struggle recounted in the psychoanalytic writings of Freud and Klein. Consequently, I have also pointed out the shortcomings of the 'continuing bonds' theory of grief that attempted to highlight the ways in which relationships persist after death. I argue the continuing bonds theory promotes a one-sided relationship, which is not so much the continuation of a relationship, but the persistence of an idealised vision of the deceased person. The continuing presence of the deceased person's identity is a construction that the bereaved person creates and adapts to their everyday life, reinforcing the individualistic notion of the subject the theory set out to criticise. The continuing relationships bereaved participants had with their deceased partners and relatives continued to develop and change. Further, being able to adapt the deceased person's identity meant the living person could regain control over the relationship that was not possible when the person was alive. This was a way of overcoming the ambivalence that existed within the relationship before death.

My aim has been to demonstrate the importance of analysing grief as a socially constructed experience that is influenced as much by government policy as it is childhood attachment issues. To counteract the emphasis on psychological understandings of grief I expanded my analysis beyond the psychological canon of grief literature to examine developments in mental health policy and political and economic reforms, concurrently with developments in bereavement care practice and research. Only by expanding the types of perspective that come to bear on grief and its recovery can grief detach itself from the association with 'naturalness,' which ironically might allow for the 'reality' of grief to come into view. Incorporating a variety of perspectives has enabled a better understanding of the paradox of grief, so that the bereaved person is viewed in such a way that acknowledges the relational and social nature of subjectivity. It also demonstrates how grief—and death—is a continuing concern across the disciplines, and not only within psychology.

Why 'Non-recovery' Matters

In the introductory chapter, I described my interest in exploring the experiences of people who fail to recover. My aim was to analyse non-recovery as a possibility, to bring the concept of not recovering to the fore. In this endeavour I was supported by the archaeological and genealogical methodology of Foucault who sought to bring hidden histories into view. My aim was not to make a judgment on what non-recovery might involve and how the experience might feel, merely to bring the possibility under analysis. Furthermore, in arguing for the possibility of non-recovery my intention was not to advocate suffering. The question remains—why highlight the option of failing to recover: why does not recovering matter?

Recovery discourses privilege happy emotions and happy citizens, disregarding and labelling problematic the experience of the person I have endeavoured to revive in this book: the embodied, relationally formed person who experiences bereavement, suffering, and periods of unhappiness, and who may not perform autonomously but is often ambivalently tied to people dead and alive. When recovery promotes a vision of the subject that ignores how people exist in relation with one another, not recovering matters because it reveals the ways in which people are always already vulnerable and non-sovereign when faced with the other; how in a sense people are already incomplete and failing to recover when recovery means detachment, self-integration and autonomy.

To recover has become an obligation in a society where grief is understood within time limits and where 'prolonged' grief is defined as an economic 'burden' and a political issue. The complicated, prolonged griever is a problem for the normal routines of modern western living that prioritises neo-liberal values such as efficiency, productivity and autonomy. In this framework, non-recovery emerges as a negative, where not recovering is only ever a rejection of recovery, and consequently what recovery represents. The shape of non-recovery is formed out of the shadow of what recovery is not, representing the point of failure or resistance.

As explained in the Introduction, Kauffman's (2008) description of 'no recovery' stimulated my interest in analysing the concept of non-recovery. In his essay, Kauffman explored what it might mean if there was no recovery from grief, proposing a world in which no one recovers. No recovery was not a transitional state but a condition of human existence. I have suggested that non-recovery is not only a suspension in liminality but can become a way of living. While the Grief Recovery Method encouraged bereaved people toward the never-ending pursuit of completion, my interest in non-recovery has been to explore what happens when people remain 'incomplete' or get 'stuck' in grief. Getting stuck presents a problem to linear models of grief, and to the linear course of recovery. The practitioners described the "movement" clients would experience as they worked through their grief, and the problematic 'stuckness' clients experienced when they were "unwilling" to "move forward". Stuckness was thus framed as an unproductive place of "nothingness", yet I have suggested that stuckness be viewed not simply as a place out of which to move.

Grief could force someone to exit his or her sense of 'normality' or assumed world, but in turn I suggest the liminal space might become the new 'normal' space. For example, in Van Gennep (1960) and Turner's (1969) description of liminality, liminality is only a phase in the rite of passage that is followed by reintegration in society. The bereaved participants experienced everyday life cyclically rather than linearly, where plans and routines were carefully crafted on a day-by-day basis, yet the future was hard to manage and envision. The period of 'non-recovery' may have been only an impasse, but for many of the bereaved participants, grief brought with it a new sense of time and space in which they had learn how to live with ambiguity and uncertainty.

Non-recovery might signal the lack of ritual to guide people back towards recovery. But as I have sought to demonstrate it might also signal the reality that what comes to be considered as 'non-recovery' is in constant negotiation and liable to shift. Recovery and non-recovery are both temporary trajectories across the liminal space that can be renegotiated. Non-recovery is not just a negative space of nothingness, nor is it static, but a place of dynamic movement. As described in

Chapter 6, the 'recovered' and 'resistant' identities were equally transformations in identities, albeit headed in divergent directions. Recovery is a performance, or as Kauffman described a 'symbolic' gesture, that is achieved by successfully fulfilling the markers of normality. Yet these markers of normality continue to shift and change. Failing to play the game and performing grief the wrong way could incur a moral judgement from others, and the bereaved person could find him or herself discredited; on the other side of the boundary.

Non-recovery in contrast denotes the failure to measure up to the 'good life,' highlighting how recovery has become an obligation of the individual to live a certain way, producing a narrowing of perspective in the different ways people might live out their lives. Yet, the pursuit of normality or the good life requires constant work. In the search for recovery and 'completion' bereaved people were driven to write and rewrite 'completion letters,' carry out 'grief work,' and complete the 'tasks' and 'stages,' all in the name of their own freedom. Aware of the threat of becoming 'discredited' in their performance of grief, bereaved people maintain a nervous relation to normal, compelled only by the 'cruel' promise of recovery.

The 'Complicated Griever': Construct or Reality?

In this book I have explored the debates around 'complicated' and 'normal' grief that were taking place in grief and bereavement research and practice. The increasing psychiatric concern for 'complicated' and 'prolonged' types of grief marked a key shift in bereavement care and practice. What I found was that in bereavement practice 'complicated' grief remained a contested and negotiated term. Rather than a self-evident diagnosis, practitioner definitions of 'complicated grief' were at times conflicting, ambiguous and vague. The fact that understandings of grief and recovery were undergoing this constant process of negotiation, whether in the counselling room or the home of the bereaved person, revealed how grief and recovery were open to interpretation. For some participants what constituted grief and recovery was very clear to them, but for others less so. How different people within the liminal space of grief drew the boundaries between normal and abnormal grieving, successful and unsuccessful recovery thus became a central focus of the book.

However, this ambiguity became problematic methodologically as I sought to capture the account and experience of the 'complicated griever.' At the outset of the study I chose not to focus on one specific type of bereavement. As a result, the liminal space of grief was wide open with which to pose the question: what type of grief gets complicated? As detailed, speaking to practitioners surfaced conflicting definitions, or definitions that were subtle and vague. From the accounts of bereaved people, grief was something experienced and managed in an individual manner, where identities of 'recovered' were actively pursued, or else a settling into a new identity that rested neither in 'recovered' or 'unrecovered.'

I could only find the 'complicated griever' if I became complicit with the diagnostic categories of 'complicated' and 'prolonged' grief. Yet I struggled to adhere to the category of complicated grief if it was not an identity with which the bereaved person themselves identified. Furthermore, the methods I chose to employ—qualitative interviews—required participants who could articulate their experiences of bereavement and feelings of grief. The ability to construct a narrative around one's feelings of grief enabled a level of coherence in the interviewees' accounts, even if that narrative continued to change. For example, I recognised following the interview with Jamie, who refused to be recorded and who struggled with knowing what to say in the interview setting, that the complicated griever rested in these silences, and the inability to articulate their experience.

What initially felt like a failure to fulfil my research aims soon became a significant finding in its own right in that I realised that dividing lines between normal and abnormal while seemingly definite and clear in theory were conflicted and ambiguous in practice. But further, my own choice of method was inadequate in capturing the experience of complicated grief that out of necessity was constructed on the silence of the complicated griever. The psychiatric diagnostic categories of 'prolonged grief disorder (PGD)' and 'persistent complex bereavement disorder,' are identified by external symptoms and self-report measures that ask respondents to identify with pre-determined statements. Perhaps by employing these tools I could have identified among the participants those at 'risk' of developing, or experiencing, complicated grief. The diagnosis of complicated grief makes the problem of grief manageable and provides a clinical solution. But without these tools—and the willingness to use them—I alternatively sought to question the role of the boundary between 'normal' and 'complicated' grief and how the boundary frames grief into two contrasting experiences. Both what happens in policy and practice and how people make sense of grief in their own words, construct the boundary between normal and complicated grief, either by reaffirming or rejecting it. I chose not to reaffirm this boundary and the categorisation of grief into normal or abnormal forms. Instead I chose to destablise the truth claims supporting these notions of grief and of recovery to consider how people might come to inhabit grief differently, and move in and out of categories.

I have come to realise that whatever the 'reality' of the experience of the complicated griever, it occupies the silences behind the discourses around grief. However, in making the silenced person visible the researcher faces the problem, as I did, of actively constructing a silent consciousness that did not already exist. The articulation of previously hidden silence is, I suggest, changed in the act of narration, and further transformed in the researcher's interpretation and representation of those stories. In other words, the research process can make the abstract become concrete, but how and what stories are produced requires vigilance in order to avoid the loss of authenticity and the reinforcement of oppressive discourses. Ultimately as a researcher in this enquiry, I played an equal role in the construction of the complicated griever, by being forced to assume that complicated grief was a quantifiable and thus researchable phenomenon. What remains to be understood is what happens when people come to identify with the category of complicated griever and speak from a place of complicated grief. How people might inhabit the diagnosis will impact on how complicated grief continues to be defined and measured. Furthermore, once a person speaks as a 'complicated griever' their identity will be reconstructed in the telling of their account. This might cause the person to move across the boundary from 'normal' to 'complicated,' and back to 'normal.' But, I suggest, on what side of the boundary the person is located will not only be a judgment of the person who speaks.

The Future of Bereavement Research and Practice

The debates around the 'medicalisation' of grief persist as the ICD publishes its eleventh edition with the inclusion of PGD, suggesting the nature of bereavement care and practice will continue to evolve in the UK. Further research is required to track these changes as they take place on a political and policy level, examining how bereavement care becomes situated in ongoing changes to mental health care. As PGD becomes a recognisable diagnosis it will be crucial to explore whether and how people come to receive a diagnosis of PGD, investigating the points of contestation that may arise in the act of diagnosis. It is not clear how people will respond to such a diagnosis, and whether people might come to embrace the label as a legitimate form of identification. Will a diagnosis of PGD enable people to make sense of difficult grieving experiences? Will people turn more towards medical understandings of grief rather than literature, poems and stories? Certainly, contemporary researchers are actively pursuing the biological underpinnings of grief, undertaking neuroscientific studies to understand grief in terms of brain chemicals (O'Connor 2005, 2012). The excitement around exploring neuroscience to help explain mental disorders (Rose 2013; Fitzgerald and Callard 2014) suggests that the focus on the brain to supply the answers for grief will only increase. The study of grief thus continues to be redefined, albeit from a scientific or professional point of view. Examining the views and experiences of the bereaved person will be crucial to understanding the implications of these developments, particularly those considered to be experiencing 'complicated' or 'prolonged' grief.

Furthermore, research needs to attend to the types of treatment people will undergo to 'recover' from PGD and complicated grief. There would need to be consistency across the bereavement care organisations to implement such treatment, and as detailed in Chapter 4, this is a consistency which is currently lacking. Drawing from my findings on bereavement care practitioners, an increasing emphasis on psychiatric diagnosis may serve to widen the gap between the therapeutic approach of a person-centred volunteer-delivered bereavement counselling service and a clinical model of bereavement care. This poses the wider question of who has responsibility over the management of grief. The responsibility for 'complicated grief' is clearly situated in the hands of the professionals, and yet the emphasis on grief as 'natural' has meant historically, bereavement care has separated itself from a 'medical model.' I suspect that with the introduction and implementation of psychiatric diagnosis of PGD that the purpose and goals of bereavement care will become increasingly uncertain and divided (Pearce and Parkes 2017).

I have argued that psychological approaches have dominated the experience and recovery from grief, which consequently has reduced the possibility for other ways of understanding and managing grief. But further, I have questioned the need to manage grief in the first place. Drawing out the implications for practice from this book, therefore, rests on the hesitancy to make universal claims about grief and what should be done about recovering from it. Yet clearly there is a need to address individual and collective suffering in a modern western society such as the UK, where its population arguably are experiencing conflict and confusion over how best to live with feelings of grief. The bereavement counsellors I met at Caris bereavement service presented a model of care that benefited by being an open-ended service that allowed for clients to 'work through' the difficulties of grief and was facilitated by counsellors who were trained in a variety of approaches which meant grief was understood and dealt with from a wider perspective. While in my view, these factors enabled a better approach within the already existing aims and intentions of bereavement counselling, this book has argued for a need to challenge and critique the constructed need and obligation to recover, around which therapeutic discourses and interventions also have been constructed to remedy.

Acknowledging the possibility of non-recovery from a practice perspective involves acknowledging that the method can fail the person.

Shifting responsibility away from the individual and moving away from describing recovery as a result of the 'willingness' of the client, I argue is crucial for promoting a model of care in bereavement services, rather than a (superficial) over-emphasis on individual choice (Mol 2008). To arrive at this point practitioners and the models they employ need to acknowledge that a failure to fit the model is not necessarily a failure to achieve recovery, or a form of resistance. Bereavement care practice needs to become aware of how managing grief is linked to societal norms and political and economic concerns that do not necessarily have the interests of the bereaved person at its centre. However, as I have demonstrated the boundary between individual and political concerns is increasingly unclear, as contemporary government policy has continued to utilise a discourse of individual well-being, which in principle aims to place the individual at the heart of policy.

Only by acknowledging the ways in which recovery has become an obligation of the modern individual, along with an array of other modern demands such as maintaining happy emotions and being a hard-working citizen, can new ways of practicing, living and experiencing grief be considered. When recovery, completion and happiness are no longer positioned as the ever out-of-reach goal to which each individual is encouraged to desire and achieve, can bereavement care practice embrace the liminal space that grief can provide, rather than erasing it in the name of normalisation.

References

Árnason, Arnar. 1998. "'Feel the Pain': Death, Grief and Bereavement Counselling in the North East of England." Unpublished Doctoral thesis, Durham University.

Fitzgerald, Des, and Felicity Callard. 2014. "Social Science and Neuroscience Beyond Interdisciplinarity: Experimental $entanglements." *Theory, Culture & Society* 32 (1): 3–32.

Kauffman, Jeffrey. 2008. "What Is 'No Recovery?'" *Death Studies* 32 (1): 74–83.

Mol, Annemarie. 2008. *The Logic of Care: Health and the Problem of Patient Choice*. Oxon: Routledge.

O'Connor, Mary-Frances. 2005. "Bereavement and the Brain: Invitation to a Conversation Between Bereavement Researchers and Neuroscientists." *Death Studies* 29 (10): 905–922.

———. 2012. "Immunological and Neuroimaging Biomarkers of Complicated Grief." *Dialogues in Clinical Neuroscience* 14 (2): 141–148.

Pearce, Caroline, and Colin Murray Parkes. 2017. "Bridging the Divides in Bereavement Research: A Conversation with Colin Murray Parkes." *Mortality* 22 (3): 181–193.

Rose, Nikolas. 2013. "The Human Sciences in a Biological Age." *Theory, Culture & Society* 30: 3–34.

Turner, Victor. 1969. *The Ritual Process: Structure and Anti-Structure*. Chicago: Aldine.

Van Gennep, Arthur. 1960. *The Rites of Passage*. London: Routledge & Kegan Paul.

Appendix A: Tables of Participants

See Tables A.1, A.2, and A.3.

Table A.1 Bereavement care professional participants

Name	Role	Organisation
Wendy	Bereavement service counsellor/coordinator	Caris Islington bereavement service
Linda	Bereavement service counsellor/coordinator	Caris Islington bereavement service
Charlotte	Bereavement counsellor	Caris Islington bereavement service
Matthew	Bereavement counsellor	Caris Islington bereavement service
Claire	Bereavement counsellor	Caris Islington bereavement service
Kelly	Bereavement counsellor	Caris Islington bereavement service
Sarah	Early Intervention Project Manager	Cruse
Jane	Early Intervention Project volunteer	Cruse
Susan	Bereavement support worker	Cruse
Marion	Bereavement support volunteer	St Christopher's Hospice

(continued)

C. Pearce, *The Public and Private Management of Grief*,
https://doi.org/10.1007/978-3-030-17662-4

Table A.1 (continued)

Name	Role	Organisation
Tony	Trauma counsellor, Senior supervisor for hospice bereavement service	St Christopher's Hospice
Ellen	Senior member	Grief Recovery UK
Pamela	Bereavement service co-ordinator	Local bereavement service in London

Table A.2 Bereaved participants

Name	Age at interview (yrs)	Type of bereavement	Length of bereavement (yrs)
Anne	46	Husband fell out of a window	4
Tania	41	Husband died of sudden brain haermorrage	2
Laura	51	Husband died suddenly of ruptured aorta	2.5
Saadhia	30	Mother died after long illness	4
Jamie	34	Sister died in accident when he was 16 Mother died when he was 24	18 10
Paul	64	Wife died after long illness	1
John	63	Wife died of cancer	9 months
Rose	63	Husband died of heart attack	26
Helen	64	Grandfather when 7 years old Parents later in life	57

Table A.3 Former or current mental health service users

Name	Role
Eva	Former mental health service user. Former Recovery College peer worker
David	Current mental health service user
Donna	Worked on women's suicide crisis helpline

Appendix B: Bereavement Organisations—Detailed Information

The participating organisations present examples of bereavement care at national and local level, each with different forms of public support and funding, training and methods. Below I provide further background on the participating organisations.

Cruse Bereavement Care

Cruse Bereavement Care is the largest national charity in the UK dedicated to the provision of bereavement counselling and the training of bereavement volunteers. Cruse's mission, as stated on its website, is to ensure that all bereaved people have somewhere to turn when someone dies. Cruse was founded in 1959 and was originally dedicated to the support of widows (and very different levels of support beyond emotional) but now offers mainly emotional support to adults and children who have experienced any form of bereavement. Cruse support largely consists of one-to-one counselling: according to their figures 29,803 bereaved people received such support in 2014. Cruse currently has 5700 volunteers who deliver bereavement support. The charity relies upon government grants and donations to fund their services but Cruse

C. Pearce, *The Public and Private Management of Grief*,
https://doi.org/10.1007/978-3-030-17662-4

also has considerable interest in participating in research and position themselves as being at the forefront of bereavement care and practice. This is shown in their Early Intervention Project, which was launched in 2013 and funded by the Department of Health to target people at risk of 'Prolonged Grief Disorder.'

Caris Islington Bereavement Service

Caris (Christian Action and Response in Society) is a charity that provides a bereavement service to those who live in the borough of Islington, in North London. The bereavement service was established in the early 1980s, as a deanery project by the Anglican churches in Islington, managed by the deanery 'Social Responsibility Committee.' CARIS Islington resolved to become an ecumenical project, although most of its funding relies on the support of local churches. Caris provides training for volunteer counsellors, all of whom are already undertaking or have completed other formal counselling qualifications. The service Caris provides is open-ended and maintains around 40 counsellors and approximately 180 referrals a year of which half become clients. Caris also runs a cold weather shelter as a parallel project that provides nightly accommodation to over 100 homeless people in total in participating churches. Caris carried out their own research into what they discovered were notable links between homelessness and bereavement, publishing a report in 2010 (CARIS Islington, 2010).

St Christopher's Hospice

St Christopher's Hospice was founded by Dame Cicely Saunders in 1967 and is widely regarded as the first modern hospice. It is located in Sydenham, South East London. St Christopher's is a charitable organisation that relies on donations. St Christopher's bereavement services consist of one-to-one and group support delivered by volunteers who receive training. I interviewed a bereavement support worker and bereavement service senior supervisor at St Christopher's. I also attended a bereavement support group to present my research, which led to one further participant in the study.

Grief Recovery UK

Grief Recovery UK is a not-for-profit organisation, which is the UK branch of the Grief Recovery Institute founded in the USA. The Grief Recovery Institute was born out of the Grief Recovery Handbook, which was created by John W. James who had developed his own unique strategy for recovery from loss following the death of his young son. The Handbook (James and Friedman 2009) declares: 'It's not counselling, it's not therapy, it's not an alternative treatment.' The method is described as an 'action program for moving beyond death, divorce and other losses including health, career and faith.' It comprises a series of trademarked steps and activities that promise 'completion' and recovery from loss. Grief Recovery UK actively trains 'Grief Recovery Specialists' and support is delivered in a group or one-to-one setting.

Index

C. Pearce, *The Public and Private Management of Grief*,
https://doi.org/10.1007/978-3-030-17662-4

The manufacturer's authorised representative in the EU is Springer Nature Customer Service Centre GmbH, Europaplatz 3, 69115 Heidelberg, Germany. If you have any concerns regarding our products, please contact ProductSafety@springernature.com

Printed and bound by CPI Group (UK) Ltd, Croydon, CR0 4YY
01/10/2026
02225967-0007